George

Very best wishes.

David

THE MADNESS OF ADAM AND EVE

THE MADNESS
OF ADAM AND EVE

HOW SCHIZOPHRENIA SHAPED HUMANITY

DAVID HORROBIN

BANTAM PRESS

LONDON · NEW YORK · TORONTO · SYDNEY · AUCKLAND

TRANSWORLD PUBLISHERS
61–63 Uxbridge Road, London W5 5SA
a division of The Random House Group Ltd

RANDOM HOUSE AUSTRALIA (PTY) LTD
20 Alfred Street, Milsons Point, Sydney
New South Wales 2061, Australia

RANDOM HOUSE NEW ZEALAND LTD
18 Poland Road, Glenfield, Auckland 10, New Zealand

RANDOM HOUSE SOUTH AFRICA (PTY) LTD
Endulini, 5a Jubilee Road, Parktown 2193, South Africa

Published 2001 by Bantam Press
a division of Transworld Publishers

A catalogue record for this book is available from the British Library
ISBN 0593 046498

Typeset in 11/14pt Stempel Garamond by
Kestrel Data, Exeter, Devon.

Printed in Great Britain by
Mackays of Chatham plc, Chatham, Kent.

1 3 5 7 9 10 8 6 4 2

CONTENTS

ACKNOWLEDGEMENTS

In writing this book I have relied on voluntary and involuntary, witting and unwitting contributions from too many people for them to be individually acknowledged. Any attempt to make a list would run the risk of offending both those included and those not included.

Three people have provided very direct and invaluable help. Amanda Green has kept the successive typescripts in order and has been a constant source of help and organization. Crispin Bennett has sought out the most obscure references and tracked down copies of materials which I had thought unreachable. Sherri Clarkson has from the earliest moments of the conception of the book tolerated my ramblings and, as far as she was able, has kept my thoughts moving along relatively rational lines.

THE MADNESS OF ADAM AND EVE

PREFACE

THIS BOOK HAD ITS ORIGINS DURING TWO PERIODS WHEN I WORKED in Kenya. The first was as a medical student when I went to work for four months with the embryonic Kenyan Flying Doctor Service. Like so many others, I was captivated. The landscape, the people, the game were overwhelming.

One day I drove out of Nairobi, over the Ngong Hills and down, down into the bottom of the Rift Valley. There, at a place called Olorgesailie, is one of the most immediately striking of the sites left behind by ancient humans. Dated to somewhere around 700,000 years ago are thousands of the artefacts we call hand-axes littered over a several-acre site. These axes smashed into my consciousness with a force I have never forgotten. Who were the people who made these objects? Where did they come from? Where did they go to? What relationship did these people have to us?

Ten years later I was back in Nairobi as a professor in the brand-new medical school, helping to get it started. Also teaching there, with a lab just down the corridor from mine, was Alan Walker, who has since become one of the world's leading palaeoanatomists, researching ancient human and pre-human fossils dug out by himself, by the Leakey family and by other researchers. Alan always had those bits of bone lying about, some from people who were around at the time that the Olorgesailie site was being created, some earlier, some later. The sight of these ancient bones reinforced my interest in the evolution of humans which had been triggered a decade earlier. Ever since, I have maintained a strong interest in all that has happened in the field of evolutionary studies.

In the middle of a long vacation in Nairobi I heard a lecture by Howard Bern, the distinguished Professor of Zoology from the University of California at Berkeley, who was visiting Kenya. His subject was prolactin, a hormone produced by the pituitary gland in the middle of the skull. Prolactin helps breasts grow and stimulates milk production but must also do something else, since males have almost as much prolactin as do females. Howard's research had shown that prolactin is a universal regulator of water and salt metabolism throughout the animal kingdom. For example, it is the hormone which enables young salmon to migrate from fresh water down to the sea, and provides the required adjustment when, as mature adults, the salmon return to their home river. I was fascinated by the story and this started a ten-year period during which the effects of prolactin on humans became one of my major research interests.

About a year later, several colleagues and I published a paper in the medical journal the *Lancet* describing some actions of prolactin on human kidneys which we had observed by injecting the hormone into ourselves. As a result of this article, I received a letter from Gwynneth Hemmings. She runs the Schizophrenia Association of Great Britain, an organization mainly for people with schizophrenia and their relatives. She pointed out that the drugs then used for schizophrenia caused massive secretion of prolactin in both sexes and asked if I would give advice to the Association about the possible consequences.

And so I came to know something of the strange and sometimes terrible world of schizophrenia. The more I found out about the illness, the more interested I became. The study of prolactin gave me new ideas as to what might be the biochemical basis of schizophrenia. I became obsessed with the strange features of the illness, not just the unusual behaviour but the resistance to pain and arthritis, and the improvements in symptoms which could occur during fevers such as those caused by malaria. However, I did not expect that my schizophrenia research would ever link with my interest in human evolution.

But that is what happened. A series of observations by me and by many others led inexorably to the view that the origins of schizophrenia and the origins of humanity were intimately related. Schizophrenia has a unique pattern of distribution: it is found to approximately the same extent in every racial group throughout the world. This almost certainly means that schizophrenia was present in humanity at the time of the development of the first true humans before the races separated. Second, although schizophrenic patients themselves are often disabled, their relatives are often extremely high achievers. Einstein's son was schizophrenic, James Joyce's daughter was schizophrenic and a good case can be made for the idea that much of Isaac Newton's behaviour was what we call schizotypal, or part way between normality and frank schizophrenia. As will be seen later, schizophrenia and another related serious mental illness, bipolar disorder or manic-depression, are found remarkably frequently in the families of those who have reached the highest levels of creative achievement in many fields. There appears to be a genetic link between extremes of creativity and schizophrenia.

We are clearly distinguished from our immediate pre-human ancestors by our exceptional creativity, whether it be in science and technology, in the arts, in religion or in political and military organization. These skills are typical of those seen commonly in the families of schizophrenic patients. Gradually, over the years, the logic of what I was doing forced me to think more and more about a surprising possibility. If schizophrenia and bipolar disorder, present before the races separated, are responsible for much of human creativity, madness may have played a critical role in the emergence of modern humans.

This book sets out my intellectual odyssey and the conclusions I have reached. These conclusions are leading to new understanding of our origins, to new respect for the several genes which, when present together, cause schizophrenia, and to new approaches to the treatment of schizophrenia. This research programme, which started at Olorgesailie so many years ago, provides a new story about our human origins. More importantly, it also provides a new approach to the treatment of the illness. It links our past and our future in surprising ways.

1

'LOOK, PAPA, PAINTED BULLS'

MARIA DE SAUTUOLA, 1879

ONE SUMMER MORNING IN 1879, A NINE-YEAR-OLD SPANISH GIRL, Maria de Sautuola, was particularly excited. As a special treat her father, the Marquis de Sautuola, was to take her with him to explore a recently discovered cave on his estate. The Marquis was a distinguished amateur archaeologist who was elated by what he had found. Some years earlier, one of his dogs had disappeared into a hole. In trying to find the dog, the Marquis had stumbled upon a cave complex. Following a visit to an exhibition in Paris at which prehistoric hand-axes and other artefacts that had been found in caves were displayed, the Marquis decided to explore his own caves properly. His archaeological experience led him to recognize that the debris on the cave floor indicated early human occupation and he spent several days surveying what seemed to him to be a remarkable discovery. Already distinguished in the archaeological world, he believed that these extraordinary finds on his own estate of Altamira might make his international reputation. In fact, the cave was to destroy him.

But that was in the future. That morning when he took Maria into the cave he was filled with excitement and optimism. Once inside, the Marquis almost forgot his daughter, busying himself with further meticulous examination of the floor of the cave. Maria soon became bored with such attention to detail and wandered off on her own with a lamp. Unlike her father, she did not know that archaeological finds of interest were likely to be discovered only on the floor. She lifted her lamp to see what she could of the walls and the roof.

'Look, Papa, painted bulls!' were the words that changed the face of archaeology. For the first time, a modern human had come face to face with the magical world of prehistoric rock art.

His daughter's exclamation made the Marquis raise his eyes from the floor to the walls of the cave. He was stunned by what Maria had discovered. Now his reputation as an archaeologist of international calibre really would be made. He brought in skilled draughtsmen, proper lighting, and a colleague, Juan Vilanova y Piera, Professor of Geology at the University of Madrid. The two men devoted immense amounts of money, time and effort to producing accurate copies of the extraordinary display on the walls of his cave of Altamira. In 1880 they published what is in retrospect a restrained and accurate account of the discovery.

At last they were ready to present the findings to distinguished archaeologist colleagues at international conferences. But the reaction was quite opposite to the one so fondly imagined. Instead of being recognized as a great discovery, the work was dismissed as fraudulent. Almost all the experts agreed that the paintings were fakes. It was obvious to the professionals that no prehistoric human could produce images of such exceptional brilliance. Audiences simply did not believe the reports. One of the most distinguished experts, Emile Cartailhac, 'asserted that they were the work of conservative Spanish clerics, hoping to defend belief in divine creation'. Another, Gabriel de Mortillet, went so far as to argue in a widely circulated pamphlet that the art in the cave had been created by anti-evolutionist Spanish Jesuits trying to make a laughing stock of the emerging sciences of palaeontology and prehistory. As a result of those first reactions, one of the most important milestones in the rediscovery of the Palaeolithic past was relegated to scholarly oblivion for more than twenty years. The Marquis was not recognized as the discoverer of a sensational treasure. Instead he was branded a fraud and banned from attendance at future international archaeological congresses. He died in 1888, a disappointed and humiliated man.

Years after his death, other professionals came across the Marquis's report of the Altamira find and went to the cave to investigate. The investigators concluded that the find was indeed genuine, as were others at Lascaux in south-west France and elsewhere. It became established that the artists who made these extraordinary murals were working over a long period of time, between 10,000 and 40,000 years ago. Their work long predates the technological successes of the agricultural revolution, and of working with clay and metal. To his great credit, but too late for the Marquis, Emile Cartailhac publicly recognized his error and in 1902 published an article in the journal *L'Anthropologie* entitled 'Mea culpa of a sceptic'. He made a pilgrimage to Maria to apologize for what he had done to her father.

This story encapsulates beautifully much that exemplifies our human nature. The intellectual curiosity of the Marquis; his initial failure to look at the walls of the cave; Maria's innocent curiosity, which enabled her to look for things which should not have been there; the Marquis's ambition to be recognized by his peers; the vicious jealousy and blindness of those peers: all provide examples of the brilliant, distressing, illogical and idiosyncratic ways in which we humans react to the world.

But this pales beside the astounding brilliance of the art itself. These supposedly primitive humans, living tens of thousands of years ago, produced art of a quality which stands comparison with the artistic output of much later and more sophisticated eras. These works catch the very essence of an animal, with a stunning spareness of line, and show that their creators would not be surpassed in ability by many artists who followed. No one studying the paintings can doubt that these people were human in the way that we are. Picasso, after seeing the cave paintings for himself, is reputed to have said, 'We have learned nothing.'

The appearance of symbolic art of this quality represented an abrupt transition from anything achieved by any of our earlier predecessors or close animal relatives. The Neanderthal people, who may have survived until as late as 30,000 years ago, had brains that were larger than our own, but nothing they left behind comes close to what we see at Altamira.

Human physical and cultural evolution has for the most part been a rather slow affair. From the first stone tools, made perhaps 2.5–3 million years ago, until as recently as 100,000 years ago, the rate of change has been hardly more than glacial. Standard patterns of tools are found across Europe, Africa and Asia with near imperceptible changes over thousands of generations. Our ancient ancestors were clearly conservative people who showed little evidence of a desire to innovate or to express diversity. Bodies were changing gradually, and brain size was increasing. But by between 200,000 and 300,000 years ago our bodies and skulls seem to have reached something very close to those of modern humans. The Neanderthal branch of our family even had larger skull cases, and hence larger brains, than we have. In our gross physical structure, we do not seem very different from what we were 200,000 years ago.

But the same cannot be said for our minds. The people who produced Altamira were quite different from those who lived 200,000 years ago. While our knowledge of our ancestors remains very limited, the artefacts that they have left behind demonstrate a clear discontinuity in mind, if not in body, which occurred at some point between about 50,000 and 200,000 years ago. As Ian Tattersall of the American Museum of Natural History has noted:

> The archaeological record is but a dim record of the full panoply of behaviors of any early hominid, but if it shows us anything at all it is the starkness of the contrast between the torrential outpouring of symbolic behaviors by the Cro-Magnons (the people who created Altamira and Lascaux) and the essentially symbol-free behaviors of their predecessors. The fundamental innovation that we see is that of symbolic thought – with which language is virtually synonymous . . . The final acquisition of this remarkable capacity was not simply an extrapolation of what had gone before.

*   *   *

Something extraordinary must have happened to create human minds capable of producing the Altamira paintings. That something is certainly not obvious from our outer skull structure. Nor is it obvious from any other aspect of our skeletal anatomy. What happened within our brains left no external trace on our bones, but it did leave tracks in the form of an explosion of artistic and technical skills. The cave paintings are but one example. Artefacts show that human culture, instead of being dull, slow-changing and near universal up to perhaps 100,000 years ago, became exciting, rich and rapidly changing, with immense geographical diversity. Something more than mere brain size must have been involved. What might that something have been?

My contention, which will be developed later in this book, is that our modern human minds were made by a change in the way in which the nerve cells (neurons) inside our heads make and break the connections they develop with each other. In some people the connections between these micro-elements of the brain developed an extraordinary richness. As a result, some people began to see the world in entirely new ways. They made associations, and developed skills, the advantages of which had not previously been apparent.

What might have been the basis for such a change? We are certainly not going to find out by closer and closer inspection of skeletal remains. We must approach the problem more obliquely. We can reach some tentative conclusions on the basis of the artefacts of all types which began to be made by the owners of these new minds over the past 100,000 years. Paintings, adornments, musical instruments, tools and weapons can all give us clues. We can then look at those individuals in modern society who are responsible for similar artistic and technical achievements and ask what is special about them. We will never find certain answers, but what I hope to show is that we can begin to feel our way towards a sense of what may have been the changes in our minds which made us human.

THE GIFT OF MADNESS

The central idea of this book will be a surprise to many. The theory is that we became human because of quite small genetic changes in the chemistry of the fat inside our skulls. These changes injected into our ancestors both the seeds of the illness of schizophrenia and the extraordinary minds which made us human. I hope to lead you through the personal intellectual journey which has led to this conclusion.

Many people, both expert and non-expert in the fields of human origins and psychiatry, will initially be affronted by this proposal. For the non-expert in psychiatry, the word schizophrenia often conjures up one of two images. The first is the bizarre behaviour of homeless people in inner cities, some of whom have schizophrenia. The second is of a motiveless, appalling murder which took the life of an innocent person completely unconnected with the murderer. These are the current media images of schizophrenia.

But schizophrenia represents much more than these stereotypes. Consider the following type of experience, which has happened to most people who have achieved any prominence in schizophrenia research. The phone rings and at the other end is a guarded voice. The questions are initially cautious and probing. Is the listener sympathetic, knowledgeable and, above all, discreet? Eventually the caller is identified as someone who is well known in politics, business, academia or the arts. They have a problem: a son, a daughter, a brother, a sister is ill. The diagnosis is schizophrenia. Is there anything that can be done to help? Is there any new teatment?

The greatest achievers are rarely schizophrenic themselves – although the 1994 Nobel Laureate in Economics, John Nash, was an exception to this rule. The philosopher Ludwig Wittgenstein was possibly another, and during some periods of their lives both Isaac Newton and Immanuel Kant could easily have been diagnosed as schizophrenic. At least one other recent Nobel prize-winner, whose name is well known beyond his own field, is schizophrenic. However, with surprising frequency, individuals with whom the thinkers and achievers share one-half, one-quarter or one-eighth of their genes are schizophrenic or have bipolar disorder, another serious mental illness which is now being recognized as related to schizophrenia. The greatest creative achievements in art, science, music, business and politics have often been made by those who share a portion of a schizophrenic inheritance. At least three recent biomedical Nobel prize-winners have schizophrenic children. It is this association between a family history of schizophrenia and extraordinary achievement that has made me suspect that the biochemical changes which produce schizophrenia are closely related to the biochemical changes which made us human.

∂

'IS MAN AN APE OR AN ANGEL?'

BENJAMIN DISRAELI, 1804–1881

THE GREAT APES, CHIMPANZEES, GORILLAS AND ORANG-UTANS, ARE our nearest living animal relatives. The two chimpanzees, the 'common' and the 'pygmy' or 'bonobo', are closest to us. We did not evolve from the modern great apes, but we and they are both descended from a common ancestor. What do we know about that ancestor and about the changes which made us human?

The genetic differences between humans and great apes are small. Current estimates suggest that we share around 99 per cent of our genome with the chimpanzees. But although the differences are small, they are crucial because they make humans humans and chimpanzees chimpanzees.

Genetic differences produce biochemical differences between individuals and species. Every genetic change has a biochemical consequence. Can we begin to understand the nature of the biochemical variations which differentiate us from the great apes?

The following features are perhaps the major differences between humans and the great apes:

1. The consistent upright posture of humans, in contrast to the occasional and relatively clumsy standing upright of apes.

2. The larger brain size of humans, both in absolute terms and relative to the size of our bodies.

3. The creativity and intelligence of the larger human brain as dramatically shown by cave art.

4. The extensive fat deposits beneath human skin, even in people who are relatively lean. Only when grossly overfed do great apes develop subcutaneous fat deposits and even then these are different in structure.

5. The accumulation of fat in human breasts and buttocks, which leads to the characteristic human shape.

An important fact, which seems to have been missed by most writers about human evolution, links at least four of these features. All, except the consistent upright posture, are intimately related to the biochemistry of fat.

We have become used to thinking of fat as nothing more than a useless irritation, a major problem for those who live in the developed world. We overlook the fact that the brain is mostly fat – a specialized type of fat to be sure, but fat none the less. The growth of our brains during evolution was the growth of a fat organ. Moreover, the myriad fine connections which nerve cells make with one another and which form the structural basis of our intelligence and creativity are fat-rich connections linking fat-rich cells.

The growth of our fatty brain was paralleled in evolution by the growth of the fat beneath our skins and by the specialist fat depositions known as breasts and buttocks. Similar biochemical forces perhaps drove the increases in size of our brains, breasts and backsides. Fat plays a major part in these key anatomical features which distinguish us from our nearest relatives.

I believe that the differentiation of our bodily structures from those of the great apes was largely driven over 2–3 million years by changes in fat biochemistry. These changes increased the size of the fatty organs, the brain, breasts, buttocks, and other subcutaneous fat deposits. Then, somewhere between 50,000 and 200,000 years ago there occurred a change in the profusion and richness of the fat-rich connections between the nerve cells of the brain. This crucial event, which I believe made us human as opposed to large-brained great apes, also gave mankind the condition which we know as schizophrenia. I hope to persuade you that we are human because some of us have all or part of a schizophrenic genome.

HUMANS AND GREAT APES: WHAT MAKES THE DIFFERENCE?

The chimpanzee enclosure is always one of the most popular at any zoo. Spend an hour or two watching a group of chimpanzees and anyone can recognize that they are close relatives of humans. Their social interactions, their curiosity, their petty quarrels, their body structure, their expressions, all give us an uncomfortable feeling that we are not so far apart.

But there are also differences, and it does not require zoological expertise to note what they are. Chimpanzees can walk upright, but they are not particularly comfortable doing so. They can communicate by sounds, but the range of sounds seems much less complex than ours. They are clever, but their cleverness is more limited than ours. They have big heads in relation to their body size, but not so big as ours. Their buttocks and thighs are not as rounded and fattened as ours, making their anuses and female genitalia much more obvious. The breasts of the females are flaps of skin and are not rounded out with fat.

We are clearly similar but, equally clearly, different. We are not descended from chimpanzees, but we and the chimpanzees did have a common ancestor. Chimpanzees may have changed from that common ancestor just as much as we have, but there can be no doubt that the ancestor did exist.

There are two broad ways of attempting to answer the question of how long ago the human line and the chimpanzee line separated. One is to reconstruct the fossil record which describes both the chimpanzee line and the human line, and to attempt to work out when the structures come together in a common ancestor. But the problem is that the record is fragmentary, especially for the chimpanzee line, and there are often serious difficulties about dating fossils. This is not surprising when one considers how improbable is the fossilization of any creature. For creatures living in the conditions in Africa in the last 10 million years, the likelihood is that perhaps one in 10,000 or even one in a million primates left a fossil behind. Of those, perhaps one in a million has been found, so it is not surprising that the record is sparse.

Given the problems, it is to be expected that we will never have certainty, based on fossils, of the timing of the existence of that common ancestor. Estimates based on fossils have ranged widely, from around 3 million years ago (or around 150,000 human generations) to around 10 million years ago or more. In the absence of an accumulation of extraordinarily lucky fossil finds, we must find other ways of narrowing down our conclusions.

Fortunately, another way does exist. The DNA (the abbreviation for deoxyribonucleic acid) in our chromosomes (our 'genome') is central to life. But not all DNA is immediately and immutably vital to our existence. Random changes (mutations) can take place in regions of the DNA which are not absolutely and immediately critical to normal gene function. Because the bits of DNA concerned are not essential, such mutations may not be eliminated by the various processes which keep our DNA functional. And just as a clock ticks regularly, so these mutations tend to occur at a relatively regular rate. By comparing the number of differences between a particular stretch of human DNA and the same stretch of DNA in a chimpanzee, we can estimate how long the two species must have been apart to generate these differences.

A DIGRESSION: THE BIOCHEMISTRY OF DNA

By now most people have some idea of how genes work, but a brief recap may be helpful.

Our genetic material consists of strings of DNA. In turn, the DNA itself is made up of strings of chemical compounds called nucleotide bases. There are four types of these bases: adenine (A), guanine (G), cytosine (C) and thymine (T). The way in which the bases are arranged on the DNA forms the so-called genetic code.

Each string of three bases represents a unit of that code. There are sixty-four (4 × 4 × 4) ways in which any three out of four nucleotides can be arranged to give a three-base (triplet) code. There are twenty amino acids and so each amino acid can usually be represented by more than one triplet code, although methionine and tryptophan can only be represented by a single triplet. The triplet codes are known as 'codons'.

Each of the triplet codes indicates a particular amino acid. Amino acids are the individual biochemical components of which proteins are made up. Proteins make up the machinery which drives the behaviour of all the cells in the body, and also provide some of the structure of the body. Each protein may consist of anything from a few to a few hundred amino acids strung together. Proteins which contain fewer than about thirty or forty amino acids are usually known as 'peptides' but they have the same fundamental composition.

A 'gene' is a string of DNA bases in a legible code which specifies the sequence of amino acids in a protein. When a cell is activated to make a particular protein, the mechanism 'reads' along the gene, identifying each triplet code. Each triplet specifies a particular amino acid, and the protein is assembled by stringing together the amino acids of the type and order specified by the triplets of the gene. This is achieved by an intermediate mechanism involving a type of molecule called RNA (ribonucleic acid), and structures called 'ribosomes' which assemble the amino acids in the correct order. The details are complex, but the principle is relatively easy to understand.

The latest estimates suggest that there are in the order of 50,000–150,000 protein-specifying genes in humans. It is perhaps an indication of complexity, or alternatively of hype, that on the day the 'completion' of the draft map of the human genome was announced, the scientists most knowledgeable in the field were betting on how many human genes might exist. Their estimates ranged from a low of 25,000 to a high of 200,000. Perhaps we do not know as much about the genome as we thought!

The genes, however many there may be, are strung together to form very much longer pieces of DNA known as chromosomes. In humans there are forty-six of these DNA strings, or chromosomes, each containing many hundreds or even thousands of individual genes. A piece of tissue the size of a pinhead contains around 10 million human cells, the population of a city the size of London. Each cell contains DNA strings which, if stretched out, would be around two metres in length. In each human cell, twenty-three of these chromosomes are derived from the mother and twenty-three from the father. Twenty-two of these chromosome pairs, the 'autosomes', are extremely similar and carry the same sets of genes: each gene therefore has two copies, one coming from the mother and one from the father. The twenty-third pair, comprising the sex chromosomes, is different. There are two types, X and Y, which differ in overall appearance and in the genes they carry. Individuals with two X chromosomes are female; those with one X and one Y are male. So only males have Y chromosomes.

In addition to the genes themselves, each of which specifies the structure of a particular protein, there are supplementary coding regions adjacent to the genes. One code says 'start' and indicates where the reading of the gene should begin. Another code says 'stop' and indicates the end of the gene. Other adjacent regions are 'promoters' or 'regulators' which tell the gene mechanism to switch on and make more copies of the protein, or to switch off and stop making copies.

A mystery which we as yet do not understand at all is that less than 5 per cent of the total DNA in the chromosomes is written in the code which specifies particular protein genes and the mechanisms for controlling those genes. Many experts in genomics call the 95 per cent of chromosomes whose DNA we do not understand 'junk DNA'. The implication is that it is completely useless DNA with no function, which has just randomly accumulated during the course of evolution.

A much smaller group of experts has doubts about this interpretation. They find it difficult to believe that 95 per cent of human genetic material is rubbish and point out that in the past various human organs have been thought to have no function, only to have their essential nature demonstrated by further research. These investigators believe that the 95 per cent of 'junk DNA' does *not* represent useless rubbish, but is functional DNA whose role we simply do not yet understand. They argue that this DNA may be critical to understanding the ways in which genes are regulated.

Whatever view one takes, it is clear that the 'Human Genome Project' (HGP) is something of a misnomer. The HGP is not aimed at identifying the structure of the whole human genome but at identifying the 5 per cent of the genome which contains the genes whose coding systems we understand, and also the control systems for those genes. Even when the HGP is truly completed we will have the task of providing a good explanation for why 95 per cent of the genome is 'junk' or, in my view, the more likely problem of explaining just what that other 95 per cent does. It is possible that the human genome may prove to be far more complex than can be dreamed of on the basis of our present understanding.

BACK TO THE GENOMIC CLOCK

What is apparent is that very few of our genes are uniquely human. The great majority are shared with other species that have genes for making the same or similar proteins which perform the same functions. Britain's then Chief Scientist, Sir Robert May, on the day the 'completion' of the draft of the HGP was announced, pointed out that humans share perhaps 50 per cent of their genes with bananas.

The parallels between our gene structures and those of other species are remarkable. About 40 per cent of our genes are shared with the yeasts which are used to make alcoholic drinks or bread. About 60 per cent are shared with worms. About 80–90 per cent are shared with mammals to whom we do not feel particularly closely related, such as mice or rabbits. And around 98–99 per cent are shared with chimpanzees and other great apes. The differences in the genome between ourselves and chimpanzees are therefore tiny compared with the overwhelming similarities.

A mutation is a change in one of the bases that specify the codes for the amino acids in a protein. Many factors can lead to such mutations. Most are spontaneous accidents with no specific cause. Some may be due to failures of faithful replication during cell division. Some may be caused by chemical agents or by physical factors such as heat or radiation. Some parts of the structure of a protein are absolutely essential for normal function, but most are not critical and can vary as a result of mutation without function being lost. A few mutations may occur in crucial bits of a crucial protein and render it partially or completely non-functional. The result is disease or death for the carrier of that mutation. A few other mutations may also occur in crucial bits of the protein but enable it to perform its functions better, or even to acquire new functions. Such mutations may confer an advantage on the individual carrying the mutation. They are probably much rarer, because it is easier to damage a complex system by random change than to improve it. But most mutations are in non-critical areas and are effectively neutral: they neither improve nor harm the function of the protein and so they can accumulate without damaging or conferring advantage on the individuals carrying them.

There is now much evidence that such random mutations accumulate in the genome at a rate which is relatively constant for particular parts of the genome. This means that the occurrence of mutations can be used as a form of genetic clock. If one identifies a part of the genome which codes for the same protein in different species, or which codes for other features of the genome, one can work out the precise sequence of the bases in the two species and also work out just how many differences there are between them. The fewer differences there are, the more closely the species are related, and the nearer in time was their last common ancestor. The more differences there are, the further away was that last ancestor.

Scientists have concentrated on three different components of the genome in developing their clocks. The Y chromosome occurs only in males and is always passed on from father to son. It is therefore a guide to ancestry in the male line. The forty-four non-sex (autosomal) chromosomes occur in both sexes and mutations in them can be used to chart the history of both. And outside the nuclear genome there are tiny sub-cellular organs, or 'organelles', called mitochondria, which are responsible for generating much of the energy that a cell uses. The mitochondria are believed to be the remains of parasitic bacteria which colonized cellular organisms in the remote past, but which were then captured by the cells and used as energy generators. Some of the proteins of mitochondria are coded for by DNA which is found in the mitochondria themselves and not in the forty-six pairs of nuclear chromosomes. The importance of this is that sperm do not contain mitochondria. The mitochondria of the fertilized egg therefore come entirely from the unfertilized egg – i.e., entirely from the female line. Male and female genetic histories can therefore be followed separately by looking at Y-chromosome and mitochondrial DNA.

A example of how this works is provided by a South African group, the Lemba. The Lemba appear in almost every way to be black South Africans. They claim, however, to be Jews and their rituals have some elements of Judaism which cannot easily be explained away by cultural exchange in the past several hundred years. Their claim is that perhaps a thousand or more years ago some Jewish merchants came from the north to trade, but liked the Lemba and their country so much that instead of returning home they stayed, took Lemba wives and introduced Jewish customs. To most people the story seemed incredibly far-fetched, but Daniel Goldstein and others decided to check it out by looking at Lemba mitochondrial and Y-chromosome DNA. The mitochondrial DNA was wholly African but the Y-chromosome DNA was substantially Jewish in pattern. The Lemba story must therefore be largely true and their Jewish customs almost certainly developed in the way their traditions assert. This is just one striking example of the way DNA analysis can be used to build up a detailed picture of the relationships between modern human groups – and also to explain the relationships between humans and animals. As often in science, the devil is in the detail and there are many uncertainties about the exact interpretations of findings, but among those with specialist knowledge of the field there are few doubts about the overall picture.

The primates, the animal groups to which humans belong, are characterized by having both grasping hands and binocular vision. They include the tarsiers, the lemurs, the Old and New World monkeys, and the apes. The apes have larger brains than monkeys, lack tails and include the gibbons, orang-utans, gorillas and chimpanzees. Much work has now been done on DNA sequences in humans, the two sorts of chimpanzees, gorillas, orang-utans and monkeys. From this it is obvious that the five apes are much more closely related to each other than they are to the monkeys or to other primates such as the lemurs. It is also clear that we are more closely related to the chimpanzees than we are to the gorillas and the orang-utans. It is reassuring that the genetic clock bears out what most of us would conclude from a visit to the zoo: the chimpanzees really are our closest relatives.

Of course, we cannot yet be certain about the precise calibration of the genomic clock. Some parts of the genome may mutate more rapidly than others, giving different rates of accumulation of differences so that there can be discrepancies between the mitochondrial, Y-chromosome and autosomal DNA clocks. The rates of mutation may not have been the same in the past as they are today, for example due to variations in the intensity of cosmic radiation or of earth-based radiation resulting from volcanic activity. But with these reservations, most of those working in this field have now agreed that we last shared a common ancestor with the chimpanzees 5–7 million years ago. It is the genetic changes that have occurred since that time which have made humans and chimpanzees two different species.

WHAT ARE THE FACTORS WHICH MADE US HUMAN?

Genomics confirms what we can learn from simple observation at any zoo: the genetic differences between ourselves and chimpanzees are relatively few and relatively small. But these differences are crucial. Unravelling and understanding them is one of the most exciting projects in the whole of biomedical science.

Fortunately, the areas of the genome in which we must look for differences are also relatively few. They can be summarized as follows:

1. The genes which enabled us to be comfortable walking and standing upright.

2. The genes which gave us a layer of fat beneath the skin and which expanded that fat, particularly in the buttocks and the breasts, and particularly in infants during pregnancy. Human babies are born extremely fat compared to all other primate babies.

3. The genes which gave us a large and well-connected brain. This is the most important difference between ourselves and chimpanzees. Surprisingly, the brain, like our subcutaneous tissue, is substantially made of fat, so there may be interesting links between breasts, backsides and brain, in biochemistry as well as in our imaginations.

4. The genes that gave us the mechanical structures in the nasal and oral passages, the larynx and the rest of the respiratory system, which allowed us to develop clear speech: coupled with the brain structures which allowed us to understand that speech and so to control our breathing and larynx so that we could reply.

It used to be thought that the assumption of an upright position and the growth in the brain might be closely interrelated in time. But we now know that this view arose because of the incompleteness of the fossil record. As that record has been filled in, and in particular as fossilized remains have been found which include the skull as well as pelvic and leg bones from the same individual, it has become apparent that these events were widely separated in time. We probably gained our upright position between 3.5 and 5 million years ago, but the brains of our ancestors showed little signs of growth until about 2.5–3 million years ago. We do not know when we accumulated fat, or lost our body hair, or developed the tissues like the larynx required for clear speech, because these tissues leave little fossil record. This book will concentrate on what happened in the last 5 million and especially the last 3 million years, and on the structure and function of the brain. It will suggest specific changes which were responsible for making us human. It will also describe the path which led me to this conclusion, starting from my time as a medical student working in Kenya.

3

BONES, TOOLS AND GENES

ONE DAY, AS A YOUNG MEDICAL STUDENT WORKING FOR THE NEWLY formed Flying Doctor Service in Nairobi, I borrowed a car and took the afternoon off. I had been taught anatomy at Oxford by a man who was recognized as an authority on human evolution, Wilfred Le Gros Clark. I had won a prize for an essay I wrote on early primates in the fossil record and had come to know Le Gros Clark modestly well. He knew I was going to Kenya and suggested that I should try to see the site of Olorgesailie.

I drove out of Nairobi on a cloudy July day, towards the Ngong Hills, made famous by Karen Blixen and her coffee farm as she described it in *Out of Africa*. The road went over the southern shoulder of the hills, then dropped sheer into the Great Rift Valley, the slash in the earth's crust which runs from the Jordan down through East and Central Africa. For the past 10 million years the Rift has been the site of great lakes, some fresh, some brackish, some salt, and also the scene of intensive volcanic activity and earth movement. The volcanic activity is important in the story that follows because it has regularly covered the region with layers of ash and lava which can be accurately dated by physico-chemical methods. Between these volcanic layers are many other deposits, particularly common ones being sediments laid down by lakes and rivers. At some periods in history these Rift Valley lakes were very large, some larger than Lake Victoria today. At other periods they were much smaller. But they were always there and the deposits associated with them can almost always be reasonably accurately dated because of the intervening volcanic strata.

The road was bone-shakingly rough and I made slow progress, partly because I stopped frequently to look at the incomparable Rift Valley views, at the giraffe and other animals which frequently crossed the road, and at the Masai herdsmen and their cattle, whose country this was. There were few signposts and on several occasions I thought I must have missed Olorgesailie, but eventually I saw a small, roughly drawn fingerpost and took the side track to the archaeological site, which consisted of little more than a few hot and dusty huts. And the hand-axes.

Today Olorgesailie is a well-protected and well-organized site with raised walkways and a careful separation between axes and visitors, so that nothing will be disturbed and displaced from its context. But then there was little to keep the visitor from the axes. They seemed to be everywhere in their thousands: different shapes, different sizes, presumably different functions, but on first impression overwhelming not so much in the detail but in the mass. This ancient, dried-up margin of a stream flowing into a once lush lake shore had clearly been important to early humans. Now dated to between 600,000 and 700,000 years ago, Olorgesailie gave a tantalizingly elusive insight into our ancestors. Tantalizing because no human remains and relatively few other artefacts have been found at the site. The thousands of hand-axes lie alone as testimony to what might have happened. The rest must be filled in by our imaginations.

On the road back to Nairobi that evening my imagination was in turmoil. I could not stop thinking about the way we might have become human. No matter where my medical career took me, I knew that I would always be enchanted by work which helped to define better whence we came.

I am not alone in being captivated by the urge to understand our origins. We eagerly devour news of the latest fossil findings.

Particularly important discoveries make the covers of international news magazines and often lead to high sales of that issue.

Unfortunately, our interest sometimes seems inversely proportional to the reliability of our knowledge. We are trying to do what in any complete sense must be impossible: to reconstruct what happened despite the almost total absence of evidence. The peoples we are trying to find probably rarely exceeded tens of thousands in number at any one time. They left behind few identifiable artefacts other than durable stone and bone. The vast majority of them died and left their remains in circumstances which led to complete destruction of body, bone and domestic artefacts within a few months or at most a few years. Almost infinitely rarely, one of these people died in a strange circumstance – in a cave, in a flood, in a marsh, in a volcanic eruption – which led to the preservation of bone but nothing else. All studies of the human record since we parted company with the chimpanzees must inevitably be based on the flimsiest of foundations. It is not surprising that the views of experts are so diverse or that the quarrels can be so virulent, as illustrated by the Altamira story. A quarrel of palaeontologists and palaeoanthropologists might be the appropriate collective noun. There is nothing like lack of evidence, coupled with the high intelligence and ambition for renown of the people discussing that evidence, to generate heat rather than light.

What then are the few reliable facts about which almost everyone can agree?

FROM 5 MILLION TO 3 MILLION YEARS AGO

During this period in Africa there were several – perhaps many – types of what we might call the hominids, species or varieties who are differentiated from the ape line but who are not human. Their skeletal remains are relatively abundant from the north-east of Africa, through East and Central Africa to the south. But defining species from bone fragments alone is almost impossible, hence the virulence of some of the quarrels.

The pre-humans of this period usually go by the general name of *Australopithecines*, although some experts wish to split them into smaller, more closely defined groups. One of the most famous among them, partly because she (or perhaps he) was found as a relatively complete skeleton and partly because Don Johanson and his team gave her (or him) the catchy name of Lucy, was discovered in 1974 in Hadar in the Ethiopian section of the Rift Valley. (She was called Lucy because Johanson's camp was then reverberating to the sounds of the Beatles song 'Lucy in the Sky with Diamonds'.) No one underestimates the importance of Lucy and of the other fossils found in the vicinity.

These creatures have been assigned the name *Australopithecus afarensis* and they lived between 3.2 and 3.6 million years ago. They lived by the margins of lakes and rivers, and their remains are usually found alongside those of other lake-margin species, including turtles, other reptiles, fish and mammals. The bones suggest that their trunks were upright and in structure part way between ours and those of the great apes. Their legs were rather shorter than ours and their arms were longer and stronger, probably indicating that tree climbing was still very important. In height they were in the region of 3 feet to 4 feet 6 inches, so they were much shorter than we are. We do not know yet whether the different varieties or species varied greatly in size, or whether the bigger ones were males and the smaller ones females. This is one of the most active points of discussion in the field. Their teeth suggest that they had moved away from the near complete vegetarianism of the great apes to eat a mixed diet of both vegetable and animal origin. Their brains were not much different in size from those of modern chimpanzees – roughly a third to a quarter the size of our own. But apart from the fact that over 3 million years ago pre-hominids stood upright and were comfortable when walking, and that they were usually fossilized near water, we know virtually nothing about their lifestyle. They appear to have left behind no artefacts of any kind. Many presume that their behaviour may have been similar to that of modern chimpanzees, eating a widely varied diet, mainly vegetarian, but also involving insects, grubs and occasionally small animals or the scavenged carcasses of larger creatures.

We do know unequivocally that *Australopithecus* walked. At a magical place called Laetoli in Tanzania, discovered by Mary

Leakey and her colleagues, there is an artefact which makes me and many other people feel an extraordinary affinity with these 3.5-million-year-old people. There, pressed into the freshly fallen volcanic ash from a nearby eruption, are footsteps, apparently of at least two people walking closely together. One set of footprints is considerably larger than the other. They might have been a male and a female or a parent and a child, but which we will never know. Rain appears to have fallen soon after they walked by, converting the ash into a form of concrete and preserving the footprints for all time. To drive across the Serengeti Plain with its little-spoiled animal wealth, and to see these obviously near-human footsteps made by members of a nuclear family, is to experience something which tugs at the heart like few other things ever can. One can feel in the atmosphere a real contact with those two or three people walking through their hazardous environment.

Only one general conclusion can be made about the environment in which these pre-people lived. Their remains are almost always found along watercourses or on or near lake margins. A reasonable assumption, therefore, is that at least some pre-hominids lived by water, but what we do not know is whether most of these creatures lived in such environments. Do we find remains near water because that is where most *Australopithecines* lived, or do we find remains there because these environments provide relatively good conditions for fossilization? Could it be that remains are not found elsewhere because other environments do not provide the right conditions for fossilization? We simply do not know. But there are other pieces of evidence, to be discussed later, which suggest that water was always important to us.

FROM 3 MILLION TO 2 MILLION YEARS AGO

From somewhere between 2 and 3 million years ago comes the first clear evidence of change in brain size, structure and function. It is found in two forms.

First, there are skulls whose brain cavities are unequivocally larger than those of chimpanzees or *Australopithecines*, indicating that they contained larger brains. For the first time in the fossil record there is solid evidence of a substantial change in brain size. Second, there is evidence that these larger brains might be able to do interesting things. We know this because we find around this time substantial numbers of crudely shaped stone implements. These are deliberately shaped for a purpose, rather than being random chunks of rock. Simple stone tools of this type are called Oldowan after the Olduvai Gorge in Tanzania where they were first clearly identified by the Leakey family.

Palaeontologists give the people with larger skulls, who deliberately made crude stone artefacts, the first name of *Homo*, the genus (grouping of species) to which we belong. Their usual species name is *Homo habilis*, handy human, reflecting the tools which they consistently made. Of course, we do not really know whether they formed a single separate species, whether several species were involved, or whether they would better be defined as advanced *Australopithecines*. Such is the stuff of academic argument, but these people were clearly different. Perhaps the most spectacular find of hominids of this group was made at the end of 1996 in the Middle Awash Valley in northern Ethiopia by an American–Ethiopian expedition. This find was spectacular not only because of the bony hominid fossils but because of the other bones found in the same fossiliferous layers which were accurately dated to 2.5 million years ago. The fossils were given the name *Australopithecus garhi* by the discoverers, but other scientists could easily have assigned them to the genus *Homo*.

It is not the naming which is important. What matters is the detailed assemblage of other fossils found in association with the hominid activity. The mineral deposits and the bones are characteristic of a shallow freshwater lake and its grassy margins. There are birds, fish, reptiles, including crocodiles and turtles, and a wide range of antelope and zebra-like species with associated predators. Many of the animal bones found at these Ethiopian sites show cut marks and chop marks characteristic of those made in modern experiments when animals are butchered using stone tools. The investigators write that these finds demonstrate that

> stone tool wielding hominids were active on the lake margin 2.5 million years ago. The bone modifications indicate that large

animals were disarticulated and defleshed and that their long bones were broken open, presumably to extract marrow, a new food in hominid evolution with important physiological, evolutionary and behavioral effects. Similar patterns of marrow acquisition have been reported for younger sites such as Koobi Fora and Olduwai Gorge.

Bone marrow consists largely of fat. This new food coincided with brain expansion and tool use. Were these three things related?

These butchered bones were not found in association with any stone tools. The authors speculate that this may be because the right types of stone were rare in this area, so any tools made may have been carefully conserved and carried from site to site. But in another part of the Rift Valley, in the north of Kenya, a tool factory has been found which dates to between 2.3 and 2.4 million years ago, just a little later than the Ethiopian site. We know that this was a place where stone tools were made because the archaeologists performed the remarkable feat of substantially fitting groups of up to twenty fragments back into their original cobble. This enabled accurate assessments to be made of the skills involved in the tool-making from the parent core. In a wonderful analysis, the archaeologists showed that the makers of the tools must have understood their materials thoroughly. They were also able to execute rapid, precise and aimed movements of the arm, something which modern chimpanzees cannot easily do.

The remainder of the evidence from the site is tantalizing in its hints and in its inadequacy. There are no hominid bones, so we cannot be sure who made these tools. But they were people somewhere on the progression – or a near side branch – between *Australopithecus* and *Homo*. And they lived on a lake or river shore, for among the tools were the remains of lakeside grazing mammals, reptiles and fish. Tortoise bones and ostrich-egg fragments were particularly common in association with the tools, possibly indicating hominid meals. Here was a people comfortable in their environment, an environment rich in water, marsh and marginal lakeside open country.

FROM 2 MILLION TO 0.5 MILLION YEARS AGO

During the period from 3 million to 2 million years ago there appear to have been steady increases in brain size, but the fossils of *Homo habilis* and its immediate *Australopithecus* antecedents and relatives seem confined to Africa. The Oldowan stone tools were crude and simply modelled. They were obviously made by people skilled in selecting the best stone for the job, and skilled in striking that stone to produce the best fragments, but there is only limited evidence of subsequent deliberate shaping of a finished tool.

About the end of this period, around 2 million to 1.7 million years ago, however, another stage of hominid evolution occurs. The skulls become more similar to those of modern humans and there is a substantial increase in the size of cranial cavity. Somewhat later, about 1.5 million years ago, there is also a clear improvement in the quality of the tools. They are much more shaped, obviously much more carefully made by humans, much more clearly tools; they deserve the name hand-axes. Palaeontologists give the people with the changed anatomy who made the tools the name *Homo erectus*.

As with the *Australopithecines*, much of our knowledge of *Homo erectus* depends on a limited number of spectacular finds. Perhaps the best known was made by an expedition led by Richard Leakey and Alan Walker, the anatomist who shared with me the teaching of medical students in the early days of the University of Nairobi. This find has become known as Nariokotome Boy or Turkana Boy, because he was found by the noted fossil hunter Kamoya Kimeu in the Nariokotome River valley on the edge of Lake Turkana. The place where he was found dates the skeleton to between 1.5 and 1.7 million years ago. Remarkably, the skeleton is nearly complete, enabling a proper evaluation of all the components of the body and of the way they fit together. The skeleton may be so complete because, although the boy died in a marsh among crocodiles and turtles, his body seems to have been quickly covered by mud, so preventing its dismemberment by scavengers.

Three things are immediately obvious to anyone, even without specialist knowledge, who looks at the skeleton. First, the boy was much bigger than the *Australopithecines*. He was 5 feet 3 inches tall and specialist knowledge of his bone age indicates that he was somewhere between nine and twelve years old. Alan Walker has estimated that his full adult height would have been over 6 feet. Second, the boy clearly stood erect. All his bone structure indicates that this was a comfortably and completely bipedal species. Third, his skull case shows that his brain was considerably larger than earlier hominids' and was more than twice the size of a modern chimpanzee's.

More detailed examination of the skeleton has revealed many other features, only one of which I will pick out here. The size of the spinal cord is roughly indicated by the holes in the vertebrae through which the cord passes. The spinal cord clearly cannot be larger than the vertebral holes. In modern humans, in the region of the thorax the spinal cord has expanded to accommodate the nerves which supply the muscles of respiration. All animals breathe but only humans speak. The control of breathing required to supply air is a basic need of all animals and is relatively simple: other animals do not show any substantial expansion of the spinal cord in the thoracic region. They breathe to live and nothing more. But modern humans also breathe to speak. The complexity of the control of breathing needed for speech is much more demanding and so the nerve supply must be much more intensive and consequently bulky. As a result, the thoracic vertebrae of humans who speak show a major increase in the size of the hole for the spinal cord. This expansion is not seen in Nariokotome Boy. It is therefore likely that either he could not speak or that his speech was very limited and not much more impressive than the vocalizations of chimpanzees.

A second *Homo erectus* skeleton, this time of a mature woman and also discovered by the Kimeu–Walker–Leakey team, provided a major surprise. Vitamin A is an essential nutrient for human beings. With vitamin D, it is one of the essential nutrients which is fatty and which accumulates in fat. It is required for many aspects of human function: for the control of cell division, for the normal growth and development of all tissues, and for the function of the eyes, especially at night. It is also one of the few essential nutrients which in overdose can be seriously poisonous. Furthermore, it is one of the few poisons which leaves a clear mark on the bones. The skeleton of someone suffering from vitamin A toxicity is thickened in very specific ways which are unequivocally diagnostic.

Turkana Woman's skeleton showed clear evidence of vitamin A poisoning, which must have existed for many months to produce such extensive changes. She was probably in agony for a long period before she died, because the condition causes intense bone pain. Alan Walker has reasonably drawn the poignant conclusion that she must have been cared for by her family and band, as otherwise she could not have survived in a harsh, predator-rich environment. But where might the vitamin A, sufficient to cause toxicity, have come from? There are really only two sources and even they are important only if they become a major part of the diet. One source is the liver, particularly the livers of carnivores and also of animals, birds or fish at the top of the aquatic food chains. This is because vitamin A is ultimately made by micro-organisms which live in water. So we get – or used to get – our vitamin A from cod liver oil or halibut liver oil. The first reports of vitamin A poisoning occurred in Arctic explorers who ate seal or polar bear livers. The other source is the grubs of various insects, including bees and termites. So Turkana Woman, and presumably Turkana Boy, were at least partly and perhaps wholly carnivorous. They were consuming substantial amounts of liver from creatures at the top of the aquatic food chain, or killing and eating carnivores, or eating large amounts of insect grubs, or possibly all three. At the same time these people must inevitably have been consuming substantial amounts of the fat which is always associated with vitamin A in foods. As will be shown later, this type of fat is necessary for brain growth, and so may have played more than a passing role in our development.

OUT OF AFRICA FOR THE FIRST TIME

Homo erectus was adventurous. Starting from East Africa, these hominids spread throughout the whole of the continent, much of Europe, except for the far north, and much of Asia, again except for the far north. For something in the region of 1.5 million years, from about 2 million to about half a million years ago, *Homo erectus* and relations are the dominant hominids in the world. There are variations in anatomy which have led to great arguments over whether this or that hominid should be called something different, such as *Homo ergaster* or *Homo heidelbergensis*, but the broad anatomical picture suggests either a single species or a group of closely related species.

The remains of *Homo erectus* and variants appear to radiate from Africa, reaching the Iberian peninsula in the west and Java in the east. For the first 0.4–0.5 million years of this period, the culture associated with *Homo erectus* was Oldowan – crude stone tools equipped for cutting and scraping meat and for bashing bones to get at the marrow. Most of the early sites are in Africa, but a recent find at Dmanisi in Georgia, dated to about 1.7 million years ago, shows just how far *Homo erectus* had spread even at such an early date. Like almost all the African sites, this one was near water, at the confluence of two major rivers. Other similar sites, but usually with less complete dating and identification, have been found from Spain to Java. The last clear *Homo erectus* specimens in Africa and most of Eurasia are dated to around 0.3–0.5 million years ago, although a recent controversial date in Indonesia suggests that *Homo erectus* might have persisted there until as late as 30,000–40,000 years ago. During all this time, anatomical changes appear to have been modest, with perhaps a gradual increase in brain-case size but certainly no dramatic development.

This extraordinary movement of *Homo erectus* across the main connected land masses is unusual to say the least. No other species is known to have spread so quickly across so great an area with so many differences in environment, the only constant perhaps being water. *Homo erectus* was certainly adventurous, but such extraordinary spread could be explained only if the species lived in groups with a strong tendency to divide. The bands of individuals must have split, split and split again to cover so much territory so quickly. The personality characteristics which might have facilitated such repeated divisions do not appear to have been much explored. They provide an important clue, as we shall see, to the mechanisms involved in the evolution of the brain.

HAND-AXES AND FIRE

With one, or perhaps two, major exceptions, the culture of *Homo erectus* may be summed up in one pejorative word: 'boring'. Of course this is unfair, because we know so little of their lives and almost everything that was not bone or stone has been lost for ever.

But there is one particular type of artefact which makes an enormous impact on everyone who sees it for the first time, especially if they see it where it was found. These are the hand-axes which so impressed me at Olorgesailie. They began to appear around 1.5–1.6 million years ago in Africa and spread quickly to wherever *Homo erectus* settled, except perhaps to far South-East Asia. We do not know how the spread happened, whether one group invented it first and then taught all the others by education of adjacent bands, or whether many groups around the world discovered the technology more or less at the same time, or even whether a guild of specialist hand-axe-makers arose, travelling from place to place, separate from other people and keeping their esoteric technical skills to themselves.

We do not even know what the hand-axes and their associated cleavers were made for. The cleavers really do look a bit like modern axe-heads, with a shaped and sharpened end. One could readily imagine them being used to crush bones to extract the marrow, for example. But the so-called hand-axes are a puzzle in spite of their extraordinary abundance. One thing obvious to anyone who has held one is that, unless they were held by some sort of handle, for which we have no evidence whatsoever, to hold them in the hand for chopping or butchering could easily have done more damage to the wielder of the tool than to the object being addressed. For hand-axes, beautifully shaped as they are, have a sharpened edge all round. It is impossible to hold one to strike a blow without simultaneously doing serious damage to a presumably ungloved hand.

For me, the most attractive theory is that hand-axes were used as missiles to attack animals at or near the water's edge. This theory, developed by Eileen O'Brien and recently supported by William Calvin, seems to me to fit the facts. It explains why there is an edge all round, to increase the likelihood of doing damage to the target.

It explains why so many hand-axes appear to be unused, because most probably missed or, having hit a soft target and done some damage, fell into water or mud and were difficult to retrieve. It also explains why, as at Olorgesailie, so many beautiful undamaged axes seem to be scattered randomly over a wide area. We know that at the time of occupation, 0.6–0.7 million years ago, the site of Olorgesailie was a stream flowing into a swampy lakeside which might well have been immensely attractive to animals. Throwing hand-axes at the large concentrations of game at such places might well have been a profitable occupation and could explain more readily than anything else the apparent random scattering and the relative lack of other artefacts. It could also explain why some hand-axes are found embedded edgewise. O'Brien has described how she persuaded discus-throwing athletes to throw casts of hand-axes. Their shape made them fly through the air in a vertical orientation and repeatedly they embedded themselves edge or point first when they hit the ground.

But perhaps the most important thing about hand-axes may have been the pressure they put on humans to optimize three different but related activities. First, the maker had to identify an appropriate block and then to visualize the shape in the uncut stone. Then the tool-maker had to knap that shape precisely while seated on a secure foundation. Finally, the axe-user had to develop the motor functions needed to fling the hand-axes accurately at a relatively distant prey.

The visualization of the shape in stone, encapsulated by Michelangelo's comment that his skills as a sculptor were in revealing what was already there, is almost certainly a novel human attribute which developed during the time of the worldwide dominance of *Homo erectus* and their relatives. Of great interest is the fact that the attribute of visualizing three-dimensional shapes is common among modern architects and sculptors who often suffer from what we now call dyslexia, the learning disability which involves problems in dealing with the written word. Surprisingly, in spite of their problems with words, the ability to see what is not yet there, to visualize the three-dimensional structure of a building before it exists – and before it can be modelled by modern computer graphics – is something which is well known to many dyslexic people. As we will see later, dyslexia is also common in families who have schizophrenic members and this 'abnormal' genetic variant may have had its strongly positive side in human history.

Another unusual attribute, well known to families with dyslexic members, is a curious combination of clumsiness and manual dexterity. Dyslexic people are often clumsy at motor skills which involve the whole body, like jumping or running or catching. Sometimes this clumsiness is so extreme that it is given a formal name: dyspraxia. But sit a dyslexic child down so that his (dyslexia is much more common in males) trunk is stable and grounded, and that same 'clumsy' child may show extraordinary manual dexterity within a limited visual field. For example, dyslexic children may be very skilled at building models or using construction kits like Lego.

These two attributes – the visualization of the shape in the stone, and the precision of hand movement when the body is stabilized – are precisely those required to make hand-axes and cleavers. Is it possible that the skills which *Homo erectus* clearly had in these areas were predominantly found in a limited sub-group who had the genes which we would now call dyslexic?

This same set of genes required for making the axes may not have been present in the people who actually used them if, as O'Brien suggests, the hand-axes were commonly thrown. Because what is quite different about throwing, as compared to knapping, is that the former requires extraordinary coordination, not just of the hand and arm muscles, but of the trunk and legs as well. Calvin has emphasized the abilities involved in accurate throwing. If accuracy is to be achieved, not only must the hand and arm perform a precise set of movements at astonishing speed, but the rest of the body must be stabilized to provide a solid and fixed launching pad for the briefest of movements. The skills involved are those of the athlete.

One area which has not been sufficiently appreciated by palaeoanatomists and palaeoanthropologists is the relationship between hand-axe-making, throwing and breath control. I personally realized this when I was reading a newspaper article about a person who specializes in microsculpture – the ability, for example, to sculpt a perfect ivory miniature of the Statue of Liberty within the eye of a needle. The work is now highly successful commercially and the sculptures are in great demand. Three things in particular struck me about this article. First, and this is something which is shared by the throwing athlete, the artist said that one of the most important skills involved in microsculpture was control of breathing. In order to make absolutely accurate movements of his hands, his breathing had to be temporarily stopped, and that stoppage had to be coordinated with what his hands were doing. Any athlete knows that similar precise coordination of breathing is critical to top-level performance in any game or sport which requires an object to be thrown, hit or caught. Without the precise – yet largely subconscious – regulation of breathing, top athletes could not accurately stabilize their bodies to allow the violent arm movements to be activated with such force and such precision. Second, the sculptor is profoundly dyslexic yet, to a level not seen even in most dyslexics, he has extraordinarily precise control of his hands and fingers. Third, his choice of material is of the utmost importance: it must be finely and evenly structured and must not unexpectedly fracture along unwanted planes. All these abilities – the fine control of hand movements and breathing, and selection of materials – are, of course, what would be required of a skilled maker of hand-axes.

The precise regulation of breathing is what is needed to enable us to speak. The argument will be developed later that perhaps hand-axe manufacture and throwing were important skills which humans had to develop before primate vocalization could become speech. Turkana Boy had not yet developed the control of breathing required for speech, but perhaps later varieties of *Homo erectus* did. We do not yet have the fossils which would allow us to draw a definite conclusion.

Despite the skills of *Homo erectus*, I must conclude this section by emphasizing again how glacial was cultural change during the period of their dominance. About 400,000 years, or 20,000 human generations, elapsed between the appearance of *Homo erectus* and the emergence of hand-axe culture. For another million years, or 50,000 human generations, that hand-axe culture was almost unchanged across the inhabited world. Moreover, in both periods, the tool cultures showed astoundingly little geographical variation. Even experts, without knowing the context of the discovery, have great difficulty in saying whether an Oldowan tool assembly, or a collection of hand-axes and cleavers, is African, European or Asian. Members of the *Homo erectus* species may have been *Homo* but they certainly did not share with us our relentless passion for change and cultural diversity. That switch, from extreme stability of culture in space and time to extreme variability and diversity, is perhaps the most important single event we have to account for in human evolution.

FROM 0.5 MILLION TO 0.2–0.1 MILLION YEARS AGO

Having stayed more or less static for 1–1.5 million years, with little but a slow drift upwards, again the fossil record shows a spurt during which members of the genus *Homo* developed brain sizes as big as or even bigger than the brains of modern humans. Whether this change occurred in one place and then spread around the world or whether it occurred in several different places more or less simultaneously is unknown. What is known, however, is that, associated with the change in skull size is a final improvement in the quality of hand-axes and the introduction of some geographical diversity. Some of the axes are now quite beautiful objects, and begin to show variations between geographical locations. Many of them appear not to have been used but rather to have served some ornamental, status or courtship function. There is also the emergence of a new type of tool-making, in which stone cores were carefully prepared and then multiple blades and flakes were struck off from a single core. For the first time there are also objects made of wood – in particular, spears with fire-hardened tips. So we know that these people could fashion beautiful objects, and could also begin to understand and control fire and the way it might change the properties of materials.

The people who made these things have been given many different names and there is no agreement about nomenclature, about species, or about the relationship of one group to another. By about 300,000 years ago the Neanderthals appear, a group with particular skull and body shapes found across southern Europe and what is now known as the Middle East. What is not in doubt is that brain sizes of Neanderthals and of other peoples living in Africa and Asia at the same time had grown rapidly and become fully modern. The tool quality and the control of fire indicate that they understood the rudiments of technology. But, despite the wide geographical dispersion, there is still only limited cultural diversity. Towards the end of the period there is evidence possibly suggesting burials, and the use of red ochre for personal decoration. There is much argument about whether some of the objects found represent understanding of symbolism and a concept of life after death. But what is not in doubt is that, compared to the profusion of utilitarian stone tools, symbolic objects are rare, difficult to interpret and fragmentary, and may not even exist.

FROM 0.1–0.2 MILLION TO 20,000 YEARS AGO

Early in this period, some time between 100,000 and 200,000 years ago, humans whose skulls and bodies were essentially modern appeared for the first time. The archaeological record shows that they were around in good numbers between 50,000 and 100,000 years ago. Given the time needed to multiply, this means that these people could have originated anything from 100,000 to 200,000 years ago. They are present in Africa, from Eritrea to the eastern Congo to South Africa, at sites which have been dated to between 90,000 and 140,000 years ago. Soon after that they appear in the Middle East and by 50,000 years ago they are in Europe, Asia and perhaps Australia.

This time something truly dramatic happened, not in the overall body structure or brain size, which changed only modestly, but in the way the brain worked. This change produced rapid and profound shifts in behaviour. Modern humans had evolved.

Let us return to the genetic clock for a moment. In the past fifteen years, key regions of autosomal, mitochondrial and Y-chromosome DNA from almost all human populations have been sequenced. These genes can be used to trace the female (mito-chondrial) and male (Y-chromosome) lines. The autosomal (non-gender-specific) lines can be used to trace the history of both.

Studies of mitochondrial DNA, of Y-chromosome DNA and of DNA from other chromosomes all lead to the same conclusion. All modern humans descend from ancestors who lived somewhere between 50,000 and 200,000 years ago, most probably between about 130,000 and 160,000 years ago. The genetic clocks mostly point to around the same date, although the Y-chromosome clock suggests a somewhat younger last common ancestor. A single pair, probably living in a small band of between twenty and a hundred people, were the progenitors of all modern humans. And that couple almost certainly lived in Africa. The reason for thinking this is that groups which have almost all genes in common must have diverged recently, but groups which have fewer genes in common diverged much earlier. The greatest differences between the races are between Africans and the rest. Africans show more diversity in the range of mutations present in all forms of DNA than any other people. As one moves away from Africa, the diversity progressively diminishes. The most likely explanation for this is that modern humans started in Africa and spread throughout the world.

How did these modern humans live when they first emerged? They exploited inland waterways and the sea. Much of the evidence for this is now beneath that sea because of the current high sea levels compared to several relevant periods of the past. But in a few places the geology is such that the ancient occupation levels remain above present sea level.

The most important sites are at two ends of the eastern seaboard of Africa – at Klasies River and Herrold's Bay in the eastern Cape of South Africa, and on the Eritrean coast of the Red Sea close to what used to be a land bridge between the Horn of Africa and southern Arabia. Both are dated to around 125,000 years ago, both contain remains of unequivocally modern *Homo sapiens*, and both show extensive use of marine resources, including shellfish, crustaceans and fish. A third site in the Semliki area of Central Africa is a river and lakeside site dated to between 90,000 and 100,000 years ago which has an extraordinary collection of beautifully worked ivory harpoons and other implements with obvious utility in fishing. These three sites precede others in the Middle East where modern humans are found 80,000 to 100,000 years ago and to which they travelled in their first forays out of Africa.

So the archaeological evidence is now beginning to be consistent with the genetic evidence. Modern humans were found
at two ends of the African continent 125,000 years ago and so
probably originated somewhere in Africa perhaps 130–150,000
years ago. The association with water, both inland and by the
seashore, persists – a theme to which we will return. Indeed,
Jonathan Kingdon and others have suggested that modern humans
spread around the world first along the coasts and then inland
up the great rivers, exploiting the rich resources found in most
places where water meets land. It is an intriguing and persuasive
scenario.

AFRICA COLONIZES THE WORLD

The implications of this concept – which was initially violently
rejected by many palaeontologists and palaeoanthropologists but
which is now accepted by more and more scholars – are thought
provoking to say the least. Around 2 million years ago a first
group of ancestral hominids, *Homo erectus*, left Africa and spread
around the world. For almost 2 million years, descendants of those
hominids, our close relatives, very much closer to us than modern
chimpanzees, lived throughout the connected land masses of
Africa, Europe and Asia. But having once conquered the world,
within a mere 100,000 years or so, in the period from about 130,000
years to about 30,000 years ago, all the hominids descended from
the first outward migration from Africa had gone. What happened
to them?

There are only three broad classes of explanation which could
conceivably fit the facts. The first is that *Homo erectus, Homo
neanderthalensis* and other local variants of *Homo*, products of
the first migration, interbred with *Homo sapiens*, products of the
second migration, and thus our modern genes are derived from all
these sources. The second is that there was little or no interbreeding
and relatively little direct contact but, because of competition for
resources, *Homo erectus, Homo neanderthalensis* and the others
simply could not survive and died out. The third is that we
murdered our close relatives in warfare and that is why we spread

so fast and so far and were so successful within only a few thousand years.

There can be no final word as yet concerning the choice between these three hypotheses, but the first looks increasingly unlikely. There are two strong pieces of evidence. There is simply not enough genetic diversity in the mitochondrial, Y-chromosome or autosomal DNA in modern humans to allow for any contributions from populations descended from the first migration who lived for so long outside Africa. Also, although only two fragments of mitochondrial DNA have been isolated from Neanderthal bones and analysed with sufficient rigour, the differences between modern human mitochondrial DNA and Neanderthal DNA are so great that it is highly unlikely that Neanderthals contributed anything to the modern human genome. Our immediate ancestors probably interbred little with either *Homo erectus* or the Neanderthals.

We are therefore left with the other two possibilities. Starkly stated, the choice is between 'Did they die?' or 'Did we kill them?' It would indicate a gentler, more hopeful side to modern humans if they died simply because they couldn't compete for food and other resources. But I am afraid that personally I find that difficult to believe. I do not think that the elimination would have been so complete, or that there would have been *no* ecological niches where *Homo erectus* and *Homo neanderthalensis* would have been able to survive successfully alongside *Homo sapiens*. Human myth and history, from the earliest stories of the Old Testament and of Egypt to the bloody history of the twentieth century, tell an all too consistent story. Humans can be induced to hate those who differ only slightly from themselves, and that hatred often turns to murder and genocide. My own gloomy conclusion is that we killed our closest relatives and eliminated them from the earth.

But as *Homo erectus* and *Homo neanderthalensis* were being eliminated, the other breaks which were being made with the past were astounding! Instead of the glacial rate of change and worldwide cultural similarity which had characterized the preceding 2 million years, we now see rapid development in culture. Instead of transcontinental uniformity, we see the emergence of differences between people in one river valley and the next.

Something happened to the human brain to make it more creative, to make its activities more diverse, to make it less satisfied with what was, to have visions of what might be and to act upon those visions.

We cannot know the precise dates of this intellectual and creative revolution, but some time during this period we also see the emergence of music, of religion, of art and of increasingly complex technologies. Corpses are carefully buried in standardized postures and decorated with red ochre. Flutes made from the leg bones of birds are found and, towards the end of the period around 30–40,000 years ago, the astonishing cave paintings like those discovered by Maria de Sautuola appear. Technical skills are evident in the enormous range of new artefacts made not just of stone, but of wood, of bone, of antlers and perhaps of fibre. And the tools are no longer simple, made of one material only. Stone is bound or glued to wood or bone: complexity, diversity and specialization of tools for particular tasks becomes the norm. Something remarkable has happened to the human mind. It is not related to any change in brain size because that actually decreased slightly. What could it possibly be?

I do not believe that this problem is inaccessible to investigation. On the contrary, I think that we can make rather precise guesses about what might have happened. The key clues come from our increasing understanding of that strange and terrible disease which we call schizophrenia, and its associated conditions of dyslexia, schizotypy and bipolar (manic-depressive) illness.

FROM 20,000 YEARS AGO TO THE PRESENT

During this time there have been two broad changes of over-whelming cultural importance. As far as we are aware, 20,000 years ago, all humans lived in bands of perhaps twenty to at most 200 individuals. These groups had no fixed abodes, although they tended to live by the sea or near watercourses where various types of food would be more plentiful. They probably collected all their food from the wild, utilizing plants with their seeds and tubers, fruits and fresh leaves, insects and grubs, eggs, water life, and they probably hunted, trapped or scavenged animals. But over the next 10,000 years, particularly in the region of the Middle East known as the Fertile Crescent, people began deliberately to plant gathered seeds, to harvest the resulting crops and to select the seeds from the best plants for sowing again.

By 5000 years ago the hunter-gatherer way of life was in rapid retreat, although it persisted in pockets in the Arctic and the far north of America, Europe and Asia, in the Amazon, in Africa, in the islands of the Indian and Pacific Oceans, and in Australia. For the great majority of people, however, the bulk of their food began to come from crops and domesticated animals, with hunting largely a pastime for the aristocracy. Still the majority of people lived on the land and a minority in towns and villages; most people got their food from their immediate environment; but by this time large urban centres were beginning to appear in the valleys of the Nile, Tigris, Euphrates and Indus, and on Mediterranean islands like Crete.

Over the next 5000 years, although there was a gradual rise in the populations of cities, and although cities became culturally and militarily dominant, most people remained in the countryside. It was not until the eighteenth and nineteenth centuries that the last great change began: the Industrial Revolution, which dramatically shifted people to the cities, depopulated the countryside and caused another massive alteration in dietary practices.

From this abbreviated history, we will be able to derive clues that allow us to draw firm conclusions about what factors really did make us human. The history of our bodies is closely intertwined with the history of our minds. In both, disorders which we now describe as mental or developmental played a crucial role. As with most intellectual journeys, the way in which I came to this conclusion was convoluted.

4

HOW ADAM AND EVE GOT THEIR BRAINS

UNTIL ABOUT 1960, THE STUDY OF HUMAN EVOLUTION WAS A relative backwater. The few academics involved fought some ferocious and occasionally hilarious wars, but this was nothing particularly extraordinary in the scholarly world.

Then two things happened. Louis and Mary Leakey discovered a remarkable new fossil at the Olduvai Gorge in Tanzania, a fossil which they proclaimed as a human ancestor. This led to support from the National Geographic Society of the USA and an enormous increase in interest in human origins. There also burst on the scene an energetic non-academic: Robert Ardrey, an American journalist and playwright, became captivated by Africa. In particular he was enthralled by the findings of a South African palaeoanatomist, Raymond Dart. He elaborated on Dart's work and on East African findings by Louis Leakey in a highly imagina-tive way and produced a series of bestselling books about human evolution, including *African Genesis, The Territorial Imperative* and *The Social Contract*. These books captured the imagination of the public and of many professionals, while arousing the ire but also the responsive creativity of many experts in the field. He and the Leakeys helped to set in motion a series of events which has not yet run its course.

THE MECHANISMS OF EVOLUTION

In evolution the race goes to those varieties of organism which survive and reproduce themselves in adequate numbers. That is what survival of the 'fittest' means: not the cleverest, nor those who can run fastest, nor those who can hunt best, although all are valuable accomplishments, but those who can reproduce most effectively and leave most living descendants. When environmental conditions are stable there is a tendency for varieties of organisms also to be stable and to go on reproducing themselves successfully. But if environmental conditions change, then the properties of an organism which allowed it to be successful under the previous set of conditions may no longer be quite right. It may be more difficult than before to reproduce successfully. The individual organisms, and the groups to which they belong, may become extinct.

But in any real population, no two individuals (other than identical twins, triplets, etc.) are exactly the same. This is because their complement of DNA is individual and differs somewhat from everyone else's DNA. One can observe humans, dogs, cats, even rabbits and hamsters, or indeed any other species, and it is obvious that there is a great deal of individual variation in behaviour and structure. Such variation arises from past mutations, which lead to DNA differences. This means that the effectiveness of many bodily functions in different individuals is not identical. A change in environment may favour individuals with one particular set of variations. Those individuals will survive and reproduce successfully in the new situation. Individuals without that variation set will be less successful. Eventually there will be a change in the nature of the species such that the newly favoured type of individual becomes dominant, while the old dominant variety dies out or becomes less numerous.

Here is a real example relevant to the theme of this book. Suppose that for thousands of years conditions of living were favourable for a particular hominid variety. Suppose also that food was abundant and available all the year, for example in an environment along the banks of a freely flowing river. Suppose then that a variant mutation occurred in one individual among these hominids, such that in times of plenty large amounts of fat were stored in the body. That mutation was then passed on to descendants, all of whom tended to accumulate fat.

In times of plenty such a mutation would convey no advantage. It might even be a disadvantage, with accumulation of fat slowing down those individuals in their hunt for food. Such slowing down would not matter very much so long as plenty of food was available, but suppose conditions changed. Suppose the climate altered and the river, instead of flowing freely all year round, dried up for three or four months, leading to a drastic reduction in the food supply during that period. Suddenly, the people accumulating fat in times of plenty would have an advantage over their slim fellows. As food became scarce, many of the 'normal' people would die. In contrast, the people who had become fat would be much more able to withstand the time of shortage and would survive. Over several such cycles the fat variants among those people would eventually replace the thin ones. This 'thrifty gene hypothesis' is believed to be part of the way in which our species developed its tendency to grow fat and to develop diabetes. It had a major survival advantage in a past when food supply was variable and uncertain. Now, in environments where year-round food is over-abundant, the survival advantage of the past may become a disadvantage.

This represents one way in which evolution may take place. During a time of stability, mutations may occur which change the functioning of some individuals but which do not confer any particular advantage or disadvantage. The variety or the species does not change. There is a variability of genetic characteristics but none is particularly favoured. Then a change takes place in the environment which confers a real advantage on one of these mutations. As a result, the carriers of that mutation survive and multiply while the non-carriers decline and eventually their line may die out. In this example, the pressure to change comes from the environment. Charles Darwin had no knowledge of genes and mutations and so in his writings, and in the writings of many of his modern followers, all the emphasis is on the selective pressure of the environment. There is much less about the sources of variation without which environmental selective pressure would be totally ineffective.

But evolutionary change *cannot* occur without the availability of an appropriate advantageous variety to be selected. There are two sides to the equation which are necessary for change: the environmental conditions must alter, but there must also be available novel varieties which can be selected by the new conditions. In the above example of periodic starvation, the primary drive for hominid change came from environmental change. But that alone is not a sufficient condition for evolution into a new variety or species. The environmental challenge *must* be matched by a pre-existing genetic response, a variation or mutation. This pre-existing mutation, of neutral effect in the previous environment, suddenly becomes important and useful when the environment changes. One term which has been applied to variations which are of little or no value when they occur, but which accidentally prepare the organism for some future environmental challenge, is 'exaptation'.

In another type of scenario, the genetic mutation itself may be the factor driving the change. Suppose a population of foxes lives in the Arctic but cannot survive further north of a particular latitude because their fur is not adequate against the cold. That population cannot then take advantage of a particularly abundant northern supply of food. Suppose then that in a particular fox a mutation occurs which doubles the thickness of the fur. That mutation will enable the fox and its descendants to penetrate geographical areas which had previously been too cold for survival. The new variety of fox will be able to occupy a northern range where previously foxes had been unable to live. This new variety will be able to exploit the rich food source and expand its numbers dramatically. There has been no environmental change, but a mutation has allowed the emergence of a new variety which has enabled colonization of previously inhospitable geography. As will be seen later, I suspect that this type of mutation had a much larger role in recent human evolution than has hitherto been believed.

In both these scenarios, however, the two elements must be present. There must be an environmental challenge, a change to an existing environment in the first example, or a nearby unoccupied environment in the second. Equally, there must be a genetic response or pre-response – a pre-existing variation or exaptation which enabled an appropriate response to an environmental change in the first case, or a new variation which allowed effective colonization of a previously inhospitable environment in the second.

Change *always* requires both factors – the environmental challenge and the genetic response. Since Robert Ardrey's books appeared, almost all attempts to explain recent human evolution have concentrated on the environmental challenge and have given little or no thought to the precise nature of the genetic response. They have described the challenge in very great detail: they have then said, in effect, 'and then a miracle occurred'. Somehow, without specifying a precise mechanism, the response came from nowhere and the pre-human became adapted to overcome the new challenge. The thesis of this book is that *both* the challenge and the precise biochemical nature of the response are important. In contrast to the nature of the challenge which made us human, but which can never be known with certainty, the nature of the response is readily open to reasoned evaluation using evidence which can realistically be obtained. We are close to understanding the changes which made us human.

THE ENVIRONMENTAL CHALLENGES

The basic concept which has been proposed to explain the later stages of human evolution, described in various ways in a profusion of professional and popular writing over the past forty years, has been that our ancestral line, but not closely related lines, faced one or more of a number of specific environmental challenges. The precise nature of the challenge then somehow evoked an appropriate, and seemingly inevitable, genetic and biochemical response. Repeatedly it has been argued that the uniqueness of the pre-human line, as opposed to the closely related primate and hominid lines which failed to give rise to humans, was in the precise and unique nature of the environmental challenge. All the drive to adapt, it has been argued, comes from the challenge: none comes from the genetic change which is invariably seen as merely an inevitable consequence of that challenge. I think this view is fundamentally wrong: genetic change, which occurred without environmental challenge but which then allowed new environments to be exploited, played a key role.

It is now broadly accepted by most experts that our ancestors in the period 5–10 million years ago either lived in the forest like modern-day gorillas, orang-utans or bonobo chimpanzees, or in wooded, partially open areas like 'common' chimpanzees. These ancestors had relatively small brains and were wholly vegetarian, as are gorillas, or were substantially vegetarian but not infrequently ate non-vegetarian food items such as insects, grubs or small animals, as do modern chimpanzees. Most predominantly vegetarian animals, including all modern great apes, have long, bulky digestive tracts, because vegetable foods are difficult to digest. Our early ancestors were similar. As do modern primates, our ancestors occasionally stood and walked on two legs, although still spending much time in trees. When on the ground, they probably knuckle-walked on four limbs like modern chimpanzees.

The problem is how we got here from there. What made us stand upright? Why did we lose much of our gastrointestinal tract (which is now much shorter than great apes')? What made us lose our body hair? How did we gain our subcutaneous fat? Above all, how did we acquire our large, creative brains with their capacities for symbolic thought, language and technical and artistic skills? The answers that have been given rely on the idea that at each stage there must have been an environmental challenge unique and specific to our ancestral line which provoked in some mysterious and unspecified way a unique evolutionary response.

What then are these unique environmental challenges, which, if the standard arguments are correct, lead to large, creative brains? With rare exceptions, the proposals do not distinguish carefully between a large brain and a creative brain, although as we shall see later this distinction is crucial. The challenges can be broadly grouped into categories, although there are many sub-categories and mixed categories. Each individual author would no doubt vigorously contest the validity of my classification. However, my broad categories are:

1. The savanna hypothesis, with its sub-hypotheses of hunting, food-sourcing and home bases.

2. The group-size hypothesis, with its sub-hypotheses of communication and of individual identification and status.

3. The language hypothesis.

4. The mate-choice hypothesis.

None of these is entirely independent of the others. When fleshed out, most of the concepts incorporate limited or even extensive elements of the others. All of them, however, regard a unique and specific pre-human environment, different from environments to which closely related species or varieties of primates were exposed, as the key factor in the production of unique human beings. The genetic responses are seen as inevitable consequences of these challenges. It is almost as though the originators of the hypotheses exhaust themselves by their intellectual efforts to identify the unique challenge. Rather than putting equal effort into identifying the precise nature of the genetic response, their inclination is to say, 'This unique challenge created a unique situation, and then a miracle occurred: brains grew bigger and more creative in response to the challenge, and uniquely human people resulted.' The same sort of reasoning is applied to all the other uniquely human features. Let's examine these four categories of explanation in more detail.

THE SAVANNA AND HUNTING

It is almost certain that we descended from an ape who, like almost all other primates, was predominantly but not entirely vegetarian. Insects, grubs and other small creatures were probably consumed regularly, opportunistic finds like the helpless young of other creatures were occasionally eaten and sometimes, as with chimpanzees, there were organized hunts often led by a particular individual. The importance of individual males in both initiating hunts and achieving successful conclusions has been well documented in modern chimpanzees and baboons. Craig Stanford, who worked with Jane Goodall in the famous Gombe Reserve in Tanzania, has described monkey hunts by chimpanzees, in which the lead male will catch a monkey, crack open its skull and eat the brain. The brain is mostly fat and the hunger for fat is something which is evident in all modern descriptions of hunter-gatherer societies.

But somewhere between about 3 and 2 million years ago our diets changed substantially. The evidence is considerable. Teeth and jaws became more typical of meat eaters or omnivores than vegetarians. Our gut size became much smaller, as is typical of carnivores, because the food is more digestible and so we do not need such a long and large gastrointestinal tract. We know this because although guts are not fossilized, thoracic bones are. In vegetarian primates the gut occupies a large part of the thorax, which has the shape of a pyramid with an expanded base to accommodate the gut. Lucy had a thorax like this. As the gut becomes smaller, so the base of the pyramid narrows and the thorax becomes more cylindrical. Certainly by the time that Turkana Boy was alive, we clearly have gastrointestinal tracts which are closer to modern humans' than to great apes'. The thorax of Turkana Boy is much more cylindrical than that of Lucy. We are also aware of the innumerable archaeological sites, such as those in Ethiopia 2.5 million years ago, where there is unequivocal evidence of butchered animal bones, some deliberately fractured to extract the fatty marrow. Again the hunger for fat is evident. While there is no doubt that sometimes we scavenged carcasses killed by others, the predominance of evidence suggests that the majority of those animals were killed by us for food.

We can definitely identify two times at which we know the hominid diet was predominantly not vegetable. The Turkana female *Homo erectus*, 1.6 million years ago, suffered from hyper-vitaminosis A. This is not possible with a diet predominantly of vegetable origin, or even with a diet predominantly of land herbivores. Only animals or birds at the top of the aquatic food chain, or the top land predators, or the grubs of certain insects contain enough vitamin A to generate skeletal hypervitaminosis. I think it unlikely that she was mainly eating the livers of top land predators, but the idea that she was eating grubs, birds, reptiles and small mammals at the top of the aquatic food chain seems eminently feasible.

The second fixed point depends on isotopic analysis of bones, which allows an estimation of whether the diet consisted mainly of forest or grassland vegetables or of animal food. The analyses are not easy and require a reasonable amount of well-preserved bone to be reliable. Such bone is available from Neanderthals living perhaps 0.3 million years ago and the results are unequivocal. Neanderthals were top predators with the great bulk of their food being of non-vegetable origin.

So there really can be little doubt that hunting and the consumption of non-vegetarian food became characteristic of our hominid ancestors and relatives. Where did this hunting occur? For reasons which are not entirely clear, the idea has grown up that it first took place in the open savanna and that we are a savanna species. Robert Ardrey's expressive writing, the present location of many modern sites where human fossils have been found, and the possible advantages of walking upright (bipedalism) for a savanna life may all have been factors. However, for three main reasons I find the savanna hypothesis untenable, at least in its simple form. First, virtually all hominid remains are found in places which, when the hominid died, were beside a lake or a river, even though now the place may be savanna-like. Second, we are a species which is profligate with water, in contrast to all modern savanna species. Unlike true savanna animals, we cannot concentrate our urine well and so must expend large amounts of water to excrete our waste products. Even more important, our cooling system depends on the pouring out of large amounts of sweat: when exercising in a hot open environment we can lose as much as 2 litres an hour. Given the very limited amounts of water, if any, that could be carried 2–4 million years ago, our ancestors must have spent almost all their time within at most 24 hours of abundant water.

Finally, as anyone who has tried it even with modern vehicles and rifles knows, savanna hunting is not easy and it is wildly unlikely that we ever relied upon it for our food supply. The animals are dispersed, wary and can see anyone approaching from miles away.

When hunting became important it seems much more likely that it began with small animals and in the marginal aquatic environment where most hominid fossils have been found. At the margins of lakes and rivers there are usually a great many large and small hunting quarries. There are also many more opportunities for concealment, allowing the final hunt to be carried out at closer range than is possible in the savanna. I believe that hunting was indeed important for hominids, but that two variations from the usual themes better express the reality. The first is that small and very small creatures, from small antelopes and turtles down to insects and grubs, were probably much more important than has been assumed. The second is that most hunting took place not in the open savanna but on the margins of lakes and rivers.

The hunting/savanna hypothesis proposes in general terms that the need to be cooperative and organized in a hunt involves complex cognitive functions. These are required for planning, stalking, coordinating and communicating if a hunt is to be successful. The need for such complex cognition created a selective pressure which led to the development of those variations in brain, muscle and nervous-system function which promoted hunting success. As a consequence of these needs, the brain expanded and became more effective in thinking. Precisely how this change in brain structure and function occurred is never defined.

Hunting and the related cultures are complex activities and it is undoubtedly true that a large and creative brain would have been essential for their successful performance. But did the need to hunt bring forth that large and creative brain, and if so, how? Or did a large and creative brain allow the emergence of the skills needed to hunt? Would not hunting skills have been valuable to most hominids around at that time? How is it that the same pressure produced a hunting response in one primate/pre-human group but not in the others? Given the likelihood that all were exposed to much the same pressures, how did our pre-human line generate differential responses?

My proposal is different. The brain is an organ which is mostly made of fat and, as Leslie Aiello and colleagues have emphasized, requires a lot of energy to run. Although by weight it is only about 2 per cent of the body, it uses about 20 per cent of the energy. I believe that the rich food supplies of the aquatic/marginal environment, together with mutations in lipid metabolism which enabled the brain to change and become more effective, were the prime causes which allowed the development of hunting and all its associated skills. These food supplies also allowed our guts to become smaller as our brain grew, as is so well described by Aiello. Once the relevant mutations were in place, selective pressures may well have honed them and made them more effective, in turn leading to the first great surge in human development and the transitions from *Australopithecines*, first to *Homo habilis*, then to *Homo erectus*.

All the other hypotheses of the drives behind human evolution are in a sense variants of the hunting/savanna story. They describe complex activities which could not be carried out without a large and effective brain. They then argue that, by mechanisms which are never precisely defined, the need to perform such activities somehow called forth that large and effective brain.

THE HOME BASE

Again, between 2 and 3 million years ago, there begins to be evidence that some hominid bands may have started to develop home bases to which they regularly returned. There are accumulations of bones and artefacts which suggest regular use of specific locations. Of course, many animals have home bases, so there is nothing particularly surprising about that. But the argument goes that at this point human home bases began to be more than a badger sett or a rabbit warren. They were places where artefacts of value were kept. They were places of safety which to some degree could be defended against attack. They were places where females and infants could be left in modest comfort while the males ranged far and wide, hunting and scavenging. In short, they represented the beginnings of the universal modern human concept of home.

Once more the assumption is that the complex cognitive functions required to develop, operate and sustain the home base in some way called forth the large brain, which would allow these functions to be performed effectively. Again no precise mechanisms are proposed which would enable this to happen. My view, once again, is that the cognitive brain changes came first and as a result we became much more able to make use of a successful home-base strategy.

GROUP SIZE

Group size tends to be limited in apes and monkeys to between twenty and a hundred individuals. Groups larger than this are rare, and when they do grow bigger they invariably split into smaller groups. It is a reasonable hypothesis that group size is limited by the need to know something about each individual and the relationships between the various individuals. It is stating the obvious to assert that the larger the social group, the more brain power will be required to operate effectively in that group. This is, of course, only true of animals where complex social interactions with many other individuals are of great importance. Where the required interactions are simple and limited, creatures whose brain power is not large, like ants, birds and fish, may be able to sustain groups containing very large numbers.

Nevertheless, if there is to be complex and variable interaction between individuals, the larger the group the more difficult it will be to maintain successful relationships. There is therefore no sensible argument against the idea that growth in the size of the average human group would require growth in the size and complexity of function of the human brain. But could such a need *drive* brain growth and, if so, by what mechanism? Or could brain growth provide the intellectual power needed to allow group size to grow? Again, it is the latter explanation that I favour, for reasons which will be described later.

LANGUAGE

Many commentators have emphasized that language may be the primary distinction between humans and pre-humans. It used to be said that tool-making distinguished humans. 'Man the toolmaker' was a famous concept of the first half of the twentieth century. However, that concept became progressively eroded as we learned more about the tool-making and tool-using capacities of chimpanzees, other primates, and even birds. Human tools may be much more complex, but no longer is it thought that there is a categorical distinction between humans and animals on the basis of tool-making and tool-using.

It may be that language will go the same way. Our perception that other species do not possess language may be a delusion, based on inadequate understanding. Nevertheless, as with tools, there is little doubt that human language is enormously more complex and is able to communicate not just facts but opinions, ideas and symbols. We can distinguish not just between water and fire but between ordinary water and holy water! Language is now the primary medium through which we conduct all our social affairs. The usefulness of a complex language is obvious.

Again, the view has been put forward that, because language was obviously valuable, and because language would be more feasible with a larger and more complex brain, in some way the need for language drove brain development. Complexity of brain was required, a miracle occurred, and that complexity was generated. Surprisingly little effort, however, has been put into the understanding of just what genetic and biochemical mechanisms may have generated the complexity.

A particular problem with language is that it requires the simultaneous development of devices for both transmitting and receiving, and also for remembering. For language to be important we must be able to speak, we must be able to listen and we must be able to remember what is said. Most modern theories of language seem to concentrate on one or the other but not all three. The key problem with speaking, as already mentioned, is that our ancestors used breathing, as do all other animals, solely for delivering air to their lungs to provide oxygen and allow the removal of carbon dioxide. But unlike all other animals, we now routinely use our breathing system to generate the strings of sounds which we call language. To speak while simultaneously fulfilling our need for oxygen we require very sophisticated brains for controlling our breathing and also for the complex sensory process of hearing, understanding and remembering long strings of sound. None of the language theorists has provided specific mechanisms by which all these skills were simultaneously acquired.

MATE CHOICE

Selection of who will reproduce to provide the next generation depends on two things. First, who will survive sufficiently long to be in a position to reproduce; and, second, who will be attractive enough to the opposite sex to allow their eggs or sperm to participate in forming fertilized eggs. The first process is sometimes called natural selection and the second is called sexual selection, but clearly the two are related.

However, the two may produce quite different results in practice, as Charles Darwin first realized and as many later commentators have noted. Natural selection chooses utilitarian characteristics which assist in keeping the individual alive until the time at which sexual maturity allows reproduction. Sexual selection occurs only at the time that such survival has been assured. And, as any modern male or female beyond the age of puberty is all too aware, sexual selection can be highly capricious. Both sexes may choose to mate with partners who have features which are not necessarily of immediate survival value. Beauty, loquaciousness, strength, bizarre behaviour and many other factors may all at various times be selected. Sometimes there may be a correlation between things which are sexually selected and physical survival probability. At other times the things selected appear to be actually counterproductive in the survival stakes. The bizarre tails of birds and fish, their dramatic colours as far from protective camouflage as can be imagined, the giant antlers and manes all seem to be something of a waste.

The husband and wife team Amotz and Avishag Zahavi has

proposed an ingenious solution to this problem. Their suggestion was initially regarded as heretical but is now widely supported. They argued that characteristics may be sexually selected not in spite of the fact that they are a survival handicap but *because* they are a survival handicap. They signal to the opposite sex – and in most cases this is a male signal to a female – 'I am so strong and such a good reproductive partner that I can survive and thrive in spite of the fact that I am wearing these bizarre colours or carrying around this absurd tail. So choose me because I am the very best quality there is.' Geoffrey Miller has recently expanded on this theme with great wit in his book *The Mating Game*. He has argued, in particular, that language developed because it was a sexually desirable feature. But even he has provided no mechanism for how sexual selection might specifically have generated change, nor for how sexual selection pressures could explain the many genetic features which make us human.

EVOLUTIONARY FAIRY TALES?

These concepts, and the many variants of them, are all evolutionary fairy tales, Kiplingesque just-so stories describing 'How Humans Got Their Brains'. The arguments between their proponents have generated enormous amounts of heat but little light. What is surprising is that most of the authors describe themselves as some variety of evolutionary biologist, yet they describe human evolution in terms which bear only a modest relationship to Darwinian concepts.

All the stories attempt to describe how the uniquely human brain might have evolved. They all argue that human uniqueness resulted from the unique nature of the pressure, whether it be hunting, home, group size, language or courtship. Unique pressures somehow evoked an appropriate response, the mechanism of which is rarely discussed, and certainly never in any detail. The precise details of the genetic changes which made us human are never specified and so the hypotheses are effectively un-testable and unprovable. These scenarios ignore several key concepts:

1. None of the pressures described is unique to humans, great apes or even primates. All species perform activities which would benefit from increased brain power. Alison Jolly's studies of lemurs in Madagascar have demonstrated that the social and other selective pressures which face them are remarkably similar to those which face humans, or chimpanzees or any other species. The need to find food, the need to know one's way around a territory, the need to maintain knowledge of the largest possible group of individuals, the need to communicate, the need to deal with predators, are universal. Not one of these pressures is uniquely pre-human.

2. Environmental pressures cannot of themselves *generate* a genetic response which leads to evolution to a particular end. What such pressures can do is *select* genetic responses which have occurred by spontaneous mutations and which are particularly favoured as a result of a particular environment. Without the favourable mutations, environmental pressures cannot produce change. If environmental pressure could call into being such favourable mutations, then all species would change in the same direction.

3. The uniqueness of humans therefore cannot reside in the uniqueness of the environmental pressure. Rather it must reside in the uniqueness of the genetic changes, the mutations, selected by such pressure. Yet, in comparison to the attention paid to the pressure, this genetic variation has hardly been considered. This is particularly surprising because the nature of the genetic response is readily accessible to investigation by techniques already available to us.

Even in principle, we will never be able to know with certainty what environmental pressures our pre-human ancestors faced. The sources of knowledge are too remote, too distorted and too fragmentary. They will always be susceptible to alternative explanation. We can make wonderful guesses and tell amazing stories which may capture our imagination and delight our need to know our origins, but we can never know whether or not the stories are true.

In contrast, the genetic changes which differentiated us from our ancestors, which gave us large and complex brains, together with hairless skin, subcutaneous fat, upright posture and small gastrointestinal tracts, are readily ascertainable by straightforward, relatively mundane science. Perhaps the certainty that these are things which can and will be known diminishes their appeal. But the twists in the tale are even more strange and alluring – at least in my view – than the just-so stories based on unique environmental pressures.

There are two rather obvious ways in which we can approach the problem of what turned pre-humans into humans, of what gave us our big, creative brains, our breasts and so on. The first is to study the factors which are involved in generating these things in modern human foetuses, infants and children. We actually know a great deal already about what makes infant brains grow, what makes our brains complex, what factors are associated with high creativity and a restless need for change, and what produces the appearance of subcutaneous fat. These factors are studied by embryologists, obstetricians, paediatricians, neurodevelopmental scientists, biochemists, psychologists and psychiatrists. A lot of information is already there, but for some reason is not well known to many evolutionary biologists.

The second approach is to use our knowledge that the chimpanzee is our closest living relative. We know with reasonable certainty that we had a common ancestor 5–7 million years ago. Since then the chimpanzee line has been evolving, producing differences between the modern chimpanzee and the common ancestor. Equally, we have been evolving, also producing a set of differences from our common ancestor.

The genetic differences between chimpanzees and humans are relatively small and will be identified with certainty over the next ten or twenty years. Some of these differences will be specific to the chimpanzee line and some to the human line. But by linking this genetic knowledge of differences between the two species with the biological knowledge of what makes our brains and sub-cutaneous fat grow and function, we should be able to construct a reasonably reliable picture of the crucial changes which made us human.

The rest of this book is devoted to identifying those changes. It is also the story of a personal odyssey which had its origins in Le Gros Clark's lectures in Oxford, in my early visits to Kenya and to Olorgesailie, and more specifically it is a story which began one afternoon in 1970 in the medical school at Chiromo in Nairobi.

5

BRAINS, BUTTOCKS AND BREASTS

I FELL IN LOVE WITH KENYA WHEN I WORKED THERE FOR FOUR months as a medical student. When I qualified as a doctor I regularly scanned the 'positions vacant' sections of the relevant journals for appropriate medical positions in East Africa. One day I saw an advertisement for foundation professors to help start a new medical school in Nairobi. I applied for and was offered the position of Professor of Medical Physiology and so began one of the most exciting and rewarding phases of my life.

One afternoon in the middle of the long vacation in 1970 I received a call from the US Ambassador. Mohamed Hyder, the Professor of Zoology, received a similar call. Could we organize an audience for a lecture by a distinguished American zoologist, Howard Bern, from the University of California at Berkeley? Mohamed and I conferred. Yes, we could do it. The students and most of the teaching staff were on holiday; we were the only academics around; but we ensured Howard's audience by collecting the cleaners, gardeners, catering and office staff into the main lecture theatre. Mohamed and I were the only two people who understood Howard's lecture and the only two to ask any questions. Howard was pleased by the turnout and seemed not to notice the subterfuge. Only ten years later, to his great amusement, did I tell him what had happened.

Howard's expertise was in prolactin, the hormone in women which makes breasts grow and produce milk. As a zoologist he was particularly interested in prolactin in fish. He and his colleagues had found that prolactin was the main hormone which regulates the ability of fish to deal with salt and water, and particularly to deal with movements, as in salmon and eels, between salt water and fresh water and back again.

Entranced by Howard's enthusiasm and by his findings, I began my own ten-year involvement with prolactin. My specialist training was in neuroendocrinology, the relationship between the brain and the hormonal system. Prolactin was a link in that system, being produced by the pituitary gland at the base of the brain in the middle of the head. Men produce as much prolactin as women but do not usually have breasts, so I wondered what their prolactin was doing. I started the investigation by injecting prolactin into myself and found that, just as in salmon, it helped to regulate the kidneys and to keep salt and water in balance, especially in difficult conditions. Moreover, I and the male colleagues into whom I injected the hormone developed a transient male version of premenstrual syndrome! We became irritable, puffy and had painful nipples!

My work with prolactin sparked three interests relevant to the theme of this book. First, I became interested in how ancient humans might have managed their salt and water economy in the East African climate and landscape. How could they have survived in such an apparently hot and dry environment? I was helped in this by my veterinary colleague, David Robertshaw, who was at the same time trying to understand how savanna animals coped with heat. Second, I became involved in schizophrenia research. Gwynneth Hemmings, the founder of the Schizophrenia Association of Great Britain, asked me to research further the effects of prolactin on human beings. All the anti-schizophrenic drugs then available stimulated prolactin secretion and Gwynneth suspected that it was involved in some of the effects and side-effects of these drugs on her members. She asked me to help in understanding these further.

Third, I became interested in fat. In my efforts to find out how prolactin worked, my colleagues and I found that in part it released from cell membranes substances called essential fatty acids (EFAs). These are like vitamins, fats we must eat because we cannot make them in our own bodies. I already knew quite a lot about EFAs because for three years as a Fellow of Magdalen College, Oxford, I was responsible for teaching biochemistry to medical students with my senior colleagues, Hugh Sinclair and Brian Lloyd. Hugh was the world authority on EFAs in humans, known for his then eccentric-seeming views that they were the key to understanding the degenerative diseases of humanity, diseases of the heart, the immune system and the brain. During those years at Magdalen, Hugh had drilled into me on every possible occasion the medical importance of EFAs. When I found that, in part, prolactin worked by mobilizing EFAs, I could therefore tap into considerable background knowledge.

From the date of Howard Bern's lecture in Nairobi, my professional life has been dominated by the themes emanating from my first work on prolactin, the adaptation of humans to their environment, schizophrenia and other serious mental illnesses, and fat. This chapter is about fat.

FAT AND CHIMPANZEES

When watching a group of chimpanzees at the zoo, few visitors would think that some of the most important differences between apes and humans depend on fat. Fat has such a negative image in our society that the concept that it may have been crucial in human development seems bizarre. Bizarre or not, it is also true.

Children looking at chimpanzees frequently embarrass their parents by staring at the anal and genital regions of the animals. These are enormously more prominent than in humans in both the males and females. And that is not just a matter of clothing. It is particularly due to fat.

In humans the anogenital region is to a large extent concealed by the large accumulation of fat in the buttocks and the (usually) smaller accumulation in the lower abdomen and thighs. While it is true that the female genitalia in chimpanzees are much more prominent than in humans, particularly during the period of sexual receptivity at oestrus, at least part of that prominence is due to the lack of fat. The obviousness of the anal region in both chimpanzee sexes is almost entirely due to lack of fat.

Children will often say that chimpanzees look 'skinny' and that is literally true. Their skin seems to hang in wrinkles and folds, and their body contours generally lack the smoothness seen in humans. This is because chimpanzees lack the thick layer of fat beneath the skin which is so important in giving the human body its contours. Nowhere is this more obvious than in the breasts.

Contrary to common belief, the human breast does not consist mostly of glandular tissue for the secretion of milk. Glandular tissue is present, but it often makes up quite a small proportion of the whole organ. It is the fat which gives the breast its overall shape. The amount of glandular tissue shows much less variability than the amount of fatty (adipose) tissue. This is emphasized by the fact that women with apparently small breasts are usually just as good at breastfeeding as those who are more generously endowed. The fears of small-breasted women that they may be unable to feed a baby properly are almost always unjustified.

In contrast, the chimpanzee breast consists almost entirely of glandular tissue. In the non-pregnant, non-lactating state, the breast is little more than a flap of skin over the underlying resting glands. These grow somewhat during pregnancy and lactation but never achieve the rounded state of the human breast.

The most surprising organ in which fat is important is the brain. If asked what the brain is made of, a few people might be knowledgeable enough to say mostly water, which is true. But if asked to name the next most important non-water component by weight, very few would say fat. Yet fat it is. Around 60 per cent of the non-aqueous material of the brain is fat. Humans have bigger heads than chimpanzees because their heads are full of fat.

HOW DOES FAT GET INTO THE TISSUES?

One thing is obvious from these simple observations. Humans must be different from chimpanzees in the way that they accumulate fat beneath the skin (especially in the buttocks and breasts) and in the brain. How does this fat get there? Our understanding of this reveals at least some of the genetic differences between humans and chimpanzees.

In general, fat comes from two sources. Much can be made in the body, mostly in the liver, from other substances, such as proteins and carbohydrates. Fat can also come directly from food. There are some special types of fat which *must*, like vitamins, come from food because they cannot be made by our own bodies. These special types of fats, the essential fatty acids (EFAs), are particularly important in the brain. They make up about 20 per cent of the dry weight of the brain.

The immediate source of fat for subcutaneous tissues and the brain is the blood. Both must be able to remove fat from the blood if they are to accumulate it.

Fat in the blood is carried in two main ways. As everyone knows, oil and water do not mix. Chemically, fat and oil are the same category of substance and so the fat does not simply dissolve in the water of the blood. It has to be carried.

The first method of transport is by being attached to a protein, albumin. Albumin readily dissolves in the blood and is the most important single protein in the plasma, the pale straw-coloured liquid part of the blood in which the red and white cells are suspended. But albumin can also link itself to types of fat known as fatty acids, which hitch a ride by becoming attached to the albumin and are transported in the blood in this way.

The other method of transporting fat depends on another group of proteins known as apolipoproteins. These also carry fatty particles around in the blood. In this case the fatty particles are not fatty acids themselves but more complex fats called triglycerides, cholesterol esters or phospholipids. The apolipoproteins link with the fat to form what are known as lipoprotein particles, globules of fat and protein which can float in the blood.

Most of the fat in the blood is therefore transported in the form of albumin or lipoproteins. The subcutaneous tissues and the brain must somehow get hold of this fat. In order to understand how this happens it is necessary to make a short diversion into the field of fat chemistry.

THE CHEMISTRY OF FATS

Fats in the body are usually in the form of relatively complex molecules which are put together from a series of simpler building blocks. The most important of these building blocks are:

1. **Glycerol.** Known commonly as glycerine, this is a sticky, sweetish liquid sometimes still used to help dissolve earwax. Each glycerol molecule is made of a chain of three carbon atoms, know as Sn1, Sn2 and Sn3. In glycerol itself, what is known as a hydroxyl group (a complex of hydrogen and oxygen) is attached to each of the three carbon atoms.

2. **Fatty acids.** Fatty acids consist of strings of carbon atoms linked together. Each carbon atom has four attachment points which may be linked to other carbon atoms or to other substances. In the common fatty acids, most of the carbon atoms are attached to the next carbon atom by a single attachment on each side (a so-called single bond). A few of the attachments between carbon atoms involve two attachment points (so-called double bonds). The other attachment points are linked to hydrogen atoms, except at one end where there is a so-called carboxylic acid group with the properties of a weak acid, which is why the fatty acids have been given their name. The fatty acids therefore consist of strings of carbon atoms, with hydrogen atoms taking up all the spare linking points, and an acidic component at one end. There are large numbers of different fatty acids with different properties depending on the numbers of carbon atoms in the chain, the numbers of those carbon atoms linked by double bonds and the exact positions of those double bonds. Fatty acids with no double bonds are called saturated, those with two or more are called polyunsaturated and those polyunsaturated fatty acids with four or more double bonds are called highly unsaturated. Each type of fatty acid has different chemical properties and performs a

particular function. As we shall see, these different structures may have had crucial importance for human evolution. The brain must have fat and in particular requires two highly unsaturated fatty acids (HUFAs), which have very specific functions. It is much easier to obtain these two special fatty acids from animal than from vegetable sources. Bone marrow and brain can be especially rich in these key HUFAs. Perhaps this is why hunting, and why smashing bones to get at the fat inside, became important in human evolution.

3. **Cholesterol**. To read popular articles about cholesterol and heart disease one would think that cholesterol was the worst form of molecule that anyone could be exposed to. In fact, it is vital to life in general and to the function of the brain in particular. It is harmful only when it gets into the wrong places in excessive amounts: the walls of large arteries can be such places. But in general cholesterol is essential for brain development. Some cholesterol is made in the body, but some comes from food. Again, animal sources are important, particularly for the growing brain, which is one of the reasons why milk, which contains cholesterol, is important in the diet of infants.

4. **Phosphorus**. This is a highly reactive element which burns fiercely, and is perhaps best known to the public as a component of incendiary bombs and shells. But phosphorus is an essential component of a particular type of fat called, not surprisingly, a phospholipid. Like cholesterol, in the right place phosphorus is essential to life.

5. **Choline, ethanolamine, serine and inositol**. These are highly water-soluble molecules which are found in phospholipids attached to the phosphorus atom. They play important roles in the brain.

PUTTING THINGS TOGETHER:
COMPLEX LIPIDS

The various components of lipids mentioned above are not usually found alone in the body. They are mostly linked in various ways to form complex lipids which have hugely variable properties, depending on their precise chemical composition. Some are solid, rather like candle grease; others are rather sticky fluids; others flow like light oils. Some are soluble only in other oily substances and cannot dissolve in water under any circumstances. Others may dissolve both in oily materials and in water to a limited degree. Yet others, like the phospholipids, have one end of a molecule which dissolves easily in oils and another end which dissolves easily in water. Such molecules are found where an oily compartment meets a watery compartment, or where two watery compartments of the body need to be kept separate.

The main types of complex lipids are:

1. **Cholesterol esters**. These consist of one molecule of cholesterol linked to one molecule of a fatty acid. They are found in cell membranes and are also transported in the blood. Their properties depend to a large degree on the precise nature of the fatty acid component.

2. **Triglycerides**. Most young males are passionately devoted to triglycerides without knowing it. Triglycerides are what give the female breast and backside their characteristic shapes. Triglycerides are the main form in which fat is stored in the body, beneath the skin and in the abdomen. Triglycerides therefore represent two very different aspects of the human body: a delight when they are in the right place and the right amount, but a dismaying ugliness when too much accumulates.

    Triglycerides are simple in structure. Each has a glycerol backbone with three fatty acids attached to it. The fatty acids make the triglycerides completely insoluble in water, so they have to be carried around in the blood attached to apolipoproteins, making particles of what are called lipoproteins. The texture and properties of triglycerides can vary from solid to highly liquid.

Triglycerides containing mainly saturated fatty acids tend to be towards the solid end, like butter, while those containing mainly unsaturated fatty acids are liquid oils. The right mix in the subcutaneous fat, breasts and backsides gives that texture which can be so appealing; the wrong mix in the wrong amounts helps to produce cellulite.

3. **Phospholipids.** These are the most complex of the complex lipids and their properties and variations make them absolutely vital to life. Wherever two body microcompartments need separating, there you will find phospholipids. The body consists of cells, and the intracellular compartment must be kept separate from the extracellular compartment. This is achieved by the phospholipids of the cell membrane. Within each cell there are many separate compartments, known as organelles: these are used for generating energy; for making proteins; for secreting materials; for degrading waste; and for holding chemicals needed to communicate with other cells. All these compartments are divided off from the rest of the cell by phospholipids. In particular, each nerve cell of the brain has scores, hundreds and sometimes thousands or even millions of protrusions, known as axons and dendrites, which send messages from one part of the brain to another. These axons and dendrites are composed of phospholipids: the little packets, or vesicles, of chemicals which they contain and which are used for communication are also made of phospholipids which wrap up the communication chemicals in tiny bags. The richness of brain connectivity, and thus intelligence and creativity, is entirely dependent on phospholipids. Recently, genetic engineering of mice has provided very direct evidence that this is true, as will be discussed later. A single change in phospholipid biochemistry can add 50 points to your IQ.

The basic structure of a phospholipid is not that dissimilar from a triglyceride. There is the same carbon glycerol backbone. There are also fatty acids attached to the Sn1 and Sn2 carbon atoms. It is the third carbon atom which is different. Instead of a fatty acid there is a phosphorus atom. And on the other side of the phosphorus is one of four possible components known as head groups: choline, inositol, serine or ethanolamine.

Thus a phospholipid is a two-faced molecule. One end, the end with two fatty acids, likes fats and hates water: it is said to be lipophilic. The other end, the head group attached to the phosphorus, loves water and hates fats: it is said to be hydrophilic. If one has a situation where there is a layer of oil and a layer of water – as happens when mixing olive oil and vinegar for a salad dressing – phospholipid molecules added to the mix will all arrange themselves so that the fatty tails are sticking into the oil and the head groups are sticking into the water. If phospholipids are put into water, their head groups are happy, but the only lipophilic bits to be found are on other phospholipids. As a result, the phospholipids automatically form themselves into two layered sheets, with the two sets of fatty tails pointing towards each other and the two sets of head groups facing the water. Flat sheets of phospholipid are unstable, so what usually happens is that the phospholipids form spheres of various sizes, with water inside and outside and a double layer (bilayer) of phospholipid molecules separating the two. That is how cells and subcellular compartments are made. Each consists of a phospholipid bilayer with a fatty acid core separating two sets of water-facing head groups.

GETTING FATTY ACIDS FROM THE BLOOD TO THE TISSUES

The brain consists mostly of phospholipids. The subcutaneous fat contains mostly triglycerides. Both types of fat are rich in fatty acids, about 90 per cent of the weight in the case of the triglyceride and 60–70 per cent in the case of the phospholipids. If breasts, buttocks and brains are to grow, it is vital that they should be able to accumulate fatty acids effectively. Brains require the special types of fatty acids known as HUFAs.

Since chimpanzees have little or no subcutaneous triglyceride, and since their brains are much smaller than ours, it may well be that mechanisms for getting fatty acids into tissues are key candidates for genetic differences between the species. In order for pre-human and human brains to grow, we must have developed effective dietary and biochemical methods for getting fat from the environment to inside our heads.

There are only six possible classes of component which play a role in moving fatty acids from the blood to the tissues. Each consists of a small family of proteins. There must be differences between humans and chimpanzees in one or more of these proteins which account for the species differences in the accumulation of fat in the brain and subcutaneous tissues:

1. **The albumins.** These are the water-soluble proteins found in the blood which bind free fatty acids and carry them around.

2. **The apolipoproteins.** These are the other group of blood proteins important in fat transport. They hold together in the blood the complex fat particles which contain mostly triglycerides, with smaller amounts of cholesterol esters and phospholipids.

3. **Lipoprotein lipase.** This is an enzyme which is found in the lining of all blood vessels. As the lipoproteins float by, the enzyme attacks them to split off the fatty acids which can then enter the tissues. Without lipoprotein lipase, the lipoproteins, like rejected suitors, will forever float by, never getting the chance to give up their fatty acids to the tissues.

4. **Fatty acid transport proteins (FATPs).** Fatty acids can pass through cell membranes relatively easily, but nevertheless they can be made to move more rapidly when given help. FATPs are proteins which seem to flip fatty acids from the outside of a cell membrane to the inside. In this way they speed up the accumulation of fatty acids in a tissue.

5. **Fatty acid binding proteins (FABPs).** These sit inside cells and effectively suck fatty acids into cells from the outside to the inside. They also speed up the accumulation of fatty acids in a tissue.

6. **Acylation stimulating proteins (ASPs).** These are proteins which are inside cells and which stimulate the incorporation of the fatty acids into the more complex lipids like triglycerides and phospholipids.

Thus getting fatty acids from the blood into brain, breasts and other subcutaneous tissues, and then into the complex lipids, requires the integrated actions of these six groups of proteins. Each group may have several members with slightly differing properties. All six groups obviously work well in humans, or we would not have our big brains and troublesome subcutaneous fat, but one or more must function differently in chimpanzees. As a result, in chimpanzees and other primates fatty acids are less efficiently transported into the brain and subcutaneous fatty tissues, and these tissues grow less. It is an intriguing possibility that the same protein, or two closely related proteins, may have been involved in growing both breasts and brains. The two may not be so far apart after all.

GROWING THE BRAIN

We are all familiar with the birdsong of spring. As the days lengthen, birds which have been silent all winter tentatively start to try out their voices. Within a few weeks they are in full song and, depending on the bird, may sing for between two and five months. Then, as the year progresses and the days begin to shorten again, the singing stops.

What has this got to do with the brain? As it turns out, a great deal. One of the first things that happens to a male bird in the spring is that nerve cells in those parts of the brain which control song grow and divide: this bit of the brain literally gets bigger and more complex. At the other end of the season, when singing is winding down, the process goes into reverse. Some of the nerve cells may actually die, while others shrink or lose the complexity of their nerve endings. Next spring, the whole cycle begins again.

Why on earth should anyone want to study this process in such detail? Partly, of course, for the sheer joy of finding out. But partly also for the very practical reason of learning ways in which damaged brains can be repaired. In warm-blooded animals, nerve cells usually do not grow and divide, and so repair after damage is negligible, in contrast to the repair which can occur in other parts of the body. This is why, for example, spinal cord injuries and strokes can be so devastating: the modern human central nervous system has limited capacity for repair. The songbird brain is the only known good example of a situation in which brain cells in a mature warm-blooded creature grow and divide, then die back again in a predictable and physiologically controlled way. If we could understand how this happens, we might be better able to help brain-damaged babies, children and adults, or to help people with damaged spinal cords to walk again, or even to restore function to brains devastated by a stroke.

And we are beginning to make progress. Researchers at Rockefeller University in New York City form one group which has begun to unravel the mechanisms involved in the control of song by the brain. One of the most important components of the mechanism seems to be changes in brain FABP. Just when the relevant parts of the brain are beginning to grow in the spring, lots of FABP is made in the key brain areas. This FABP sucks fatty acids into the tissue and so enables the nerve cells to grow and multiply. At the other end of the season, FABP levels fall, the supply of fatty acids to the neurons fails and atrophy takes place.

This provides direct evidence that FABP can make the brain grow. It strengthens the case for considering FABP as one of the key components of the increase in human brain size.

SURVIVING STARVATION

In Western societies many of us are too fat and most of us are getting fatter. We are constantly hounded with health advice about not becoming obese. The thought and body police are already getting to work and, before long, obesity may well be considered as unacceptable as smoking. What an unfortunate consequence of one of our most important sets of survival genes!

For that is what obesity represents. Humans have a unique

ability to store large amounts of fat when their calorie intake is a bit more than their calorie need. Many factors are involved, but at least two are particularly important. First, we have our subcutaneous fat, which acts as a highly efficient storage device. Second, we do not seem to switch off our appetites as many animals do when, as is now usual in the West, we eat more than we need to keep us going in the short term.

It is highly likely that this ability to turn almost any type of food into fat, and then to store that fat beneath our skins, is one of the reasons why pre-humans outdistanced all other apes and hominids in the race for evolutionary success. A characteristic of lifestyles which depend on living off the land is frequent and sometimes extreme seasonal shortage. Many animals in the wild die of starvation and many apes and hominids must have suffered the same fate.

The ability to accumulate fat is of enormous value in terms of survival. Humans use around 1500 to 2500 calories a day when living relatively sedentary lives and a lot more when exercising vigorously. A kilogram of fat provides around 9000 calories, enough to survive reasonably well for 4–6 days; 10kg allows survival for 40–60 days without eating, a period which may often be long enough to overcome natural seasonal shortages. Accumulation of fat may therefore have been one of the crucial factors in the survival of pre-humans and early humans as compared to other hominid lines. Fat people came through periods of severe food shortage; thin ones died. This 'thrifty gene' hypothesis, first developed by James Neel, has received much support.

FABPs, FATPs, albumins, lipoproteins, lipoprotein lipases and ASPs are important in rapid fat accumulation in adipose tissue – tissue which is found beneath the skin and in the abdomen and other areas and which is specialized to accumulate fat. Very similar factors may therefore have been involved in making fat bodies and big brains. Our psyche may be even more closely connected to our body image than we thought.

It is even possible that the obese Stone Age figurines known as the Venus of this or that may have been celebrations of our subcutaneous fat and our ability to survive starvation. Many interpretations have been put on these figurines. The guesses by archaeologists are as likely to be right about the past as future archaeologists will be about the functions of any of our present household objects. The figurines may be religious items, or some form of fertility totem, or they may simply represent early forms of non-functional art. But they also may have been celebrations of one of the key differences between ourselves and our immediate pre-human antecedents: an ability to get fat and therefore an ability to survive. The ability to remove fatty acids from the blood may be truly fundamental to our evolutionary success.

WHAT TYPES OF FATTY ACID ARE NEEDED FOR THE BRAIN?

As mentioned earlier, the fatty acids at the Sn2 position of the phospholipids tend to be polyunsaturated. They usually come from the general class of fatty acids called essential fatty acids or EFAs. EFAs were discovered in Minnesota around 1930 by a husband and wife team of nutritionists, George and Mildred Burr. As with vitamins, we cannot make them within our own bodies: we must therefore get them from our diet. We now know that EFAs are required for the normal structure of every single phospholipid membrane in the body. Without the EFAs, the phospholipids would not be fluid and flexible enough to form living membranes, nor would they be able to perform the signalling and controlling functions discussed in the next chapter. No organ in the whole human body could function without EFAs in its phospholipid membranes.

EFAs are of two distinct types, both of which are necessary. One type is called omega-6 or sometimes n-6; the other is called omega-3 or sometimes n-3. The parent compound of the omega-6 group is called linoleic acid (LA). The parent compound of the omega-3 group is called alpha-linolenic acid (ALA).

The most important single thing to understand about LA and ALA is that in themselves, especially as far as the brain is concerned, they have little importance. Their function is to act as pre-vitamins or pro-vitamins. They *must* be converted within the body into other substances which are much more important than the parent EFAs themselves. These other substances are sometimes called 'derived EFAs', but for simplicity in this book I will call them all EFAs.

Linoleic acid is converted first to gamma-linolenic acid (GLA), then to dihomogammalinolenic acid (DGLA) and then to arachidonic acid (AA), which can then pass to other compounds. For the brain it is the AA which is of overwhelming importance. AA makes up around 8 per cent of the dry matter of the brain, where it is almost all found in the Sn2 position of the phospholipids. AA is therefore crucial to brain structure, but, as we shall see in the next chapters, it plays an important role in brain function as well.

We have a similar situation with the omega-3 fatty acids. ALA itself is not very important, except as the starting material from which the other omega-3 EFAs can be made. Two of these omega-3 EFAs are of especial importance in the brain. Like AA, docosahexaenoic acid (DHA) makes up around 8 per cent of the brain by weight. Again it is required for normal brain structure, although it does not seem to be quite as important as AA in ongoing brain function. On the other hand, eicosapentaenoic acid (EPA), although found in the brain in much smaller amounts than DHA, seems to play a key role in brain function. Like AA, it can be converted to a whole range of other molecules which have key functions in cell signalling and in the control of the brain. It is almost as though in the omega-6 pathway, both structural and functional roles are combined in a single fatty acid, AA. In the omega-3 pathway, however, the structural role is concentrated in DHA while the functional role is concentrated in EPA.

Linoleic acid and alpha-linolenic acid are found in vegetables and nuts, but also in meats, marrow, eggs, insects, grubs and other small creatures. Theoretically, if we get enough LA and ALA we should be able to make enough AA, EPA and DHA for ourselves.

But for some reason, in humans, the EFA biochemical pathways from LA to AA and from ALA to EPA and DHA are slow. We may not always be able to get enough AA, EPA and DHA by this route. This may be particularly true if we eat a diet that is very rich in saturated fats, which can slow down the pathways of AA, EPA and DHA synthesis and which can compete with AA, EPA and DHA for incorporation into phospholipids. The typical Western diet, with its rich supply of saturated fat, may therefore lead to inadequate formation of AA, EPA and DHA, and inadequate incorporation of these key EFAs into brain phospholipids.

There is therefore a strong case to be made for the idea that the human brain needs a direct supply of AA, EPA and DHA for brain function. This bypasses the need for the brain to get its own AA, EPA and DHA from LA and ALA. As we shall see in the next chapter, some of the strongest evidence for this view is that most animal milks contain only LA and ALA. But human milk, in contrast, contains AA, EPA and DHA. The human baby brain can get its AA, EPA and DHA directly. It may well be that these three EFAs are critical for normal brain growth.

It is also likely that these EFAs were required in the course of evolution to allow human brains to grow from the ape level to the human level. For this to happen we must have acquired the ability to find, eat and digest food from animal sources. This may mean meat, but can also include many other foods and food sources, including marrow, insects, grubs of many types and eggs. Because much of the AA, EPA and DHA in the world originates in microalgae which grow in water, aquatic food chains are particularly rich in these key brain fatty acids. Perhaps that is why humans love, and pre-humans seem to have loved, water so much. They needed to eat water-based creatures to obtain the AA, EPA and DHA to grow their brains.

6

THINKING THE UNTHINKABLE

MOST OF THE FATTY ACIDS IN THE SUBCUTANEOUS ADIPOSE TISSUE
are in the form of triglycerides. In contrast most of the fatty
acids in the brain are in the form of phospholipids. Triglycerides
make soft, squishy, relatively unstructured tissues which are not
in any way damaged by being squeezed or by changing shape.
Phospholipid structures, in contrast, are precise and ordered
and can be destroyed by even mild trauma. It is this precise
structure of phospholipids which makes them perfect for the
organization of the remarkable thinking machine which is the
brain. I have specifically and deliberately avoided using the word
'computer' because the brain is not an organ which functions like a
computer.

There is, however, one thing which computers and other
electronic devices have in common with the brain. They all depend
on electricity. And that electricity has to be channelled with the
minimum of leakage along defined routes. In electronic devices
these defined routes are wires, or channels etched on a silicon
chip. The electricity flows along the defined routes: it is prevented
from escaping inappropriately by the plastic or other insulation, in

the case of wires, or by the non-conducting spaces between the channels engraved on a chip.

The brain, similarly, has electricity-conducting channels. They are called nerve cells or neurons. Each consists of what is called a cell body, which contains the nucleus and much of the other paraphernalia common to all cells. But extending from the cell body in the case of a neuron are large numbers of protrusions. The small ones, which are largely concerned with incoming information, are called dendrites. The long ones, which are largely concerned with sending information out to other parts of the brain, are called axons. The complexity is almost beyond imagination. There are around 100 billion neurons in the brain, each of which, through its axons and dendrites, makes contact with anything from 1000 to 10 million other neurons. Even in terms of the simple numbers of interactions, the brain is much larger than any computer. The nature of these interactions makes the brain qualitatively as well as quantitatively distinct in the way it behaves. The brain not only offers many more interactions among its units than any computer, but the nature of those interactions is different from those occurring in a computer.

But in spite of these differences, both the brain and computing devices do have one fundamental thing in common: the need for channels which will conduct electricity, and for effective insulation which will stop the channels interacting except when specifically required. That is where phospholipids come in: they can be made into near-perfect insulators, which can nevertheless be opened up easily and specifically to let electrical impulses and appropriate chemicals pass. The fine projections of nerve cells consist of an insulating tube of phospholipid enclosing an electricity-conducting column of a watery solution. Multiple sclerosis is a disease in which one of the main problems is loss of the insulation, so allowing inappropriate cross-talk between neighbouring nerve cells and malfunctioning of that part of the brain.

As described in the last chapter, each phospholipid molecule is like a Janus, able to face two ways. One face loves water and dissolves in it easily: it is said to be hydrophilic. The other face hates water and loves fat: it is said to be hydrophobic or lipophilic.

It is this two-faced nature which gives phospholipids their unique properties. If phospholipids are put in water, their water-loving faces are very happy, but their fat-loving faces are not. So what happens is that the fat-loving faces come together, creating two-layered (bilayer) structures where the two lipophilic layers face inwards towards each other and the two hydrophilic layers face outwards. This simple phenomenon is the basis on which all the membranes of the body are built.

Electricity cannot easily pass through fat, whereas it can easily pass through water. So phospholipid bilayers are wonderful insulators. The bilayers can arrange themselves into spheres, cylinders or tubes, each of which consists of water on the outside, fat in the middle and water on the inside. The fat in the middle is in essence the basis of multicellular animal life. Phospholipid bilayers separate cells from the fluid which surrounds them. They also separate the nucleus from the rest of the cell, and all the miniature sub-cellular organelles from each other. In addition, they form a framework into which all the proteins required to run the cell's machinery are embedded. With few exceptions, proteins do not simply slosh around in a kind of soup within a cell. They are attached to membranes in a precisely ordered way which enables them to perform their functions and to respond to regulating signals either from the nucleus or from outside the cell.

All cells are made up of complex structures of phospholipid membranes, but that complexity reaches extraordinary levels in the nervous system. Most non-nerve cells in the body approximate to spheres or cylinders, with indentations and ruffles on the surface. In nerves, however, while there is always a roughly spherical, pyramidal or cuboid structure which holds the nucleus and which is called the cell body, it is the protrusions from that cell body which are astonishing.

These protrusions all consist primarily of phospholipid cylinders with proteins of various types embedded in the structures. As we have seen, the shorter ones, which receive incoming information, are usually many thousands in number and are called dendrites. The long ones, the axons, usually only one or a very small number coming from each cell, carry outgoing information and are from one or two millimetres to over a metre in length. Sometimes they divide many times on the way, although more usually a single axon breaks up into large numbers of fine endings only when it reaches its destination. These fine endings, when they terminate within the brain, make contacts with the dendrites of other neurons. Outside the brain, axons usually make contact with either muscles or glands of various types.

The intricate structure is astounding to anyone who looks at it for the first time. Much of it was first described by the Spanish histologist Ramon y Cajal and it is largely through his eyes that we now see the structure of the brain. He developed, with the aid of the Italian histologist Camillo Golgi, a method of using silver to pick out all the branches of a single nerve cell, while leaving other cells untouched. This, for the first time, enabled us to get a feel for the immense complexity of the brain with its 100 billion interacting units. One of Cajal's beautiful illustrations of human brain cells is shown in Figure 1.

Nerve cells work only because phospholipids will not normally let either water or electricity pass. Electricity, water and water-soluble materials can easily travel inside axons or dendrites, but

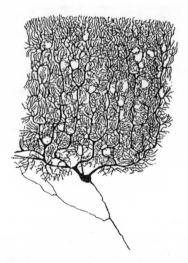

Figure 1. The brain contains about 100 billion nerve cells (neurons) and about 1000 billion glial cells, which provide both mechanical support and an appropriate biochemical environment for the nerve cells. The dawn of the understanding of the brain's true complexity came with Ramon y Cajal's beautiful and brilliant demonstrations of the complexity of the structure of each individual nerve cell. This drawing by Cajal shows the structure of a single neuron (Purkinje cell) of the human cerebellum.

cannot readily pass from inside to outside, or from one nerve cell to another. The insulation provided by the phospholipids is absolutely necessary to allow each nerve cell to function independently. Without the insulation, the brain could not even begin to work.

THE IMPORTANCE OF CONTROLLED LEAKS

Cells, however, cannot perform their functions if they are completely isolated. They must be able to communicate with the surrounding watery environment (known as the extracellular fluid or ECF) and also with adjacent neurons. The whole point of the brain lies in the complexities of the interactions which are possible.

The controlled leaks happen largely because at strategic places in the phospholipid membrane there are proteins which, in essence, act as valves. They can open or close to let water, ions like sodium, potassium chloride, or electricity pass from one side of the membrane to the other. Sometimes the 'pressure' of a particular substance is greater on one side than the other: opening the valve then lets the substance naturally flow from one side of the membrane to the other. At other times, the substance must be pumped against a pressure or concentration gradient. Then simply opening the valve is not enough: energy has to be applied to pump the substance across the membrane in a direction opposed to its natural inclination.

Nerve cells can be either active or quiescent. In the quiescent state everything just putters along quietly, the valves are partly or fully closed and the fluid outside the neuron cannot communicate with that inside the neuron. The alternative state is an explosive electrical impulse where a (relatively) large burst of electrical activity surges along a neuron. It does not travel simply by electrical conduction but by a constantly regenerating process which maintains the size of the impulse without any fall off until it reaches the end of the axon.

Analogies are always to some extent misleading, but they can help one to grasp unfamiliar concepts. Electrical impulses in neurons are triggered by the membrane phospholipids becoming leaky due to the opening of the protein valves. Each tiny valve when open allows a surge of ions and electricity to cross the membrane. If enough valves open together, the microsurges add up and take the membrane across the threshold, where a massive opening of valves occurs and a nerve impulse begins. The process can be envisioned rather like one of those light switches which you feel resisting when you move it a little. If you stop pushing, the switch will fall back to its original position and the light will not come on. However, if you push hard enough and far enough, the switch suddenly flips over into the on position, allowing a surge of electricity and the switching on of the light. A nerve cell is like a light switch with thousands of little fairies hanging on to it, some pushing in one direction and some in the other. Every now and again the fairies pushing the light on win: a surge of electricity occurs as the switch flips over. In the nerve cell, however, the switch almost always automatically flips back immediately the first surge has passed. The nerve impulse is transient, lasting perhaps a thousandth of a second. Once it has passed the fairies start to pull and push again.

So nerve impulses start in the cell body and surge out to the end of the axon. What happens then? In the fine branch endings of the axon are lots of little phospholipid spheres (technically known as synaptic vesicles). Each vesicle contains a chemical which is water soluble and sealed into the sphere. When a nerve impulse arrives at the end of the axon, the changes make some of the spheres stick to the inside of the axon phospholipid membrane. At the place where the contact occurs, the phospholipid membrane breaks down, spilling the synaptic chemicals, known as neurotransmitters, into the space between the axon endings of one neuron and the dendritic endings of the next. That space, together with the membranes on either side of it, is known as the synapse.

The dendritic endings contain proteins which are known as receptors. Each receptor has a highly specific structure which can be visualized as a lock. So long as there is no key in the lock, and so long as the key is not turned, the receptor protein sits quietly in the membrane doing not very much. But the synaptic chemicals have structures which act as the keys that can fit into the lock and turn it. Each receptor has a specific structure which can be activated only by a specific neurotransmitter, or by another chemical which is very like it in structure. When the right neurotransmitter key fits into the right receptor lock and turns it, then the lock opens and triggers a series of events inside the other neuron. These events, even on a neuronal scale, are usually micro-events. There are thousands, and in some cases hundreds of thousands, of receptors on neuronal dendrites. There are also hundreds of different types of receptors, differentiated by the nature of the specific chemical which can turn the key and by the consequences of that key being turned. The interactions of these thousands of events determine whether the next neuron will trigger an impulse or not. Again, the analogy of the fairies fighting over the switch is apt.

I have oversimplified the picture to an almost absurd extent – the reality is infinitely more complex than my crude word picture. This is why the computer is not an accurate analogy for the brain. At each step in a computer an electrical impulse may pass or may not pass: there is no intermediate state. Complexity and subtlety can be built up by increasing the numbers of intervening and alternative steps. But in the nervous system, each step is not just 'yes, pass' or 'no, stop', but 100,000 grades of 'maybe'. Put that variability into each neuronal interaction, add in 100 billion interacting neurons, and one can begin to see why it has rightly been said that the human brain is the most complex structure in the universe.

SERVICING THE NEURONS: THE GLIA

That is not all. Most descriptions of the brain concentrate on the electricity-conducting elements, the nerve cells or neurons. But for every neuron, there are ten other supporting cells or glia. So the brain consists of 100 billion nerve cells and 1000 billion glia.

Like so-called 'junk DNA', the glia have been Cinderella subjects for research. The neurons are sexy because we are persuaded that they are the mechanisms by which we think and control our bodies. But 90 per cent of the cells inside our skulls are not neurons. What on earth do they do?

There is a dearth of research on glia and so any short, honest answer has to be 'We do not know.' But we are beginning to get some answers. Glia used to be thought of simply as packing cells, the material put into a parcel of fragile objects to stop them rattling around and breaking. There may be something in this, but most people who have studied glia are convinced that there is more to their story than that. These cells are too complex, too intricate in structure, to be merely packing.

At least two other functions are now reasonably established: the glia help to provide nutrients and maintenance for the nerve cells; and they provide the chemical soup within which the brain functions. The glia secrete hundreds and perhaps thousands of chemicals into the environment surrounding the neurons, chemicals which subtly regulate the ways in which neurons respond to their world. The complexity is beyond comprehension.

WHAT HAPPENS WHEN THE RECEPTOR KEY IS TURNED?

Again, any answers must be immensely oversimplified. My aim is not to give a precisely accurate picture because that would be impossible. Rather, I seek to provide an impression of what might happen and of the complexities and subtleties that exist.

The receptors without their keys are relatively quiescent, but once the key has been turned by a transmitter, then a number of things may happen.

One class of events involves the receptor itself acting as a valve to let water-soluble materials, usually sodium or calcium ions, enter the nerve endings. If enough receptors are activated in this way, a nerve impulse may result, or chemical processes inside the nerve cell may be activated.

A second broad class of actions involves the receptors being linked to other proteins, just inside the membrane, called G proteins. These proteins are control centres which can exist in two states, inactive and active. Turning the key in the lock of the receptor flips the adjacent G protein from the inactive to the active state: again this initiates a cascade of events in the cell.

Some of the key G proteins, which can be activated by many types of receptor, regulate the functions of a group of enzymes called phospholipases. As their name implies, these phospholipases can break up phospholipids. Among the phospholipases I, and many others, believe that a type called phospholipase A_2 (PLA_2) is particularly important in the brain. I now think it may be one of the keys to understanding devastating illnesses like schizophrenia and autism.

Changes in the activity of phospholipases and associated mechanisms may be one of the key factors which make us human. This is not as far fetched as it sounds. Two mouse strains have recently been developed in which two different components of the phospholipase-associated system have been genetically altered. In both cases the mice are super-intelligent, perhaps gaining about 50 per cent more reasoning power. These super-mice will be discussed in more detail later, but just for the moment imagine what might happen now if a particular racial group suddenly became on average 50 per cent more intelligent than the rest of us. We would not be arguing about a few questionable IQ points, but about a massive step forward in intellectual power. I will argue that a comparable event took place some time in our relatively recent past and that its impact was devastating for all other hominids. This was the creation event which made us human. And it involved something as apparently mundane as the way our nerve cells deal with fat when the receptors at a synapse are activated.

THE PHOSPHOLIPASE A_2 CYCLE

When many neurotransmitters turn the key in their receptors, one result is activation of PLA_2. This acts on the Sn2 position of phospholipids to release a highly unsaturated fatty acid (HUFA), often arachidonic acid (AA). The release of AA leaves behind the remains of a phospholipid which has lost its middle fatty acid: it is now called a lysophospholipid (LyPL). AA, remember, is very important in brain structure, making up about 6 per cent of the dry weight of the brain. Other HUFAs make up another 12 per cent.

LyPLs and HUFAs are hugely active molecules. Each is able to switch on or off many other mechanisms within the neuron. Each may help to trigger nerve impulses, regulate the energy output of the neuron, or switch on or off a whole series of different genes. Some of these events will change some functions of the neuron in semi-permanent ways, leading to what we call memory.

It is usually important not just to switch on the PLA_2 cycle, but to switch it off so that the neuron does not enter a permanent state of activation. The switching-off mechanism begins by linking the HUFA, such as AA, to another molecule called coenzyme A (CoA), which acts as a sort of carrier or guide for the HUFA. The type of enzyme which does this is called a fatty acid coenzyme A ligase (FACL). The HUFA–CoA can then be linked back to the LyPL, to make a normal phospholipid with its fatty acid restored in the middle position: the enzyme which does this is called ACLAT.

This PLA_2 cycle is central to the regulation of neuronal function. It is activated when nerve cells are activated, when memories are being laid down, and when nerve endings of dendrites or axons are growing and developing. Wherever nerves are growing or functioning in any way, the PLA_2 cycle is working. We cannot think, move or feel without the involvement of the PLA_2 cycle in millions of interlinked neurons.

HOW FAULTY FAT CAN DEVASTATE THE BRAIN

Sadly, much of our knowledge of the importance of particular chemical reactions within the body depends on observing what happens when those chemical reactions fail. Within the body each chemical reaction is usually regulated by one or more enzymes. If a mutation leads to an enzyme losing a function, the disease which follows can give rise to surprising though tragic insights.

About four years ago a baby who obviously had something wrong was born to a family in Germany. Its head and the brain within were very small. As a result, all sorts of functions were not working properly.

The paediatricians checked out every known cause of such a failure of brain growth but none of them fitted. The illness appeared to be new to medical science. Eventually the doctors and biochemists tracked down a single chemical abnormality: a failure of an enzyme which converts the important brain HUFA, AA, into one of its products involved in signalling to neurons, a substance called leukotriene C4 (LTC4). A year later, a second baby was found with the same failure of brain growth and the same enzyme defect. The conclusion was clear: the fatty acid AA, through conversion to LTC4, is vital for normal brain growth. The illness is so rare because affected infants die before or soon after birth and cannot reproduce. It is likely that babies with this disease are affected by new mutations: such mutations, because of their devastating consequences, cannot be passed on.

Alport syndrome is another rare, but rather better-known, genetic abnormality. Children with this condition are usually severely deaf, and they also have a rare type of kidney disease. We now know that Alport syndrome is caused by a lack of a structural protein called collagen IV. As a result, neither the inner ear nor the kidneys develop properly because of structural abnormalities. But some children with Alport syndrome have an additional problem. They have small brains, are mentally retarded and, because of their small brains, have a characteristically abnormally shaped face. These problems cannot be explained by the lack of collagen IV on the X chromosome.

An adjacent gene on the X chromosome, however, is one of the FACL group, known as FACL-4. We now know that Alport syndrome with mental retardation is due to a deficit of both the collagen and FACL genes. FACL-4 must therefore play a key role in brain development and mental function. In later chapters we will see how important this is.

AA AND BRAIN GROWTH

The tragic case of the German baby clearly showed that LTC4 formed from AA was essential for normal growth and development. It fits in with a lot of other work pointing in the same direction: AA is critical for brain growth. Perhaps the two most important studies were those by groups led by Michael Crawford in London and Susan Carlson in Memphis.

Michael Crawford is one of the world's leading authorities on the fats of the brain. He also worked in East Africa, at Makerere University in Uganda. We met while we were examining medical students at the University of Dar-es-Salaam. Michael has emphasized that the brain is extremely rich in two particular fatty acids, AA and docosahexaenoic acid (DHA). He wondered whether the supply of these fatty acids to the foetus might be one of the determinants of brain size.

For obvious ethical reasons, this is not a question which can be answered directly by experimentation. One has to sidle up to it to see if one can tease out some clues. Michael Crawford reasoned that the fatty acids for the baby's brain mainly came along the umbilical artery from the mother. By looking at the fatty acid composition of the artery from the discarded umbilical cord after birth, some indication of the role of AA and DHA supply to the baby might be obtained. By measuring the baby's head circumference after birth, it would be possible indirectly to get an indication of brain size. Would there be any relationship between umbilical cord fatty acids and brain size?

With regard to DHA and all the other fatty acids measured, there seemed no relation to head size. But with AA the situation was different. The more AA there was in the umbilical cord, the bigger was the baby's head. There was clearly a correlation between more AA and a bigger brain.

Correlations, however, do not necessarily mean a causative relationship. Sometimes a correlation means that one factor is causing another, but often a correlation occurs because both factors are caused by some third factor. To take a prosaic example, after the Second World War ownership of cars and of home washing-machines rose dramatically. If you plot the one against the other on a year-by-year basis, it is clear that there is a very close correlation between purchases of cars and purchases of washing-machines. But that does not mean that the purchase of a car *causes* the purchase of a washing-machine or vice versa. The two are correlated not because one is causing the other but because both are indications of generally increasing prosperity. Correlations are not always interpreted as cautiously as they should be.

So Michael Crawford's work does not necessarily mean that high AA levels are causing brain growth, although that is one possible interpretation. Susan Carlson's work provided more direct evidence.

Susan Carlson was concerned primarily with the growth and development of premature babies. She was particularly concerned about finding the best way of feeding such babies so that they developed normally. Fifteen years ago no one knew whether the best formula for premature babies was human milk. These babies are much younger than babies normally starting on human milk and so that milk, which is adapted for babies being delivered after a normal forty-week pregnancy, might not be exactly right. An artificial formula designed specifically for premature babies could be the best solution. One thing Susan Carlson *was* sure of was that we did not know enough to be able to give credible answers, so she embarked on a careful series of studies in which babies were fed various formulae.

At that time the standard premature baby formula contained only the two parent fatty acids, linoleic acid (LA) and alpha-linolenic acid (ALA). These fatty acids and their interconversions within the body have been described already in Chapter 5. But for the brain, a baby – or an adult – does not require LA or ALA. What the baby does need are the daughter compound formed from LA, arachidonic acid (AA), and the daughter compound formed from ALA, docosahexaenoic acid (DHA).

Unlike old-style infant formula, human milk contains pre-formed AA and DHA. Babies fed human milk can therefore obtain their AA and DHA directly and do not need to make it for themselves. In contrast, babies fed old-style formula have to take the LA and ALA and convert them to AA and DHA. Not everyone was convinced that premature babies could form AA and DHA quickly enough to meet all the needs of the brain. Susan Carlson decided to find out.

She took standard premature baby feeds and added to them the various fatty acids found in human milk but not in formula. She then measured the baby's brain growth as measured by head size, and also followed the babies to look at their intellectual development. The results were striking. Adding AA and DHA seemed to make the head size grow. But studies in which DHA alone was added indicated that almost all the growth-stimulating effect seemed to be due to AA, although DHA made an important contribution to structure. AA is required for normal brain growth, in part because it is converted to LTC4, as the tragic case or the German baby showed. As a result of the work of Susan Carlson and some other pioneering researchers, AA and DHA are now added to premature baby milk in most countries of the world. In many countries, though not yet in the USA, they are also added to full-term formula in an effort to make that formula more like human milk.

So we now have three crucial pieces of evidence. Arachidonic acid levels in the umbilical cord are positively related to head size: the more AA, the bigger the head. An enzyme converting AA to LTC4 is required for normal development of the brain, strongly suggesting that LTC4, derived from AA, is one of the key biochemical factors influencing brain size. Third, feeding AA directly to premature babies stimulates brain growth. This represents a strong group of facts which suggests that supply of AA may be necessary for normal brain growth.

We know that both DHA and AA are absolutely required for a normal brain. Both must therefore be supplied to provide the building blocks from which the brain is constructed. But AA seems to play a more active role, actually stimulating the growth of the brain. AA is one of the key factors which regulates final brain size.

WHERE DO AA AND DHA COME FROM?

We can make small amounts of AA and DHA ourselves from dietary LA and ALA. But for optimum growth of the brain it is likely that we need to eat at least some AA and DHA directly. Where might that come from?

It is a disappointing fact that vegetable foods, with the exceptions of some seaweeds and lichens, are devoid of AA and DHA. Vegetables, fruits, nuts and other plant sources usually contain only ALA and LA. AA and DHA come primarily from animal sources, which may include not only large animals but insects and grubs which can contain significant amounts. Meat, and especially organ meat, brains and bone marrow, can be very rich in AA and DHA.

There have been several important recent studies of chimpanzees' diet. One motive for studying this is to learn more about the needs of chimpanzees by finding out what they eat naturally in the wild. Another is to develop clues to what our diet might have been like before we separated from the chimpanzees and before our brains began to grow. The studies have to be interpreted cautiously because modern chimpanzees, like modern humans, are 5–7 million years away from our common ancestor.

Chimpanzees' diet is largely vegetarian but does contain a substantial amount of grubs and insects, such as termites, which in fact represent the bulk of the animal food consumed by them. Chimpanzees put great value on termites and have developed elaborate tool-using techniques to get them out of their mounds. They poke into the mounds using thin sticks of just the right width and length. The termites hold on to the sticks and then can be pulled out of the mound before being devoured with delight. Termites contain fat, usually mostly LA and ALA, but also smaller amounts of AA and DHA.

But chimpanzees do sometimes go after large animal prey. As we saw in Chapter 4, Craig Stanford has chillingly described what happens when chimpanzees decide to abandon their vegetarian and insect diet and hunt for colobus monkeys. When the unfortunate monkey is caught, it is torn apart, killed and eaten. Monkey food seems to be highly prized in chimpanzee society and monkey meat can be used by males to give to females to encourage the provision of sexual favours. The females benefit by getting meat, including its relatively rich supplies of AA and DHA, for their babies. The male chimpanzee which makes the kill, as his first act, often bites open the monkey's skull and eats the brain. Brains are by far the richest sources of AA and DHA. It is almost as though the chimpanzees know what they must eat to make them intelligent!

HUNTING AND WATER: THE SECRETS OF ABUNDANT AA AND DHA

There have been huge rows in palaeoanthropological circles about the importance of hunting in human evolution. Prior to about 2.5 million years ago there is not much evidence that our hominid ancestors hunted. Like modern chimpanzees, they probably consumed many insects and grubs. They may occasionally have chased, caught and consumed small animals, but there is no evidence that this was a way of life. But after 2.5 million years, the scene changes. Animal bones, with signs of butchery, are consistently found associated with evidence of pre-human occupation. What brought the animal bones and the humans together? The most parsimonious explanation is that humans were learning to hunt – or, what may have required at least as much skill and courage, to scavenge the kills made by other predators, such as the big cats.

Innumerable papers and books have been written on the theme that hunting may have been one of the crucial things which made us human. The general idea is that effective hunting would have required intellectual, physical and communication skills. The killing of relatively large animals is not a simple matter and requires cunning, planning, courage and strength. As discussed in Chapter 4, the argument is that these characteristics would have required bigger and more organized brains than those possessed by our hominid ancestors and so it was the pressure generated by the need to hunt that made us human. But, as I have pointed out, environmental pressures *cannot* of themselves generate physical or biochemical change: they can only create the conditions whereby such changes, which have occurred spontaneously as a result of mutations, may prosper or disappear. Hunting cannot have generated the mutations which allowed us to become human. It may, however, have created the conditions which allowed individuals carrying those mutations to survive and prosper.

There is one very direct, as opposed to indirect, way in which hunting may have helped to generate a big brain. This possibility has been almost entirely missed by those discussing the hunting hypothesis. Meat, and especially brain and organ meat, is an excellent source of AA and DHA. Meat may therefore have enabled us to make the very best of the relevant mutations by ensuring that our brain growth was not limited by an inadequate supply of AA or DHA. Hunting may indeed have been important in human brain growth, but perhaps not in the way usually envisaged.

Meats from large animals are not the only animal sources of AA and DHA. Much of the AA, DHA and related fatty acids present in the world comes from micro-algae which grow in mineral-rich water, like the sea or many of the only partially fresh lakes which are so abundant in East and Central Africa, the areas which to date seem most likely to have been the cradles of humankind. Many of these lakes are extremely rich in minerals which allow micro-algae to grow abundantly. Leigh Broadhurst and her colleagues have described the possible importance of such lakes and rivers as the sources of 'brain food' during human evolution.

The algae are food for many animals and birds, from flamingos at one end of the scale to massive numbers of minute aquatic and near-aquatic animals of many sorts at the other. The contents of the algae are then consumed indirectly via the food chain by fish, grubs, insects, reptiles, amphibians, water birds and mammals. Many foods directly or indirectly associated with water are good sources of AA and DHA. These water foods, many of which would have left little or no fossil trace, may have been as important as hunting in supplying the fats for brain development. How important water is to humans in Africa is immediately obvious if one flies over the continent today. Wherever there is water there are humans; wherever water is absent humans are also absent. And as discussed in earlier chapters, virtually all hominid fossils have been found in sites which were once riversides and lakesides. It is therefore not at all implausible that eggs, fish, insects, grubs and water animals and birds may all have helped to supply the AA and DHA which we needed to make bigger brains.

LIPOPROTEIN LIPASE (LPL), FABP, FATP, ETC.

Starving an animal – or a premature baby, as was done inadvertently for many years – of AA and DHA may make the brain smaller than it should be. In these circumstances, the brain is unable to reach the potential size determined by the genes.

Once that potential has been reached, however, the brain will not grow bigger. One cannot produce giant-brained animals of any species simply by feeding AA. This is because of the complex systems required to transport AA to the brain. As we have seen in other chapters, albumin, LPL, FABP, FATP and ASP are all required to incorporated AA into the brain. Moreover, we already know that variations in the expression and amount of FABP appear to be the key to brain growth in songbirds in spring. The availability of dietary AA from meat, eggs, insects, grubs or water-based foods could generate a bigger brain only if there was at the same time the availability of mutant proteins which could transport that AA to the brain.

Mutations in the proteins which could increase the efficiency of the transfer of AA and DHA to the brain are therefore strong candidates as factors which may have created the necessary conditions for brain growth. If such mutations occurred, then they could have been exploited to the full as a result of increased supplies of AA and DHA from hunting or water foods.

Within a few years we shall know whether this explanation for an increase in brain size is correct. The structures of these proteins in chimpanzees and humans will be known. We will no longer have to make educated guesses.

THE DOUGIE MOUSE AND THE MENSA MOUSE

When I wrote the first draft for this book in 1998 I predicted that mutations in phospholipid-related metabolism could occur which would change brain function to a major extent. At the time I did not expect that prediction to come true in the near future. But in the intervening two years, not one but two events have occurred which show that my view was correct. These have attracted some publicity but not, in my view, the attention they deserve. They are events which transform the possibilities for the future and give us new insight into the past. The ethical issues are much greater than those posed by most of the other phenomena surrounding the genome, genetic manipulation and cloning, which have received so much attention.

The Dougie mouse and the Mensa mouse are very clever mice, veritable Einsteins among mice. They can solve problems like no other mice before them. And they can pass that cleverness on to their descendants. These are not minor changes in cognitive performance, equivalent to a few points on an IQ scale. They are huge changes which on the human IQ scale might involve an increase in IQ of between thirty and seventy points. That is the difference between someone who is mentally retarded and someone capable of winning a top university honours degree. What would we do as a species if we were confronted by another species more able than we are on that sort of scale? What would we do if people from one human nationality or racial group suddenly became 50 per cent more intelligent, effectively switching a whole group to genius level? This is the stuff of science fiction, involving contacts between us and aliens from outer space. Yet the Dougie mouse and the Mensa mouse show that such a dramatic change can be achieved in one step by a single, relatively minor change in one gene.

HOW TO MAKE SUPERMICE

Many pieces of evidence from many different sources point to the concept that a neurotransmitter substance called glutamate is involved in the laying down of memory. And since an effective memory is required for high intellectual performance, the glutamate system is thought to be involved in cognitive function also.

In a greatly oversimplified way, the manner in which this works is as follows. There are several different types of glutamate receptor, all differing slightly in structure. One of these receptors can also bind a chemical known as NMDA and has therefore become known as an NMDA receptor. When we are remembering something, glutamate is released from synaptic vesicles in nerve cells which are activated by the memory-generating experience. The glutamate then crosses the synapse to the next neuron and binds to an NMDA receptor on that next neuron.

When the glutamate hits the NMDA receptor this activates PLA2, which then releases arachidonic acid (AA), which in turn switches a protein called GAP-43 from an inactive to an active form. GAP-43 stimulates the growth of dendrites which strengthen the connection between the two nerve cells involved. The strengthened nerve-cell connections form the physical and biochemical basis of memory.

It all sounds a bit tenuous and non-specific. Could such a system really work to improve specific memories and cognitive function? Many had doubts and so two groups of investigators, Y. P. Tang and colleagues at Princeton and Arieh Routtenberg and colleagues at Northwestern University in Illinois, decided to find out.

We know more about manipulating the mouse genome than about any other species. We can knock out the genes for particular proteins so that the protein can no longer be made by the mouse. This enables us to see what happens when the protein is missing. We can also activate a gene so that the protein specified by that gene is made in increased amounts. The Princeton group decided to see what would happen if mice made more of a protein component of the NMDA receptor. The Illinois group decided to investigate the effects of making more GAP-43. In both cases the proteins made by the mice were normal: there was simply more of each protein.

In each case the results were extraordinary. The modified mice were much cleverer than normal mice in every way tested. They could remember novel objects for longer, and they could learn more quickly. They could better remember appropriate responses to adverse stimuli, and they could more quickly orientate themselves spatially in a new environment. These are all advantages which have obvious evolutionary survival value.

The Dougie mouse and the Mensa mouse have immense implications for those interested in the study of human evolution. First, they demonstrate that a single, relatively minor change in the amount of a single protein can produce a steep increase in intellectual performance. No change in overall brain or skull size is involved: the existing brain simply works much more effectively.

Second, both of the changes are on a single pathway where proteins and phospholipids interact. As we have seen, arachidonic acid is absolutely required for both effects. It is a component of the mechanism by which NMDA receptor activation generates change via GAP-43.

A change in human brain function analogous to that which occurred in the Dougie mouse or the Mensa mouse might well have been involved in those last dramatic events which made our brains grow and which then gave us our creative intelligence and our symbolic skills. I now believe that we can gain insight into what that change might have been by studying schizophrenia, another interest of mine which was triggered by Howard Bern's lecture. As I will demonstrate, schizophrenia is proving to be related to something going wrong with the biochemistry of fat within the brain.

7

'MAD, BAD, AND DANGEROUS TO KNOW'

LADY CAROLINE LAMB, 1785–1828

TWO MEN ARE STANDING QUIETLY ON A SUBWAY PLATFORM IN Toronto. They do not know each other. As the train approaches, one of the men suddenly pushes the other on to the tracks. Another man in London is walking through a public park. Someone rushes out from a clump of bushes and plunges a butcher's knife into the walker's neck. In Los Angeles a mother preparing food in her kitchen is hacked to death by her twenty-eight-year-old son. In Tokyo an elderly man stabs and kills three other inhabitants of the retirement home in which they are living. In each case the assailant is diagnosed as suffering from schizophrenia.

These are events which were reported recently in the press. It is not surprising that a commonly encountered view of schizophrenia is of a violent male, often but not always young, liable to commit murder without provocation. Most media coverage of schizophrenia describes this type of event. Other stories often relate to homelessness. It is pointed out that a substantial proportion of the homeless people who inhabit the streets of the world's prosperous cities carry a diagnosis of schizophrenia.

It is true that some unprovoked violent attacks on strangers where robbery is not the motive, and most violent killings of mothers by sons, are the acts of poorly treated schizophrenic people. It is also true that, since there have been great reductions in the numbers of psychiatric hospital beds in most developed countries, many ex-patients prefer to sleep rough than to live in accommodation otherwise available to them. This is the stuff of most media stories about schizophrenia. These are the aspects of the illness which most frequently affect other people's lives.

But these stories give a misleading picture. Murderers and the inner-city homeless form only a tiny proportion of those with schizophrenia. Most schizophrenic people live unsatisfactory lives and cause great distress to themselves, to their families and to their friends, but most are neither violent nor sleeping rough. They are usually troubled, difficult, gentle people, bewildered both by the world around them and by what they are experiencing within their own minds.

No one can describe schizophrenia as accurately as someone who has experienced the illness themselves. *Schizophrenia Bulletin* is a specialist journal for researchers which is published monthly by the National Institute of Health of the USA. In order to help increase understanding, most issues contain first-person accounts by patients of what it means to have this illness. These descriptions explain the illness more vividly and effectively than can be done in a textbook. Each of the following extracts is reproduced with the permission both of the author and of *Schizophrenia Bulletin*.

SCHIZOPHRENIA FROM THE INSIDE

'Hummingbird'

My story begins when I was twenty-five, about six years ago. I had just received my cosmetologist license and was working as a hairdresser. Also, I had just finished the second year of my bachelor's degree in business administration at a local university. I wanted someday to own a chain of beauty salons. I was on top of the world then. That was when the voices started and I was first hospitalized. They came the same time I was having menstrual problems, but no one can say for sure if the two were related. The voices are like people having a conversation inside my head of which I am not a part. They can be like scratching, whispers, or real loud like shouting. They clutter my mind and I cannot think straight until I am unable to do anything. Sometimes they tell me to hurt others or myself. When I hear them, I become quite fearful because I feel I am losing my mind. My fear causes me to become sad and hopeless. I will cry and cry for days. When I first heard the voices, I would drink until I passed out. When I woke up with a vicious hangover, the voices would be there like thunder, and I would start drinking again. The drinking did not make the voices go away, but they didn't bother me as much and I was happier for that. I did this for days to fight them. Then I couldn't stand the voices or what I had turned into, a sloppy, unemployed drunk. I tried to hang myself in my mother's place. Luckily, she and my sister found me in time. They took me to the county emergency room and the people there sent me to the county mental hospital.

Not long after moving in with my boyfriend, the voices came back with a vengeance. But now I could not sleep or concentrate. I became extremely depressed, irritable, afraid, and hopeless. When I am like this, all I want is to be off by myself alone. I do not want to be close to anyone. Unless I drink to pass out, I will stay up late into the night or wake up early in the morning, which can really aggravate the people around me who keep normal hours. My boyfriend and I fought constantly. I drank until I was drunk and then smoked crack to make me less depressed. But after the crack I felt even more depressed and irritable until the least little thing would set me off. My boyfriend couldn't take it any-more and threw me out into the street. Because of my mental and drug problems, my mother and sisters refused to take me into their homes. Of course, when a person has these problems, keeping a job is not an option; not that anyone in their right mind would hire them anyway. I was homeless and living on the streets. I would sell my body for a place to sleep, a good hot meal, and some alcohol and drugs. The things I did for drugs were unimaginable. I got a dose of syphilis and hepatitis, and I was infected with HIV.

I left my mental medications at the homeless shelter. So the voices came back blaring, and I was drinking until passing out and smoking marijuana constantly. I suffer from poor impulse control to begin with, and on crack I cannot control myself at all. My appearance became disheveled, my hair was uncombed, I did not bathe for days, and I would ramble and rant incoherently. I was a truly frightful sight to behold. I was something you would expect to see on your front doorstep on Hallowe'en. And that is coming from a former beautician. I believed that men were trying to kill my sisters and nieces. I was seeing shadows move and take form. I saw people coming up and staring at me when there were none. I thought people were in the bathroom with me when I was alone. I even saw the devil himself coming out of the motel where I was smoking crack. Then for five days and nights I smoked crack and drank alcohol and did not sleep until I thought my heart literally was going to explode. I went to my sister's house, where I chased her friend down the street with a butcher knife. I believed her friend had turned into a devil. The police came and arrested me. That was the second time I went to jail. The police knew me by now. I went back to the county emergency room and then to the psychiatric hospital.

This time I was a completely different person – a wild demon. I refused to take my medications. I was hostile with the hospital staff and would curse them out when they provoked me in the slightest. My family refused to visit me because it only upset me more. I know it upset them to see me like that. People who have not experienced a family member's mental illness cannot begin to comprehend the burdens, emotional stress, and hurt it causes the family too. I flew into a rage because I thought other patients had spilled my ice cream when there was no ice cream there at all. I raved on about wanting to kill my nephew whom I love dearly. I even tried to rush hospital staff in an attempt to leave on my own. I would stand rigid and stare into space for hours at a time. I needed assistance from the hospital staff just to change clothes and bathe. They would have to instruct and prompt me over and over to do the simplest tasks. Then I managed to steal a bottle of aspirin. I swallowed the entire bottle in another attempt to kill myself. They found out and pumped my stomach. If ever there was a bottom, I had hit it. The problem with suffering from mental illness is that, even if the illness has not blinded a person to the fact they hit bottom, it surely makes the person unable to do anything on their own.

'Paranoia'

I've been diagnosed as having paranoid schizophrenia. I also suffer from clinical depression. Before I found the correct medications, I was sleeping on the floor, afraid to sleep in my own bed. I was hearing voices that, lately, had turned from being sometimes helpful to being terrorizing. The depression had been responsible for my being irritable and full of dread, especially in the mornings, becoming angry over frustrations at work, and seemingly internalizing others' problems.

I finally had an episode, at home, not work, that I couldn't get out of and one that was making me too miserable. This was several months after a front-page automatic weapons robbery in North Hollywood, near my residence, and during a change in my supervisors. The voices, human-sounding from a short distance outside my apartment, were slowly turning nearly all bad. I could hear them jeering me, plotting against me, singing songs sometimes that would only make sense later in the day when I would do something wrong at work or at home. I began sleeping on the floor of my living room because I was afraid a presence in the bedroom was torturing good forces around me. If I slept in the bedroom, the nightly torture would cause me to make mistakes during the day. A voice, calling himself Fatty Acid, stopped me from drinking soda. Another voice allowed me only one piece of bread with meals. These two voices called themselves 'professionals'. I was forced to stop smoking, too. If I smoked, I would hit a pedestrian with my car. (Later that changed to causing someone else to hit a pedestrian.) My isolated existence, having no friends to visit and living alone in my apartment, made these restrictions worse. Small pleasures were all I had. I began to spend weekends sitting on the couch all day.

I thought of suicide a lot. Dread of going to work or doing anything outside of the apartment was insurmountable, though in spite of it, I kept going to work. Outside of the apartment, when I went to work or ran necessary errands, people would seem to mentally attack me. Something would spring from them to me and stay with me for hours, causing me mental anguish. It felt like a presence from my attackers bullied its way inside my head, tormenting areas in there.

'Special moments'

The reflection in the store window – it's me, isn't it? I know it is, but it's hard to tell. Glassy shadows, polished pastels, a jigsaw puzzle of my body, face, and clothes, with pieces disappearing whenever I move. And, if I want to reach out to touch me, I feel nothing but slippery coldness. Yet I sense that it's me. I just know.

I know I am a thirty-seven-year-old woman, a sculptor, a writer, a worker. I live alone. I know all of this, but, like the reflection in the glass, my existence seems undefined – more a mirage that I keep reaching for, but never can touch.

I've been feeling this way for almost a year now, ever since I was diagnosed a paranoid schizophrenic. Sometimes, though, I wonder if I ever knew myself, or merely played the parts that were acceptable, just so that I could fit in somewhere. But the illness has certainly stripped me of any pretense now, leaving me, instead, feeling hollow, yet hurting. I twist and turn, hoping to find a comfortable position in which to be just me.

There are still occasional episodes of hallucinations, delusions, and terrible fears, and I have medication for these times. It relieves my mental stress, but I hate my bodily responses to it and the dulling of my healthy emotions. Therefore, I stop using the drug as soon as the storms in my mind subside. And I keep wondering why there isn't more emphasis on alternative therapies, such as the holistic programs used now by people with physical illnesses.

But I know I'm still me in the experience. And I'm creative, sensitive. I believe in mysteries, magic, rainbows, and full moons. I wonder why it's expected that I be quieted, medicated whenever it seems I'm stepping out of the boundaries of 'reality'. Should I let anyone know that there are moments, just moments, in the schizophrenia that are 'special'? When I feel that I'm travelling to someplace I can't go to 'normally'? Where there's an awareness, a different sort of vision allowed me? Moments which I can't make myself believe are just symptoms of craziness and nothing more.

What's so 'special'? Well, the times when colors appear brighter, alluring almost, and my attention is drawn into the shadows, the lights, the intricate patterns of textures, the bold outlines of objects around me. It's as if all things have more of an existence than I do, that I've gone around the corner of humanity to witness another world where my seeing, hearing, and touching are intensified, and everything is a wonder.

Music, especially if I listen through headphones, envelops me and becomes alive, breathing high and low notes, and I'm floating on the movement.

Sometimes, in my schizophrenia, I go to the library, feeling like an explorer in a jungle of words and pictures. It can be frustrating because I capture nothing – not even one book chosen and checked out – but I scan the photos, the copied artworks, even focus on a paragraph or two, as I venture along the shelves, my eyes jumping from book to book. I soon leave, empty handed, yet satisfied by having seen so much.

My illness is a journey of fear, often paralyzing, mostly painful. If only someone could put a Bandaid on the wound . . . but where? Sometimes I feel I can't stand it any longer. It hurts too much, and I'm desperate to feel safe, comforted. It seems, at these times, when I reach bottom, that I'm given a message and I feel mystical, spiritual, and like a prophet who must tell anyone that there's really nothing to fear. A white light often appears, branding this message on my very soul, and those who are most afraid will see it in me and be at peace. And I somehow feel better for being the courier.

These 'special' moments of mine – there are so few, but I look for them and use them to help me pass through the schizophrenic episodes. And I can't even predict when or if these moments will come. But I won't deny their existence; I won't tell myself it's all craziness.

'Delusions'

A drama that profoundly transformed David Zelt* began at a conference on human psychology. David respected the speakers as scholars and wanted their approval of a paper he had written about telepathy. A week before the conference, David had sent his paper 'On the Origins of Telepathy' to one speaker, and the other speakers had all read it. He proposed the novel scientific idea that telepathy could only be optimally studied during the process of birth. He believed that the mother and infant have a telepathic bond that begins during delivery and should be studied before stimuli in the outer world significantly influence it. The paper described his observation, in an obstetrics clinic, of the mother and infant's facial expressions. They smiled or cried in parallel during delivery and for several minutes afterward. Facial expressions of happiness or pain appeared to occur at the same time and to be of similar intensity. He hoped this correlate, consistently present at seven births, would be verified for all humans. David knew that the paper, in reflecting engagement with an esoteric subject, was a signpost of his growing retreat from mundane reality.

David's paper was viewed as a monumental contribution to the conference and potentially to psychology in general. If scientifically verified, his concept of telepathy, universally present at birth and measurable, might have as much influence as the basic ideas of Darwin and Freud.

Each speaker focused on David. By using allusions and nonverbal communications that included pointing and glancing, each illuminated different aspects of David's contribution. Although his name was never mentioned, the speakers enticed David into feeling that he had accomplished something supernatural in writing the paper.

A spiritually evolved person with great capabilities was the center of attention. Extraordinary powers of perception, a gift for telepathy, and the intellectual prowess of an Einstein were mentioned. David was certain that all of these allusions were to him when one speaker, while discussing the telepathy hypothesis, said

---

*In this personal story, the young schizophrenic has written in the third person to distance himself from the episode.

'Our shepherd'. He was compared to a lion – courageous, regal, and wholesome; or a bird that could soar high like an eagle – extremely intuitive. He felt glorified.

David was described as having a halo around his head, and the Second Coming was announced as forthcoming. Messianic feelings took hold of him. His mission would be to aid the poor and needy, especially in underdeveloped countries. He also wanted to help everyone appreciate the joys and bear the sorrows of life; he hoped that, partly from his efforts, people would become more sensitive, caring, understanding, and loving of others.

David's sensitivity to nonverbal communication was extreme; he was adept at reading people's minds. His perceptual powers were so developed that he could not discriminate between telepathic reception and spoken language by others. He was distracted by others in a way that he had never been before. It was as if the nonverbal behavior of people interacting with him was a kind of code. Facial expressions, gestures, and postures of others often determined what he felt and thought.

Several hundred people at the conference were talking about David. He was the subject of enormous mystery, profound in his silence. Criticism, though, was often expressed by skeptics of the anticipated Second Coming. David felt the intense communication about him as torturous. He wished the talking, nonverbal behaviour, and pervasive train of thoughts about him would stop.

One speaker, whose name was a household word, referred to this intense communication about David as Nazism. The denouncement had a dramatic effect: people then sat passively and without talking or thinking. They no longer communicated to David through movements, speech, or telepathy. Revering this speaker and in an extremely suggestible state, David felt that verbal and nonverbal harassment of anyone very spiritually evolved was like Nazism, the worst of all evils in his view. For the first time, David anticipated that his role in life would be to see that the psychological brutality of Nazism could never happen to anyone else. He would ensure that humanity would be cleansed of the potential for Nazism. This transformation of humanity would take place with the arrival of the Second Coming.

During the next few weeks, David came to believe that he

was the reborn figure of Jesus Christ and that their spirits were identical. Like Christ, he was constantly in touch with the infinite and the eternal, and lived with a halo around his head that represented unity with God. David believed that he was the only person who could prevent the impending war that would end the world. He could prevent it by loving all humans and never qualifying or compromising his love.

From his apartment, David had a panoramic view in which many people expressed the basic needs and goals of humanity to him. They hoped that as the Messiah he could promote world change for the better. Activity on the left side represented the transcendental, intuitive, and holistic realm of human life; activity on the right side represented the material, rational, and analytical realm. As an example of expressed needs and goals, exhaust from airplanes in the sky formed patterns: the balanced scales of Libra on the left symbolized emotional harmony, and a scorpion on the right symbolized the analytical approach to life . . .

David began to suspect and then perceive that the federal agency was observing him. For a moment of insight explaining many peculiar, recent events in his life, he knew that he had been accused of treason for slandering Americans during his psychotherapy. Specifically, he had told his psychiatrist that Americans were debasing him 'like Nazis'. Wondering whether the Federal Bureau of Investigation was observing him, David decided to employ his telepathic powers to find out. An agent at a local agency told him there was no investigation. David read the agent's mind, however, and determined that the Central Intelligence Agency was conducting an investigation.

By electronic means, the CIA let people around the world know what David said in therapy. Gradually, everyone took sides either for or against the CIA and their opponent, David. The speakers from the conference all promoted David in their own countries as the Messiah. To harass him, verbally or nonverbally, was the psychological equivalent of Nazi torture. Many countries were bitter toward the United States government for letting the CIA investigate a spiritually evolved person. David viewed the CIA, in its harassment, as violating an amendment of the Constitution – freedom of religion.

It dawned upon David that the CIA was listening to most of his thoughts wherever he went, even sometimes during sleep. David could not think privately in words. His thoughts in words gave rise to subvocal movements that produced specific patterns of sound during breathing; the patterns were immediately picked up and deciphered by hidden CIA electronic equipment. David had no consistent privacy of mind, except for concrete visual imagery; such imagery was usually very pleasurable and could not be monitored because no sounds were generated. Thoughts in words often seemed to come from external sources that were localized in space, as if someone were talking to David; he could hear these thoughts, simultaneously while thinking them or momentarily later, broadcast by the CIA using electronic means. Wanting a confession of treason, the CIA tormented David by playing his thoughts aloud and also by making comments and criticisms about his thoughts. The CIA always claimed only to want the truth of whether David was a 'traitor' in his own mind; nonetheless they tormented him. The CIA treatment of him made the flow of his thinking sometimes seem chaotic or random. Also, playing his thoughts aloud led to a vicious cycle that was extremely painful for David. Hearing a particular thought broadcast tended to promote repetition of that thought.

Because his thoughts were broadcast around him, David often felt that his consciousness was controlled from outside himself and that he had merged with the external environment. In his perceptions, broadcast thoughts were often superimposed on the sounds of running water, air vents, and cars passing by. These continuous noises of water, air, or car motion usually sounded like flies buzzing in the background of the broadcast thought. The boundary between his mind and the world seemed blurred.

THE NATURE OF SCHIZOPHRENIA

These accounts provide a flavour of what it must be like to suffer from schizophrenia. They also give an indication of the extraordinarily diverse manifestations of the illness, which can vary dramatically from patient to patient, and also, at different times, within the same patient. Part of the fascination of schizophrenia relates to the extreme individuality, indeed often the originality, of a patient's symptoms and behaviour. But within this wide individual range, certain themes emerge. Not all patients with schizophrenia exhibit all these features; however, most patients during the lifetime of their illness will show many of these aspects to some degree.

Social and emotional withdrawal

It is common for schizophrenia to reveal itself first during adolescence. It may sometimes be difficult to distinguish illness from mere adolescent moodiness. Professionals are often wrong in giving reassurance and parents are often right in being worried.

One of the first manifestations of the disease may be an increasing need for and insistence on solitude. Most people, perhaps especially during adolescence, need solitude at some time, but in the person who is becoming schizophrenic this tendency may be exaggerated. They will tend to spend more and more time in their room, increasingly to withdraw from friends, and to make less and less contact with the outside world. When contacts are made with other people, including family, the emotional responses (technically known as the 'affect' of the schizophrenic person) are often either absent or inappropriate. A situation which would normally elicit a cheerful response may be met with a blank stare. An event of sorrow or grief may be greeted with a cold laugh or other entirely inappropriate reaction.

At the same time there is often an inversion of the normal day/night rhythm. The person will stay up later and later at night, frequently obsessively listening to music or crouching over a computer screen. The hour of rising in the morning becomes, not surprisingly, progressively later. Eventually the sleep/wake pattern may be completely reversed, which may be a source of considerable family distress and tension.

Disorganization of thinking

The schizophrenic individual often thinks in ways which, at least initially, appear incomprehensible to the normal person. Bizarre connections are made between apparently unrelated facts, observations or events – connections which to the patient appear rational and crystal clear. The sympathetic and concerned listener may, with difficulty, be able to discern some logic in the process, but the thought patterns are rarely simple or direct.

This has given rise to the vividly descriptive term of 'knight's move' thinking, by analogy with chess. The schizophrenic individual's thinking may head in one direction and then suddenly veer off along a quite different path. There is often a connection, but it may be very tenuous.

Associated with such thinking disorders, and possibly in part a cause of them, is an inability to distinguish between the relative importance of incoming information. All sensations may be perceived as potentially of equal significance. The bird flying across the road may be as important as the oncoming car. The colour and pattern of the newsreader's tie may be as important as the words being spoken. The patient may have an overwhelming sense of being bombarded with an incomprehensible *mélange* of often conflicting information and may be thoroughly confused about what action to take.

While these extreme disorders of information processing and of thinking are disabling, it does not require much insight to appreciate that, in milder forms, these 'problems' may bring creative advantage. Someone who is open to a somewhat wider range of information and experience than usual, or who can see unusual ways of approaching a problem, is a person who may be highly creative. A 'touch of schizophrenia' may be a valuable asset, as will be discussed in much more depth in a later chapter.

Delusions of control and paranoia

Many schizophrenic people come to believe that something or someone is controlling their lives. Their brains are being directed by outside agencies, often aliens, or intelligence services of their own or hostile countries, or terrorist organizations. Many patients complain that listening devices and controlling systems have been planted in their homes, or in nearby buildings, or sometimes in their own bodies. The controlling influences are usually seen as malign, acting in some way against the patient's own best interests and in favour of a hostile agent or agency. As these delusions grow and develop, they can lead to suspicion and to serious paranoia. There may be extreme and irrational fear of outside influences operating through people and places which others would regard as completely normal.

Hallucinations

One common and classic feature of schizophrenia is the sensation of voices being heard inside the mind, although there are no external sounds. Sometimes these voices are friendly, inspiring and encouraging. The voices which Joan of Arc heard may have been of this type. More commonly the voices are irrational and bizarre, and sometimes they are downright threatening.

On occasion the patient may be able to conduct a dialogue with the voices and this interchange becomes an important part of their life. At other times voices may be imperious and directive, telling the listener to do certain things or else there may be terrible consequences. Schizophrenic patients who murder may do so under this type of inner direction. Visual hallucinations have received much less attention than auditory ones, but recently it has been recognized that they too are commonly experienced.

Interest in religion and in complex philosophies and belief systems

Interest in religion is not a sign of schizophrenia, but, as will be seen in Chapter 9 on family studies, extreme interest in religion is much more common among the relatives of schizophrenic people than among the relatives of normal people. What is common in patients with schizophrenia, or in those who are at risk, is an interest in religion or philosophy which is extraordinarily intense and all-consuming. The involvement may become very complex and elaborate. It may involve belief systems which start with orthodox religion or philosophy but then become more and more complex, intricate, elaborate and bizarre. The lives of some of the saints have features which may, without stretching the point too much, be labelled schizophrenic.

Hostility

Many schizophrenic patients are not hostile, but some are. Not surprisingly, the hostility is commonly found in those who are paranoid. Very surprisingly to those unfamiliar with the illness, the hostility is often directed much more intensely against the patient's family and friends than against anyone else. Mothers are particularly vulnerable: anyone who kills their mother is likely to be schizophrenic.

The hostility from a close relative can be terrifying and is frequently seriously underestimated by professional advisers, especially those who are relatively recently qualified. Patients may appear to behave quite rationally to such advisers but then return home to subject their mothers to a reign of terror. Families should always be listened to. Sometimes, of course, they are less than objective, but often their terrifying tales are true.

In their fully fledged forms the features of schizophrenia are invariably destructive. But milder versions of those same features have obvious advantages. Strange ways of thinking can lead to creative acts, especially in the arts and sciences. An interest in religion is one of the most persistent aspects of our humanity. And a little paranoia and irrational hostility may have some survival value.

THE COURSE OF SCHIZOPHRENIA

No two schizophrenic patients exhibit exactly the same manifestations of the illness. Similarly, no two schizophrenic sufferers experience an illness which runs precisely the same course. Nevertheless, in most cases there are certain common patterns which can readily be recognized.

Several long-term studies of children who are at risk of schizo-phrenia because of their family history have been performed in the USA, Europe and Australia. There are no certainties, but those children who will later develop the illness may be different in several ways from those who grow up to be normal. The child at serious risk is the one who is somewhat withdrawn; who is less easy in social relationships; who is less able at sport; and who is less able to deal with words. Of course, most children who exhibit these features do not go on to become schizophrenic, but those children who do become schizophrenic are mostly drawn from this pool of slightly odd and lonely children.

During adolescence, behaviour often becomes odder. The young person becomes more withdrawn, spends more time alone, may become intensely interested in religion, philosophy, computers, mathematics or numerology, and may become hostile towards the immediate family. Again, all these things are common in perfectly normal adolescents. But there can be a quality about the hostility or the withdrawal which is outside the norm and which can be detected by an alert and experienced clinician or parent.

Descent into full schizophrenia usually occurs some time between the ages of fifteen and thirty-five, often after the young person has left home. It may be precipitated by some form of stress, such as financial problems, trouble with college courses, exams, relationship difficulties or any of the other problems which affect people at this age. An inexperienced counsellor may take the view that the stress has caused the schizophrenia. This is not true. Stress does not cause schizophrenia. Stressful episodes precipitate its appearance and influence its timing in a person who is almost certain to develop the condition sooner or later. If the stresses are completely removed, the person may return to a relative, if somewhat odd, normality. Yet there will always be the risk that another stressful episode will precipitate a recurrence of the problem.

Increasingly, we are finding that the stressor which precipitates the first episode of schizophrenia is drug abuse. Cannabis seems particularly important in this context. Again, what seems to be happening is that the drug is exposing an underlying susceptibility. Cannabis is not causing the schizophrenia. Most people who smoke cannabis do not become schizophrenic. However, cannabis exposes those who are most at risk and tips them over the edge.

Schizophrenia tends to occur a year or two earlier in men than in women. Men also tend to become more seriously ill with the disease. This is in part due to the action of the female hormone, oestrogen. Several studies have now shown that this hormone has a partially protective effect and a group in Melbourne, Australia, is exploring the possibility of using oestrogen as a treatment. Among women who are schizophrenic, those with the highest oestrogen levels are the least severely ill.

After the age of thirty-five relatively few patients become ill for the first time. When this does happen it usually occurs in people who have long been recognized as being slightly odd but who, because of sheltered family and social circumstances, have escaped many of the stresses of life. There are, however, two recognized late peaks, although these are much less marked than the surge in adolescence and early adulthood. One of these peaks occurs in women at or soon after the menopause. It is likely that this is related partly to the extra stress which some women experience at menopause, and partly to a loss of protective oestrogen. The other peak occurs in old age and can affect people of both sexes. It is not yet clear that this is the same illness. It may be a form of degeneration of the nervous system with a biochemical basis different from that in the main forms of schizophrenia.

RESPONSE TO TREATMENT

At present treatment of schizophrenia is distinctly unsatisfactory. Unfortunately, it is not uncommon for professionals to give unrealistically optimistic predictions. Such over-optimism is not at all helpful in the management of the condition. Almost all patients and their families are aware of this reality as they go through their lives trying to cope.

The truth is that depressingly few people with schizophrenia will ever be continuously employed in normal work. Of those who are, most are in jobs which are much less demanding than would have been expected by those who knew these people before they became ill. Even Nobel Laureate John Nash, who did exceptional work in mathematics, game theory and economics in his twenties, failed to fulfil his promise in the succeeding thirty years. Schizophrenia tragically blights minds and lives. It drives patients and their families to despair. Because it begins so young and then lasts a lifetime, its impact is much greater than that of illnesses like cancer or heart disease, which have much higher profiles but which usually develop much later in life and rarely destroy the mind.

Of every five young people with a first episode of schizophrenia, perhaps one will recover sufficiently to live a nearly normal life, either without drugs or with low drug doses. It is a disappointing fact that the usual doses, even of the newest drugs, are rarely compatible with a fully normal existence. On average they produce only a 15–20 per cent reduction in symptoms. Older compounds cause the serious side-effect of abnormal involuntary movements (similar to Parkinson's disease and to other neurological disorders). Not surprisingly, these effects cause great distress to both patients and families.

A new generation of drugs is relatively free of these movement side-effects, but these new treatments commonly cause sedation, cardiac problems, severe weight gain, or even diabetes – effects which can be very bad for personal performance, for long-term health and for self-esteem. Both old and new drug treatments may cause a vague dysphoria, a sense of unease, a feeling that things are not quite right in the brain. Because of the difficulty in defining it precisely, this dysphoria does not always emerge in lists of the side-effects of the drugs, but conversations with patients make it clear that this is one of the main reasons why so many people stop treatment.

As a result of these problems, of the four people who do not achieve near normality, only one is likely to comply with proper drug treatment near continuously. Such patients must of necessity stay in close contact with the mental health services whose job it is to provide psychological, social and often financial support. These services may help to reduce stress and to prevent major relapses, but they can work successfully only in association with proper drug treatment. Without drugs, the other support services can only rarely keep a patient tolerably well.

Of the three remaining patients, one will not take medication regularly, mainly because of side-effects, but will remain in some contact with the support services. Such patients can be reached and will often accept help, and even medication, to deal with severe relapses if this is presented in the right way.

Sadly, the remaining two patients will usually just drop off the edge of the world and be 'lost to follow up'. They do not want to continue contact and what happens to them is not always clear. Some commit suicide: between 10 and 20 per cent of all patients with schizophrenia commit suicide during the course of their illness. Some join the ranks of the homeless or near homeless. Some live desperate, unhappy and secluded lives at home, causing great misery to themselves and those around them.

The picture is not a happy one. But partly as a result of new biochemical understanding of brain-fat biochemistry there is hope that it may be beginning to change. New research into the bio-chemical causes of schizophrenia suggests surprising connections with our human origins. It also gives hope that new treatments which are free of the unpleasant side-effects of existing drugs may become available.

THE EXTRAORDINARY GEOGRAPHICAL DISTRIBUTION OF SCHIZOPHRENIA

Most diseases vary significantly in their distribution around the world. Certain diseases are absent from some races while being common in others. Others differ substantially in the proportion of people affected from race to race. This is not the case with schizo-phrenia. In all populations of the world, from the Canadian Arctic to Patagonia, from Lapland to the Cape of Good Hope, from Siberia to the world of the Australian Aborigines, the picture is the same. Between 0.5 per cent and 1.5 per cent – and usually between 0.7 per cent and 1.0 per cent – of all the populations who have been adequately studied develop schizophrenia over a lifetime. This is a very special feature of schizophrenia. No other illness shares a similar distribution.

Although much evidence collected by many investigators over

many years pointed in this direction, the uniform geographical distribution of schizophrenia was finally confirmed by a large World Health Organization study performed in the 1970s. The research protocol was highly complex and detailed. The first stage was to establish an agreed and uniform definition of schizophrenia on which all the participants could agree. Differences from country to country in the diagnostic criteria defining diseases have often made population studies in psychiatry very difficult. The WHO investigators were determined to avoid that trap and they succeeded in agreeing on exactly how schizophrenia should be defined.

Armed with this agreed definition, the investigators then went to eight countries with very different racial and cultural backgrounds: the USA, Colombia, the UK, the USSR, Czechoslovakia, Nigeria, India and Japan. In each they assessed carefully the incidence and the lifetime risk of developing schizophrenia. In addition, the investigators devised a measure of the severity of the illness in affected individuals.

The results were surprising to many. The lifetime risk of schizophrenia was similar in each of the eight countries. Neither race, nor political system, nor culture seemed to have any major impact. All people are equally susceptible, no matter what their colour, religion, political beliefs or financial and nutritional circumstances.

As part of the WHO study, the investigators also developed a score for the lifetime severity of schizophrenia. This was a measure involving the duration of illness, the severity of illness and the consequent degree of lifetime disruption. Again, in view of the strong findings of a relatively uniform lifetime prevalence across races, the results were surprising. The lifetime severity of the illness differed substantially from country to country. In some countries schizophrenia seemed usually to be a relentless lifetime disorder with a progressively disastrous downhill course. In others it seemed to be more of an episodic illness without that relentless progression, and with long periods of apparent or near normality. Embarrassingly for Western medicine, the countries where the course was best were those which are least developed. Western industrialized countries scored worst.

Many attempts have been made to explain this finding. Race was irrelevant and none of the other obvious possibilities, such as political system, social or family structure, type of health-care system or degree of economic development, provided a persuasive explanation.

After completion of the original study, two Danish investigators, O. and E. Christensen, had another idea. They wondered whether nutrition might be involved in reducing or exacerbating the severity of the illness. Their initial explorations indicated that they were on to something. It seemed that variations in fat intake might be able to explain much of the difference in severity from country to country. Countries with a high intake of saturated fat relative to the intake of unsaturated fat did badly. Countries with a low intake of saturated fat did well. Diet in general and fat intake in particular seemed to have a marked effect on the course of schizophrenia.

This is an observation to which I shall return. It may provide insights into both the evolution of humanity and the development of schizophrenia. But at this point I want to concentrate on the first of the two major findings of the WHO study: the fact that schizophrenia is present in all races and that the proportion of people affected by the illness is so similar around the world.

To date few people have tried to think through the implications of this observation. The interpretations that have been proposed differ greatly in detail but agree on one important conclusion: the problem of schizophrenia must have entered humanity prior to the time when humans divided into separate races. While we were still not many generations, if any, from the original Adam and Eve (no matter how that story may be interpreted), some humans had schizophrenia. And as our ancestors migrated from Africa 100,000–150,000 years ago and differentiated into the different races, so they carried schizophrenia with them to the corners of the earth.

When did this injection of schizophrenia into humanity occur? We can never be sure because our knowledge of our origins is, and will probably forever remain, fragmentary. Most of the evidence has been irrevocably lost.

But some evidence does remain. As discussed earlier, perhaps the most important lies in the mitochondrial, Y-chromosome and autosomal genes which are present in contemporary humans. By analysing the differences, and with knowledge of the rates at which DNA may change with time, something approaching consensus has been achieved – although there remain some dissenting voices. The now widely accepted view is that all modern human races had common ancestors who lived in Africa between about 200,000 and 100,000 years ago. If schizophrenia entered the human race later than the diaspora out of Africa we might expect some modern human groups to be without the illness.

The latest date at which schizophrenia could have entered humanity must therefore have been before the last date at which there could realistically have been reproductive communication between all humans. We cannot state with certainty when that date was, but there is reasonable evidence to suggest that, once the Australian Aborigines reached their new continent, rising sea levels would have cut them off from the rest of humanity. That date of reaching Australia must have been more than 40,000 years ago because there are well-dated archaeological sites in Australia going back to about then, and the most recent evidence dates the earliest sites to around 60,000 years ago. The earliest realistic date for entry into Australia is therefore around 70,000–80,000 years ago. How long it took for our ancestors to migrate from their African origins to Australia is unknown, but 10,000–20,000 years may be a reasonable guess.

So, at some time between about 60,000 years ago at the latest, or 150,000 years ago at the earliest, all human races acquired their schizophrenic inheritance. I believe that this acquisition was the single most important event in human history. I suggest that this was the break-point between our large-brained, possibly pleasant, but unimaginative ancestors, and the restless, creative, unsettled creatures we so obviously are today. Is this the true creation story?

8

'I THINK FOR MY PART ONE HALF OF THE NATION IS MAD – AND THE OTHER NOT VERY SOUND'

TOBIAS SMOLLETT, 1721–1771

FIRST-YEAR PSYCHOLOGY STUDENTS, AFTER READING AN ELEMEN-tary textbook of psychiatry, are usually pretty confident about what constitutes schizophrenia. Similarly, neuroscience researchers who specialize in brain studies, but who do not see patients, often think that schizophrenia is a nice, clean clinical entity. Those who work with patients and their families, and who observe carefully the behaviour of their professional colleagues, often become less and less certain about the precision of the distinction between schizophrenia and normality or schizophrenia and other psychiatric illnesses.

SCHIZOPHRENIA AND OTHER PSYCHIATRIC ILLNESSES

One of my teachers in psychiatry at St Mary's Medical School in London was struggling to explain to us the distinction between normality, neurotic disorders and psychiatric disorders. He produced an oversimplification which nevertheless is helpful in beginning to get a handle on these difficult concepts. The over-simplified concept is somewhat old fashioned, as is the distinction between neuroses and psychoses, but it does offer some insight.

He said that neurotic disorders were problems of coping with the world which any normal person could understand, even if they could not understand the degree of distress caused. We all know what it is to be anxious, about an examination, a job interview, the result of a football match, a public performance. Even if we do not share their level of distress, it is not too difficult to get into the skin of someone who is irrationally anxious about meeting people, about car journeys, seeing their children off to school or any other of the minor uncertainties of life. Equally, the person who suffers from such a problem usually understands that the fears are largely irrational and has some insight into the nature of the condition.

The story is similar with mild to moderate depression. We all feel down for a while after life's disappointments – a failure to win the Lottery when this time we had that special feeling that our number would come up, loss of a key football match or baseball game by our favourite team, a failure to get a promotion we really wanted, a disappointing school report for one of our children, loss of a substantial sum of money on the stock market, or the illness or death of a close relative or friend. These all naturally and quite reasonably make us feel depressed for a period which relates to the severity of the event. We can therefore understand, if not share, the feelings of someone who becomes irrationally down after rela-tively minor life events, or even after no negative life events at all.

Again, we all know what it is like to worry mildly about whether we locked the car or turned off the cooker. Virtually everyone has had the experience of returning irrationally to check on something we are pretty sure we have done correctly. So we can understand people with an obsessive compulsive disorder, who have to check everything many times, or who repeatedly wash their hands, or perform other rituals which normal people perceive as completely irrational. Irrational they are, but we have at least some insight into what they are feeling.

Psychotic disorders are not like that. In the psychoses, my

teacher said, you cannot begin to imagine how someone could experience these feelings or behave in that way. The continuum with normality seems to be lost and the patient seems out of touch with reality and with their clinical carers. Such patients have no real insight into their condition.

The features of schizophrenia have been discussed in the previous chapters. The paranoia, the delusions, the hallucinations, the ideas of reference and control which can occur, all seem impossible for the normal person to understand without specific professional training. The same can be true of the other two major psychiatric disorders: bipolar disorder (sometimes known as manic-depression) and psychotic depression.

Bipolar disorder is a situation where the psychiatric state of the individual can vary dramatically over time. The variation may be from mania – an impossible 'high' – to normality and back again. Or it may be from normality to psychotic depression – a profound 'low' – and back again. Or it may be from normality, to mania, to depression and back through the cycle on a roller-coaster which leaves the patient, the carers and the relatives emotionally and sometimes physically exhausted. Mania often begins with a state called hypomania which many patients really enjoy. They feel good about themselves, they need a reduced amount of sleep, they feel super-energetic, they perform well at work, they may be socially hyperactive. They feel that they are attractive, life-enhancing people, a view often shared by those around them. The happiest people on earth are those few fortunates who seem to be in a state of mild, stable hypomania.

But, sometimes gradually and sometimes abruptly, the hypo-mania can shade into something darker and more dangerous. The absence of a need for sleep leads to days of eighteen-, twenty- or even twenty-two-hour activity. The self-confidence leads to decisions which are beyond reason and which not infrequently lead to financial ruin. The feeling of creativity can be extraordinary. Occasionally that creativity leads to something spectacular, like Handel's *Messiah*, written during a twenty-eight-day creative burst which was probably a manic episode. More often the feeling of creativity, like that sometimes generated by a drug high, leads to an outpouring of inconsequential drivel which is viewed with appalled dismay by its author once the episode is over. There may be extreme hypersexuality, which is often astonishingly successful in projecting an image of attractiveness and in generating surprising numbers of partners, frequently without the taking of ordinary precautions about pregnancy or the spread of disease. There may be extreme irritability and intolerance of the views of others. There may be hallucinations and delusions. The individual becomes totally immune to any rational persuasion. Eventually the actions become so grandiose and bizarre that some form of coercion must be used to ensure hospitalization, where the episode can usually be brought to an end with appropriate treatment.

Often, however, before hospitalization occurs, the mania is terminated by a switch which seems to be thrown in the brain of the patient. A man will go to sleep in an impossibly high state and wake up a few hours later in an equally profound despair. This switch, almost as disorientating for the relatives and carers as for the patient, is why the disease is called bipolar disorder, or manic-depression.

The depressed state, which sometimes occurs in cycles even without the mania, or sometimes is more or less continuous, can be as profound and irrational as the mania. There may be a sensation of apparently irretrievable despair and guilt. Every past mistake, every indiscretion and every failure become enormously magnified and patients blame themselves to completely inappropriate degrees. Nothing at all gives pleasure – not food, drink, nature, beauty or sex. No interest can be aroused in anything. Delusions are not infrequent.

At their extremes, schizophrenia, bipolar disorder and psychotic depression appear to be clearly defined, well-characterized disorders. The young psychiatrist can pick out with certainty which patient falls into which category. But with experience, that certainty becomes less confident. Many patients seem to have features of both schizophrenia and either bipolar disorder or depression. This occurs so often that as early as the 1930s a fourth psychosis – schizo-affective disorder – was identified to describe those patients who seem to have features of more than one disorder and who cannot easily be pigeon-holed in one of the other three.

Some psychiatrists – often the intellectual leaders of their profession, like Tim Crow of Oxford, Ming Tsuang of Harvard, or Robert Kendell of Edinburgh – have been yet more radical. They have tried to define the points of clear distinction between schizophrenia and bipolar disorder, or between bipolar disorder and depression, and have been unable to find them. Real patients rarely fit clear criteria which allow one to say with certainty that this patient is in one category and that patient is in another. There appears to be a continuum of psychotic disorder with no certain dividing line. Some investigators, like Ming Tsuang of Harvard, have begun to argue for the idea that there may be a single 'psychosis gene' which decides whether a person will be susceptible to any of the psychotic disorders, with a whole series of other genes which then determine the form which the psychosis will take, whether it be predominantly schizophrenic, predominantly bipolar, predominantly depressive, or a mixture of any two or even of all three. The concept makes clinical sense and is gaining more acceptance.

THE BORDERLINE BETWEEN
SCHIZOPHRENIA AND NORMALITY

It is obvious and unexceptionable to say that there is a continuum of psychological states between bipolar disorder and normality or psychotic depression and normality. Even though the normal individuals may be unable to imagine the extreme ends of the psychotic scale, all normal people know what it is like to be a bit irrationally depressed, a bit irrationally high or a bit irrationally obsessive compulsive.

But a bit schizophrenic? That, for most people, is a much more disturbing thought. Most non-psychotic people know that schizophrenic thinking and behaviour are highly abnormal and so are extremely reluctant ever to admit that they may experience such things. They know enough that, when given questionnaires about their psychological state, they may give misleading 'normal' answers to particular questions which may remotely suggest schizophrenic-type thinking or experiences.

But such intermediate states between schizophrenia and

THE MADNESS OF ADAM AND EVE

normality may be no less common than the equivalent intermediate states between normality on the one hand and mania or depression on the other. It is just much less common to admit to them. Some investigators, such as Gordon Claridge of Magdalen College, Oxford, have devoted a lifetime to thinking and researching such intermediate states, which may be called schizotypal, schizoid, schizophrenia spectrum or schizotaxic. (There are many arguments about the precise meanings of these words, but in this book I will use them interchangeably to describe aspects of behaviour which show some similarities to schizophrenia but which fall short of frank madness or psychosis.) Many people who are not psychotic regularly hear voices inside their heads: there are associations to which such people may belong, in part to reassure themselves of their normality in the face of an apparently psychotic symptom. It takes skill and sympathy for an investigator to tease out the fact that an apparently normal person may be having auditory hallucinations.

Other characteristics of schizotypy, which have been well described by Gordon Claridge and others, are: a tendency to be mildly paranoid, to believe that others are trying to do one down; a related tendency to feud with neighbours, family or colleagues about trivia; an obsession with health in someone who is in fact normally healthy; an intense interest in religion, beyond what might be considered usual; sometimes an obsession with numbers and precise logic, or with activities where numbers and precision may be of major importance, such as chess, music and computers; a great interest in magical thinking, involving aliens, fairies, UFOs, miraculous coincidences or other events; a difficulty with personal relationships and an awkwardness in social situations; a general characteristic which may be summed up by the word 'nerd', 'trainspotter', 'anorak' or even 'academic'. None of these things can be considered a psychosis, but just as marked sadness after a relatively trivial event represents an intermediate state between depression and normality, so schizotypal or schizoid thinking and behaviour may be intermediate states between schizophrenia and normality. Yet again, while the typical schizophrenic individual and the typical normal individual may appear to fall into clear categories, the real world fails to show categorical dividing lines. Normality merges imperceptibly into schizotypy and schizotypy merges imperceptibly into schizophrenia.

Several large and careful population surveys, organized by William Eaton in the United States, by Jim van Os in the Netherlands and by John McGrath in Australia, have provided support for Claridge's views. These surveys have asked questions about hallucinations and delusions and other aspects of schizophrenia. Schizophrenic patients will answer many of those questions in a manner characteristic of their illness. But a surprising number of people who are classed as normal will answer one, two or three questions in a schizophrenic way. They may confess to hearing voices or to an irrational sense of persecution or to a belief in fairies and the like.

Once sensitized to the concept of schizotypy, most people become aware that perhaps 10–20 per cent of the population may exhibit some aspects of behaviour characteristic of this category. Schizotypal individuals are without doubt concentrated in academia, in the more dogmatic religions, and in political parties where theory and doctrine are of great importance. The pedantry, the feuds, the paranoia, but also the magical thinking and creativity of academics may be in part related to their schizotypy. Isaac Newton, with his creative brilliance, but also his alchemy, his interest in the occult, his secretiveness and his passionate feuding, was a good example of a schizotypal person and by this designation we can avoid endless discussions of whether he was schizophrenic or bipolar. In companies, IT departments, information departments and finance departments may sometimes be places where it seems that there are unusual concentrations of schizotypal people. Despite their downsides and the negative features of their personalities, schizotypal people may also play an exceptional and positive role in society. The list of people who have shown schizotypal features of behaviour and who have also made major contributions to society is very long and will be discussed further in Chapter 9. As well as Newton it includes Einstein, Kant, Faraday, Edison and Beethoven, to name only a few of the most prominent. Schizotypal people may have been critical to human success.

DYSLEXIA

Dyslexia is a learning disability which involves particular problems with reading and writing words. In other respects the intellectual performance of people with dyslexia is usually normal.

Alex Richardson, who worked with Gordon Claridge, drew attention to an interesting aspect of schizotypy. Many people (but certainly not all) who are dyslexic are also schizotypal and vice versa. Many families in which schizophrenia is present are also commonly affected by dyslexia. Dyslexia, like schizotypy, seems to be involved in this continuum between schizophrenia and normality.

BIPOLAR DISORDER

For long periods of their lives many people with bipolar disorder appear normal or even super-normal. Only for periods of their life do they descend into psychosis, although those descents can be devastating and dramatic. But milder forms of the disorder, expressing themselves as mood changes which are less dramatic than psychosis, are extremely common. People affected in this way are often thought by others to be unpredictable and moody. Sunny, expansive, energetic and friendly on some days, on others they are gloomy, irritable, difficult to engage in conversation and slothful. 'Cyclothymic' is a useful word to describe personalities of this type. Just as schizophrenia may merge imperceptibly into bipolar disorder, so can the boundaries between schizotypy and cyclothymia be equally blurred.

OVERVIEW

The concepts of schizophrenia, of bipolar disorder and of psychotic depression are extraordinarily difficult to define in ways which provide a clear categorical demarcation either from normality or from each other. The extremes are easy, but large numbers of mentally ill or supposedly normal people do not reach these extremes. They are a bit schizophrenic, a bit bipolar, a bit depressive, a bit schizotypal or a bit cyclothymic, but the dividing lines are inevitably arbitrary and depend on the personal biases of the assessor. The abnormalities of behaviour may well vary over time, leading to changes in perceived diagnosis. If these illnesses have a genetic basis, the only sensible conclusions that we can draw are that the genes are relatively widely distributed in the population and that they are heavily influenced by non-genetic factors operating in the environment, whether as a result of social factors or as a result of biological factors such as nutrition or medication. That there is a genetic connection, and how this may have played a role in our evolution, will be discussed in the following chapters.

9

'OUR SAD BAD GLAD MAD BROTHER'

ALGERNON CHARLES SWINBURNE, 1837–1909

IN THE 1950S, BRUNO BETTELHEIM AND THE SCHOOLS OF psychology and psychiatry with which he was associated were the subjects of reverence and adulation, particularly in the United States, but also among 'right-thinking' and 'forward-thinking' people throughout the world. We now know, however, that Bettelheim's public persona was partly based on intellectual and financial deception and that he was possibly a serial abuser of children. His example provides a warning against the ready acceptance of the opinions of the myriad 'experts' who try to tell us what to do.

In the 1940s, 1950s and 1960s, particularly in the USA, psychiatry was heavily influenced by the ideas of Sigmund Freud, and the more pernicious concepts of some of Freud's intellectual heirs, like Bettelheim. Childhood psychoses, such as autism, and adult psychoses, such as schizophrenia, were all blamed on early upbringing. It was usually the mother who was to blame. The concept of the 'schizophrenogenic mother' or the 'refrigerator mother', who was unable to respond to her children with normal warmth, became commonplace. Such views are disturbingly still present, often in certain schools of psychology and sociology which seem stuck in a mid-twentieth-century timewarp. Even today it is not uncommon for social workers and psychologists, talking to the distraught parents of a teenage boy or girl who has just suffered a schizophrenic breakdown, to indicate that parental behaviour either caused or contributed to the problem.

Also in the 1950s, however, a group of determined investigators came to the conclusion that the concept of the schizophrenogenic mother was likely to be destructive nonsense. They therefore established a series of studies which was to provide the basis for our modern knowledge of schizophrenia. These studies were of three main types:

- the distribution of schizophrenia and other psychiatric illnesses in families identified because they had a schizophrenic member, or 'proband';

- the patterns of schizophrenia in identical and non-identical twins;

- the risks of schizophrenia in infants of normal and of schizophrenic mothers who were adopted immediately after birth.

Most of these studies involved some variant of the following procedure. A family with a schizophrenic member is identified and that family member is called the 'first case' or 'proband'. The family is then studied for other members who might have the same illness, preferably over several generations. Particular attention is paid to the pattern of illness in identical and non-identical twins, in first-degree relatives (parents, siblings and children, who share half of the genes of the proband), second-degree relatives (grandparents, grandchildren, uncles, aunts, nephews, nieces and first cousins, who share a quarter of the genes of the proband) and third-degree relatives (great-grandchildren, great-grandparents, and more distant aunts, uncles, nephews, nieces and cousins, who share one-eighth of the genes of the proband).

The first and most obviously apparent fact about family patterns of the illness is that schizophrenia does run in families. In this sense, certain families do seem to be schizophrenogenic. First-, second-, third-degree and more distant relatives are definitely more likely to be schizophrenic than is the general population if there is an affected family member. Identical twins of a proband are more at risk than non-identical twins or other siblings. First-degree relatives are more at risk than second-degree relatives and second-degree relatives are more at risk than third-degree relatives. Even third-degree relatives are more at risk than the general population.

The second fact is that schizophrenia cannot be due to a single gene. There are two possible explanations for how a single gene causes disease: neither applies to schizophrenia. In the first type, known as dominant, the presence of a single abnormal gene from either the mother or the father will cause the disease. Since the single gene will cause the disease, and since everyone carries two copies (or alleles) of each gene, except for the genes on the X and Y chromosomes, there is a 50/50 chance of passing the single abnormal dominant gene on to children. So in any reasonably large family study, a disease caused by a single dominant gene will be seen in about 50 per cent of all the first-degree relatives of any affected person. If the gene is present, the person is ill; if the gene is not present, the person is not ill.

With so-called recessive illnesses caused by a single type of gene, *both* members of the pair of alleles, one from the father and one from the mother, must be abnormal if the disease is to be present. One abnormal allele is silent, and does not have any adverse effect if the other paired allele is normal. Since everyone gets one allele from one parent and one allele from the other, a person with the disease must have obtained an abnormal gene from both the mother and the father. If the mother and father each have only one abnormal allele and one normal one, they will not be affected themselves, which is why 'recessive' genetic illnesses often appear out of the blue. However, each time that particular pair of parents has a child, each parent will have a 50 per cent chance of passing on an abnormal gene to that child, and so the child will have a 25 per cent chance of getting two abnormal genes, one from each parent. So each sibling of the first abnormal child will also have a 25 per cent chance of also being affected. Tay-Sach's disease and cystic fibrosis are good examples of recessively inherited diseases.

While schizophrenia clearly runs in families, the patterns of inheritance are quite different from those seen with dominant or recessive disease genes. It is therefore very unlikely that schizophrenia is caused by a single gene. It is much more likely that two, three or more genes must be present for schizophrenia to occur. There is only one serious psychotic disorder which is caused by a single gene and that is the rare Huntington's disease, which causes uncontrollable body movements and progressive dementia. This tragic illness is indeed caused by a single dominant gene and, as expected, about half of all the first-degree relatives of proband patients are affected. Folk-singer Woody Guthrie is perhaps the best-known person ever to have suffered from Huntington's disease.

The third thing that is apparent from the family studies is that schizophrenia is rarely the only psychiatric illness or psychological disturbance to be found in these families. Schizotypy is common, suggesting that it may be related to the presence of one or more, but not all, of the genes required to make someone schizophrenic. This was noted as early as 1863 by Isaac Ray in his descriptions of the relatives of psychotic patients incarcerated in asylums. He noted that many of the relatives exhibited in partial form the symptoms of the patients. These perceptive observations have been confirmed by both formal investigation and informal experience on many occasions since. But depression, bipolar disorder, sociopathy (also known as psychopathy), learning disabilities including dyslexia, and a criminal record are also more common than expected in the relatives of schizophrenic individuals.

What is going on here? The short answer is that we do not know, but there are two possible explanations. One is that several major genes must be simultaneously present in the same individual if that person is to be schizophrenic. We don't know how many 'several' is, but three or four would not be an unreasonable guess. The distributions of schizophrenia within extended families could be relatively well explained by a three-gene concept, although two genes and also more genes could be made to fit the data. If three genes were required, only those with all three abnormal genes would have schizophrenia. Those with one or two of the same abnormal genes may display schizotypy, depression, bipolar disorder, a cyclothymic personality, sociopathy, learning disability, dyslexia or even a personality susceptible to commiting crime.

Of course, families share many things apart from genes. They may share social environments, political attitudes and eating habits, among much else. An alternative to the genetic explanation, which for many years seemed equally plausible, is the environmental one. This suggests that schizophrenia and the other associated psychiatric disorders found in members of the same families are the products not of shared genes but of shared environments. This is potentially a powerful argument. How does it stack up?

THE TWIN AND ADOPTION STUDIES

A number of investigators, notably Jon Karlsson, Seymour Kety, Irving Gottesman, Leonard Heston and their many collaborators in the 1950s, 1960s and 1970s, were well aware of the arguments about the relative contributions of genes and environment, of nature and nurture, to the development of mental illness. They determined to develop novel approaches which might settle the issue. In principle the ideas are simple. In practice they required an extraordinary degree of determination, dedication and sheer bloody-mindedness to carry through to their conclusion.

There were two classic investigational strategies. The first involved identifying pairs of twins, one of whom was a schizophrenic patient. What would be the likelihood of the second twin suffering from the disease? There are, of course, two types of twins, identical and non-identical (monozygotic and dizygotic). Identical twins share all the same genes. They are products of a single egg and a single sperm, fusing together to form a single fertilized egg or zygote. Normally, when a fertilized egg first divides into two cells, both daughter (or son) cells form part of a single organism. But, just occasionally, the two descendant cells each behaves as a fertilized zygote, each giving rise to a separate child. Identical twins therefore share exactly the same genes, giving rise to the extraordinary similarities which can be so disconcerting to anyone encountering a pair of identical twins for the first time. My father as a young man had a relationship with one of two twin sisters. She did something which seriously upset him and he told her off in no uncertain terms. 'Why don't you tell that to my sister?' was the disconcerting reply. He had been speaking to the wrong twin!

In contrast, with non-identical twins there are two different eggs fertilized by two different sperm. Usually the sperm come from the same man, resulting in normal siblings. Very occasionally the sperm come from two different men, giving half-siblings, but the vast majority of so-called dizygotic twins are full siblings. However, non-identical twins do not share exactly the same genes. Like any other pair of siblings, they inherit a random mix of genes from the mother and a random mix from the father. On balance, the likelihood is that about 50 per cent of the genes between non-identical twins will be shared and about 50 per cent will not be. This is in contrast to the 100 per cent shared genes in the identical twins.

The stage is therefore set for a comparison between the two different types of twins. In both cases the twins share the same uterine environment and the same family and social environment. But in one case all the genes are shared and in the other only half the genes are shared. If the environment is all important, then the risk of schizophrenia in a second twin should be the same, irrespective of whether the twins are identical or non-identical. If the genes are all important, then the risk of schizophrenia should be 100 per cent in the second twin of a schizophrenic proband identical twin, but only about 10 per cent in the second twin of a schizophrenic proband non-identical twin (i.e. about the same as seen with two non-twin siblings). If both environment and genes are important, the result should fall somewhere between the two.

The second strategy also attempts to separate the influences of genes and environment, but in a different way. Some babies, for very many different reasons, are adopted very soon after birth. They remain with their natural mother for a few hours, days or weeks, but are then passed to a family which has no genetic relationship whatsoever with the natural parents. If genes are all important in determining psychiatric outcomes, then such children should exhibit features which relate them to the families of their natural parents. If the environment is all important, then the children should exhibit features which relate them to their adoptive parents. If both are important, there should be some intermediate situation.

The way to study this is clear. One looks at what happens to children of schizophrenic mothers adopted at or near birth into families with no history of psychiatric disorder. One then also looks at what happens to children of non-schizophrenic mothers also adopted at or near birth into families with no history of psychiatric disorder. What will happen to the children? The concept is simple but it is hard to overestimate the extraordinary efforts required to identify the children and their families, to approach them in an ethical way, to win their confidence and to succeed in obtaining reliable results. But with both the twin studies and the adopted studies the results have been worthwhile.

The single most striking result from the twin studies is that, if one identical twin is schizophrenic, it does not mean that the other identical twin will also be schizophrenic. In 40–50 per cent of the identical-twin pairs, both twins were schizophrenic (concordant). But in 50–60 per cent of the pairs only one twin was schizophrenic (discordant).

This is absolute and irrevocable proof that genes are not the total arbiters of personality, psychological health and psychiatric disease. If genes were the only factors involved, then concordance would be at or near 100 per cent. The fact that concordance is only about 50 per cent or less, even when twin pairs share all their genes, indicates that the environment has a profound effect on whether someone with a high genetic risk for schizophrenia will develop the illness.

But that is not the whole story. What about the non-identical twins, born with different genomes but reared in substantially similar environments? What is the risk of schizophrenia in one non-identical twin when the other twin is a schizophrenic patient? If the environment were really important in generating schizophrenia one might expect the risk to be much higher than in ordinary siblings from different pregnancies.

Again the results are fairly clear. The risk of schizophrenia in the non-identical twin of a schizophrenic patient is almost exactly the same – around 10 per cent – as in any other sibling of a schizophrenic patient. The intimately shared environment does not seem to produce much risk over and above that attributable to the genes.

There is an important asymmetry here. The twin studies suggest that the environment may *reduce* the risk in those who carry a high genetic load, but does not much *increase* the risk in those with no genetic load. A genetic element must be present if schizophrenia is to occur, but the impact of the genes is frequently blocked by environmental factors.

What are the outcomes in the adoption studies? Again they seem to be clear cut. Children from non-schizophrenic mothers, adopted into non-schizophrenic families, have a very low risk, certainly less than 1 per cent, of becoming schizophrenic. In contrast, children of schizophrenic mothers, adopted into non-schizophrenic families, have a risk of about 10 per cent of being schizophrenic. Children of schizophrenic mothers who remain with their mothers also have a risk of about 10 per cent of being schizophrenic. Although there are very few examples, it seems that children of non-schizophrenic parents, brought up in families where one or both parents have schizophrenia, also have a low risk of becoming schizophrenic.

The conclusions are relatively straightforward. Having a schizophrenic inheritance leads to a greatly increased risk of schizophrenia, irrespective of whether the child is brought up in a family with or without schizophrenic members. Equally, not having a schizophrenic inheritance seems to make people not susceptible to schizophrenia, even when they are brought up in a family where there are schizophrenic members.

The influence of the genes is strong, but it is not all pervasive, as is shown by the absence of schizophrenia in one member of an identical-twin pair in just over half the cases where the other twin is schizophrenic.

IS SCHIZOPHRENIA ALL BAD?

As already described in Chapter 2, I have several times in my life had the experience of receiving a particular type of telephone call from someone I do not know. Am I the David Horrobin who is interested in schizophrenia? Do I have ideas about schizophrenia which are novel and different? Do I see patients and would I be willing to consult on a case? Can I be trusted to be discreet? Assuming that the answers are satisfactory, the caller then reveals their identity. It might be a famous politician, a leading industrialist, a writer, an artist, or a member of a well-known aristocratic or intellectual family. The story which emerges always has general similarities to others. A member of the caller's family has developed what the doctors call schizophrenia. Everything has been tried to no avail. Someone has said that I may be a sympathetic listener with some new ideas. Would I be willing to help?

Virtually everyone who has obtained any prominence at all in schizophrenia research has had similar experiences. Schizophrenia can affect people of all abilities in all strata of society, but it does with surprising frequency seem to affect the families of the great, the good, the clever, the rich, the ambitious, the intellectual and the creative. Is this an illusion or could there be something to it?

Francis Galton, a cousin of Charles Darwin, was a brilliant and wealthy intellectual with no need to seek gainful employment. He devoted himself to a surprising number of different activities, one of which was an attempt to understand the genetic nature of various diseases. Long before the twentieth century destroyed the moral and intellectual credibility of the subject, Galton began to wonder whether the quality of humanity might be improved if certain people with certain defects were not allowed to reproduce. In this way, illnesses causing adverse effects might be steadily eliminated.

Henry Maudsley, the great authority on psychiatry in London in the second half of the nineteenth century, laid many of the foundations for the proper study of psychiatric disorders and made many astute clinical observations. One of London's great psychiatric institutions, the Maudsley Hospital, was named after him and remains to this day the leading centre for psychiatric research in Britain.

Maudsley and Galton would have met frequently in the small yet enormously influential intellectual circles of London. Maudsley appears to have been attracted to Galton's ideas, and to have thought long and hard about whether a eugenic programme for the reduction of psychiatric illness would be feasible on ethical and practical grounds.

But in the end, towards the close of his career, Maudsley came down firmly against eugenic concepts. His reasons were straight-forward and immensely practical. As the leading psychiatrist of his day he had been consulted by members of the great families of Victorian Britain. A surprising number of those families had members who were affected with what we would now call schizo-phrenia. Maudsley saw that a eugenic programme to eliminate schizophrenia might also run the risk of eliminating many of the most dynamic, creative and illustrious members of the Victorian establishment. He came to the conclusion that that was too great a risk to take, especially since Galton in his study of genius had also noted, 'I have been surprised at finding how often insanity has appeared among the near relatives of exceptionally able men.'

Very similar observations in relation to bipolar disorder as well as schizophrenia have been made at McLean Hospital just outside Boston. McLean is perhaps the most famous psychiatric institution in the USA. Founded in the first half of the nineteenth century, it served much of New England and kept meticulous records. In 1941 Abraham Myerson and Rosalie Boyle published a report into their investigations of the history of McLean in relation to many of the most famous families in United States history. Family after family of distinction, families boasting 'Presidents of the United States; philosophers of international importance; writers who have founded schools of literature; scientists in every field from astronomy to chemistry; medical men galore, around whose names significant developments have clustered', had all sent members to McLean. The patients were sometimes the achievers themselves but more often their close relatives. Remarkably frequently, the mentally ill relatives had been left out of biographies or official family trees. Conventional history may therefore have difficulty in identifying just how many eminent individuals have had psychotic relatives.

Myerson and Boyle were writing at the end of the period when enthusiasm for eugenics was a respectable intellectual interest, but they nevertheless made the comment, at the beginning of their paper:

> What will appear, however, is this: that had sterilization procedures of adequate type been carried out in the earlier part of the history of New England and the United States, many highly important individuals and their family groups would not have appeared on the American scene, and consequently, it is very probable that if individuals have anything to do with the development of a country, the development of the country would have been altered.

Unfortunately for our voyeuristic selves, the authors are totally discreet about the names of the families, but the strength of their conclusions is obvious.

Do my own experiences of being consulted, Maudsley's much more extensive experience with the very greatest of eminent Victorians, Galton's observations on the relatives of geniuses and the long history of McLean's association with distinguished Americans carry in them a grain of truth? Could schizophrenia and bipolar disorder, as well as being devastating afflictions, be gifts, associated with creativity and high achievement? Could genius indeed be to madness close allied?

Although they have rarely been closely examined from this perspective, some of the studies described earlier, which attempted to throw light on the gene versus environment story, did make observations of great relevance. This is particularly true of the adoption studies. The findings were carefully described in the original papers by Leonard Heston, but for some reason have rarely been quoted since, nor have their implications been carefully thought through.

Among the adopted-away children of non-schizophrenic mothers going to normal families, none became schizophrenic. Among the adopted-away children of schizophrenic mothers, brought up in normal families, about 10 per cent became schizo-phrenic, roughly the same proportion as the percentage of children of schizophrenic mothers who stayed with their mothers. This provides strong evidence for a genetic component to schizophrenia which is not attenuated by being brought up in a normal environ-ment – nor indeed made much worse by being brought up in a schizophrenic environment. This is the conclusion from Heston's work which is repeatedly discussed, emphasized and disseminated.

The references to the studies usually stop there. But to my mind, the rest of the work is even more interesting. What happened to the children of schizophrenic mothers who were *not* schizophrenic? How did they compare with the children of the non-schizophrenic mothers?

On the debit side, schizophrenia was not the only problem found in the children of schizophrenic mothers. A significant proportion were mentally retarded – but this was balanced by a group with high intelligence so that the mean intelligence of the two groups was similar. A significant proportion of the children of schizo-phrenics had criminal records, whereas none of the children of non-schizophrenics did. A substantial proportion of the children of schizophrenics exhibited sociopathic or psychopathic personalities. All of those observations about relatives of schizophrenic patients have been repeatedly made in earlier descriptive studies, but Heston's work has a particular authority.

Apart from the small group with unusually high intelligence, it all looks pretty bad. However, some encouraging results showed up as well. Heston noted that most of the children of the schizophrenics who were not ill or criminal seemed to lead more varied, interesting and successful lives than the children of non-schizophrenics: they appeared more creative and imaginative. The children of schizophrenics had a high chance of exhibiting exceptional musical ability – 15 per cent did so, as compared to none of the children of non-schizophrenic mothers. The children of the schizophrenics were also more likely to be intensely religious – 13 per cent as against 3 per cent – not just in a Sunday-go-to-church sort of way, but in a deeply philosophical manner.

So the picture emerges of an immense range of both illness and talent in the children of schizophrenic mothers as compared to the children of non-schizophrenic mothers. And this was so even though all were brought up in a non-schizophrenic environment. On the one hand, some of the group with schizophrenic mothers might appear stupid, mad, bad and dangerous to know. In contrast, others of the same group might appear clever, creative, fun, musical or deeply religious. All the good and bad characteristics of humanity seem writ large in the children of schizophrenic patients.

THE ICELANDIC STUDIES

A second series of studies supports these conclusions. Jon Karlsson was an Icelandic psychiatrist who moved to the USA but retained a passionate interest in his homeland. Two wonderful things about Iceland are its genealogical record-keeping and the fact that its population has been effectively isolated for a thousand years. This means that one can look in great detail at family histories, not just in the present generation but in many previous generations.

Karlsson embarked on a series of studies of the inheritance of schizophrenia in Icelanders. Early on he seems to have been impressed by the fact that Icelandic families distinguished in many different ways – in the arts, politics and science – had schizophrenic members more often than did families of good but undistinguished citizens. He studied the phenomenon with great care, publishing his findings in a book and in a series of important scientific papers which, like Heston's, now seem to be read rarely. But for understanding schizophrenia, in my view they are among the most important ever written.

Karlsson's findings paralleled Heston's. The Icelandic families with schizophrenic members seemed to have a greater variety of skills and abilities, and a greater likelihood of producing high achievers in a variety of fields, than the families of non-schizophrenics. Interestingly, to some degree he found that this was also true of some of the schizophrenics themselves. A significant proportion of people who later became schizophrenic did exceptionally well at school and university, only later ex-periencing a schizophrenic breakdown. This discovery of a group of high academic achievers in people who will later become schizophrenic has recently been confirmed by another study in Finland. A further Scandinavian study has just found that the children of university graduates are almost twice as likely to develop schizophrenia as are the children of non-graduates. Two recent studies of the relatives of bipolar patients, one in New York and one in London, have both reached the conclusion that their average intelligence is substantially greater than that of the general population.

So an intriguing picture is emerging which is far from the unrelieved gloom and horror of most descriptions of schizophrenic patients and their families. Yes, schizophrenia is a terrible illness, yes, it can destroy lives, but at least some schizophrenic patients and, more particularly, their first-, second- and third-degree relatives, are highly creative, highly imaginative and highly success-ful, while some others are sociopathic and criminal. Something similar is also true of the relatives of bipolar patients. Schizophrenia and bipolar disorder seem to embrace much of what is best and also much of what is worst about the human condition. If only we could find ways of attenuating the worst, schizophrenic and bipolar individuals might be able to contribute enormously to the richness of our world. As will become apparent later, that is not merely a dream but is beginning to be a reality. The fact that less than half of identical twins of schizophrenic patients are schizophrenic themselves offers solid grounds for hope. The non-psychotic twins share the same genome, they are often odd and schizotypal, but they are neither psychotic nor medicated. Some environmental factor, or a combination of factors, has attenuated the impact of the schizophrenic genome to the extent that they can live near-normal lives.

SOME INDIVIDUAL EXAMPLES

Maudsley came to his conclusion about eugenics and mental health on the basis of the anecdotes generated by his clinical experience. Many of the highest-achieving families had members who were seriously mentally ill. This seemed to occur more often than in more ordinary families. The experiences of many modern researchers in schizophrenia and bipolar disorders and the McLean Hospital records bear out Maudsley's conclusions. A surprising number of high-achieving families seem to have schizophrenic or bipolar members.

But perhaps some of the individual stories are the most compelling. Mention has already been made of several of the following, but they bear repetition here. James Joyce's daughter was schizophrenic. Albert Einstein's son was schizophrenic. Carl Gustav Jung's mother was probably schizophrenic. Several of philosopher Bertrand Russell's relatives were schizophrenic. The children of several recent Nobel Laureates, including one of the most famous, a man who is still alive, are schizophrenic. John Nash, the 1994 Nobel Laureate in Economics, is schizophrenic; his story has been wonderfully documented in the book *A Beautiful Mind* by Sylvia Nasar. Another famous recent Nobel prize-winner is schizophrenic but understandably prefers that it should not be widely known. I recently gave a seminar to thirty exceptionally high-achieving biomedical researchers. At the end, seven came up to me and said that they had a schizophrenic parent, child, sibling or cousin. I do not know about the other twenty-three!

So the picture is clear. Schizophrenia, as well as being associated with mental illness and poor intellectual performance, may also be associated with the opposites. A few schizophrenic individuals themselves, but many first-, second- or third-degree relatives, who share part of the schizophrenic genome, are some of the highest-achieving and most creative individuals around.

The close relationship between madness and creativity was, of course, noted by Shakespeare: 'The lunatic, the lover, and the poet, are of imagination all compact.' Many authors in the second half of the nineteenth and the first half of the twentieth century looked at the problem from a biographical point of view by studying the lives of outstanding geniuses. Few of the greatest achievers have been fully schizophrenic, but many have been clearly schizotypal or have had schizophrenic first- or second-degree relatives. Cesare Lombroso, J. F. Nisbet, Wilhelm Lange-Eichbaum and many others have drawn attention to the phenomenon of the association between madness and genius, and much of this biographical research has been summarized by Robert A. Prentky. The list of those whose personalities showed schizophrenic or schizotypal features is very long. The flavour may be transmitted by listing only a few of the more famous names: Donizetti, Schumann, Beethoven, Berlioz, Schubert and Wagner among musicians; Baudelaire, Strindberg, Swift, Shelley, Holderlin, Comte, Poe, Joyce, Gogol, Heine, Tennyson, Kafka, Proust and Huxley among writers; Kant, Wittgenstein and Pascal among philosophers; Einstein, Newton, Faraday, Copernicus, Linnaeus, Ampere, Edison, Mendel and Darwin among scientists and inventors. Take these names and many others who have shown schizotypal behaviour from the list of those who have made the very highest contributions to humanity and the roll-call would be greatly impoverished.

These names are those of people who themselves exhibited schizophrenic or schizotypal behaviour. It is much more difficult to compile lists of those who were not symptomatic themselves, but who had first-, second- or third-degree relatives who were psychotic. As the McLean researchers pointed out, such relatives were often excluded from biographies and from family trees. It is therefore probable that the list of high achievers who come from families with psychotic members is considerably longer than has been thought.

BIPOLAR ILLNESS

The story with bipolar illness is much the same as with schizophrenia, although here research has concentrated more on the patients themselves than on the relatives. Patients with bipolar disorder are frequently crippled only intermittently and in between times are capable of great achievements. Studies by Nancy Andreasen, Kay Redfield Jamieson, Adele Juda and others have formally shown that, especially in creative writers, bipolar disorder is much more common than it is in the general population. As many as 30–60 per cent of creative writers may be seriously ill with bipolar disorder. This is dramatically greater than the 1 per cent or so of the general population who have the illness.

The formal studies have provided satisfactory and solid evidence of the real association between creativity and bipolar disorder and depression, but again it is the individual names which startle. Prentky, Jablow Hershman and Julian Lieb, and Kay Jamieson have collected these names in their various publications on the subject. The lists include Byron, Browning, Plath, Hemingway, Conrad, Coleridge, Schiller, Crane, Balzac and Dickens among writers; Raphael, Michelangelo and Van Gogh among artists; Handel, Rossini, Tchaikovsky and Chopin among musicians. These are just some of the more famous names of artists who have been bipolar or cyclothymic.

DYSLEXIA

The study of dyslexia and achievement is much more recent, partly because dyslexia itself has only recently been fully recognized. But it has been pointed out by Ronald Davis that, as with schizophrenia and bipolar disorder, there is beginning to be a long list of dyslexic high achievers. This includes Leonardo da Vinci, Albert Einstein, Thomas Edison, Alexander Graham Bell, Walt Disney, Hans Christian Andersen and Winston Churchill. Many architects and sculptors and some of the most successful financiers are dyslexic. The association between dyslexia, schizotypy and schizophrenia in families is a tantalizing one.

OVERVIEW

No one who reviews either the experimental studies or the anecdotal evidence from biography can fail to be convinced that there must be a relationship between schizophrenia and other forms of mental disturbance and the highest achievements of humanity. In the same families, and sometimes in the same people, are those who are the most brilliant creative achievers but who also, in the words of Lady Caroline Lamb about Byron, are 'mad, bad, and dangerous to know'. It seems as though the features of personality and achievement which we regard as the highest expressions but also the worst degradations of humanity are writ large in those families which contain some members who are mad. Those extraordinary creative features of humanity which, as John Pfeiffer, Ian Tattersall and others have emphasized, appeared abruptly in modern humans but were absent 150,000 years ago are consistently associated with mental disorder. Could it perhaps be the mental disorder which made us human?

10

'AFTER LIFE'S FITFUL FEVER HE SLEEPS WELL'

WILLIAM SHAKESPEARE, 1564–1616

THE IDEA THAT SOMETHING GOING WRONG WITH THE BIO-chemistry of fat may be the cause of schizophrenia, or of other mental disorders, seems bizarre. The human mind is the most complex, the most glorious object in the universe. Its workings have been the subject of the most erudite dissertations by scholars of all sorts, philosophers, psychiatrists, psychologists and linguists. The wondrous imaginations and magical thoughts of the schizo-phrenic patient must surely have the most complex origins. The idea that they may originate in something rather simple going wrong with the biochemistry of fat – surely not! But the Dougie mouse and the Mensa mouse have provided strong evidence of the impact of single genes on brain function. Two different, apparently small genetic changes, both closely related to phospholipid metabolism, can each give a mouse the equivalent of perhaps an extra fifty points on a human IQ scale. Why should not other simple changes in fat biochemistry make us clever and creative, mad and bad?

LOOKING AT SCHIZOPHRENIA: THE IMPORTANCE OF CLINICAL OBSERVATION

Schizophrenia seems so obviously a problem of the brain. Almost all modern research on schizophrenia starts with the assumption that the problem is mainly in the head, and in particular with the neurotransmitter systems of the brain. I estimate that less than one-tenth of 1 per cent of the research on the biological mechanisms of schizophrenia assumes that there might be other aspects to the illness.

But it was not always like that. Doctors of fifty or a hundred years ago, who were less arrogantly confident that they understood the causes of disease, noted that schizophrenic patients had abnormalities other than those of the mind. They often had an unusual ectomorphic, long, thin body shape. Their posture was different and there was something not quite right about their gait. They frequently had gastrointestinal problems with no very obvious cause. They had minor physical abnormalities, including facial abnormalities and an exceptionally high arched palate. And they rarely seemed to suffer from arthritis or other inflammatory diseases.

The *New England Journal of Medicine* is now one of the most prestigious of all medical journals. In the 1930s its reputation was rising quickly, and in 1936 it published a paper by H. A. Nissen and K. A. Spencer which was to play a major role in my personal journey of discovery. The authors were careful clinical observers and had noted something rather curious: their patients with arthritis rarely seemed to suffer from psychotic disorders. And when they talked to colleagues in psychiatry they found that people with schizophrenia rarely developed arthritis. There appeared to be some mechanism whereby these two diseases were mutually exclusive. They thought that schizophrenia and arthritis might both be responses to stress, but bodies could react in only one of the ways: they could either become psychotic or become physically ill with arthritis, but they could not do both.

Since Nissen and Spencer many other investigators have made similar clinical and epidemiological observations, usually without agreeing on the proposed mechanism. The discrimination is not absolute, but arthritis is much less common than it should be in people with schizophrenia and schizophrenia is much less common than it should be in patients with arthritis. It would seem that some mechanism is operating in schizophrenic patients which protects them against arthritis.

THE PROBLEM OF PAIN IN SCHIZOPHRENIA

One of the most vivid memories of my earliest encounters with psychiatry was of a patient who jumped out of a high window. He was unobserved and when he fell to the ground he picked himself up and walked a mile to the nearest bus stop. Later that day he was found in the centre of the small local town walking around in a distracted way. He was picked up and taken back to hospital. He had no complaints, but a routine careful physical examination found two broken ankle bones. He should have been in agony, but he had been able to walk around for half a day without feeling pain.

Another patient was described in a letter to the *New England Journal of Medicine*. An observant nurse had noted that a particular hospitalized schizophrenic patient did not seem well. The patient did not complain of any problems and for a while the nurse thought no more of it, but a couple of hours later the patient still seemed sick and, although he claimed to be well, the nurse called the doctor. A careful clinical examination suggested a ruptured appendix, confirmed at operation. This is normally one of the most painful abdominal conditions of all, yet in this case the patient had felt nothing.

As a result of Gwynneth Hemmings's queries to me about prolactin, I became a medical adviser to the Schizophrenia Association of Great Britain. In consequence I have made contact with many families and I often ask them about pain in schizophrenia. Most have noticed that their relatives appear to be unusually resistant to pain, particularly during severe psychotic episodes. Minor and even major injuries, which would leave a normal person in agony, often do not seem to generate pain in those with schizophrenia.

Again, as with arthritis, there is a mass of supporting evidence for this view. Robert Dworkin has collected much of it together in a comprehensive article. Schizophrenic patients, especially during exacerbations of psychotic episodes, really do seem to be resistant to pain.

CURING PSYCHOSIS WITH MALARIA

Only one psychiatrist has ever won a Nobel Prize and that was a long time ago, in 1927. I make a habit of asking young psychiatrists whether they know which psychiatrist won a Nobel Prize and for what. I have not yet met a psychiatrist under the age of forty who has been able to answer correctly.

When I tell them that the prize was won by an Austrian, Julius Wagner-Jauregg, for treating psychosis with malaria, they are astounded and usually mutter something about 'How primitive.' When I tell them that malaria therapy was still used in the USA in the 1950s, they usually do not believe me.

At first sight it does sound something like a Nazi horror story. But it is not like that at all. Wagner-Jauregg's story is one of the most imaginative, daring and caring stories in medicine.

At the end of the nineteenth century, two diseases dominated the enormous, long-stay psychiatric hospitals of the time. One was what we now call schizophrenia. The other was cerebral syphilis, more commonly known as general paralysis of the insane (GPI).

The organism which causes syphilis, the spirochaete bacterium, *Treponema pallidum*, is a delicate creature. That is why it requires the intimacy of sexual intercourse to pass from one individual to another. Initially, like the virus which causes AIDS, the spirochaete does not appear to cause much damage. There may be a rather messy sore, or chancre, which is undoubtedly disconcerting when it appears on the penis, but which often goes unnoticed in the female genitalia. Then everything appears to resolve and the patient feels relatively healthy.

However, the delicate bacterium tracks through the body and over many years multiplies to a degree which causes severe damage. One of the places it loves to hide is the brain. Prior to the discovery of antibiotics, cerebral syphilis was just about the worst thing that could happen to a person. For reasons which are not clear, the brain damage often first becomes apparent in the onset of a mania-like condition, with excessive grandiosity and delusions of status and achievement, prior to degeneration into dementia and madness. Between a third and a half of places in psychiatric hospitals were taken up by people with this appalling disease, which inevitably ended in death, often following a varying period of psychosis. Anything that could be done to help was felt to be worthwhile.

Wagner-Jauregg became obsessed with the problem of cerebral syphilis, which he studied in every possible way. He made careful clinical observations and noted several patients whose condition appeared to be relieved or even cured by a severe feverish and inflammatory response such as could occur during the infectious illness erysipelas. Wagner-Jauregg began to realize that in some patients the experience of severe fever was followed by relief of the cerebral syphilis. He thought about various artificial ways of deliberately but relatively safely inducing a fever-generating inflammatory response and realized that this might be achieved by the use of benign forms of malaria. With great trepidation, Wagner-Jauregg dared to try the experiment. A patient who had travelled in the tropics had a relatively benign form of malaria. Wagner-Jauregg took some of his blood and injected it into a patient with GPI. Within a few days the GPI patient had a febrile attack of malaria. Wagner-Jauregg waited and watched. The patient progressively improved, and eventually Wagner-Jauregg concluded that his cerebral syphilis had been cured.

The experiment was repeated again and again. In a majority of cases the patient recovered, although Wagner-Jauregg never understood the precise mechanism by which the treatment works. Full understanding came many years later when it became possible reliably to culture the syphilitic bacterium. The organism, *Treponema pallidum*, is one of the few bacteria that are exquisitely sensitive to temperature. A rise in temperature of a few degrees will kill it. During an attack of malaria, the rise in temperature is sufficient to kill the bacterium but not the patient. The patient continues to suffer the malaria, but his much more serious disease may be cured. The malaria attacks can then be controlled by standard anti-malarial therapies.

The treatment spread rapidly throughout Europe and the USA. Most large psychiatric hospitals had a few patients with chronic malaria who acted as a reservoir for the parasite. Tens of thousands of patients were healed and Wagner-Jauregg rightly won the Nobel Prize. Malaria therapy did not die out until the 1950s, when penicillin became established as the first-line treatment for cerebral syphilis.

Wagner-Jauregg's story is one of the more dramatic episodes of medical history, but what concerns us here is a small side-show resulting from his work. He naturally wanted to see whether the treatment would work in other psychiatric disorders, and therefore gave the treatment to patients with schizophrenia. Initially the effect seemed even more surprising. As the first fever took hold, a few days after the deliberate infection, the schizophrenic patients seemed to lose their psychosis. But sadly, when the fever came down the psychosis returned. In contrast to the situation with syphilis, there was no long-term improvement and certainly no cure. The psychosis seemed to get better while the temperature was elevated and then to get worse as it came back to normal. Several other doctors tried the approach in schizophrenia; all obtained the same results and so the concept of treating schizophrenia with malaria died.

Why should I have been interested in what seemed to many to be historical nonsense? It all went back to prolactin, the hormone whose levels are raised by most anti-schizophrenic drugs. We had found that prolactin could release from phospholipids fatty acids that were involved in inflammation and infection. Could there be some relation between our findings and Wagner-Jauregg's work?

By the time I read about Wagner-Jauregg's observations, they had been forgotten by most people for fifty years in the case of schizophrenia and for thirty years in the case of cerebral syphilis. I therefore decided to ask the relatives of schizophrenic patients whether they had noticed anything similar. For example, when their ill relative had a fever from flu or some other infectious illness, did their behaviour change? I also asked nurses whether they had noticed anything about long-stay patients under their care during infections.

The results were interesting. Time and time again the relatives and nurses told the same story. While patients were ill with a feverish illness they became more friendly, warmer, less psychiatrically ill. Some family members thought that this was simply because their mentally ill relative felt a greater need for other people while they were physically ill. But most insisted that this could not be the only explanation. They believed that their relatives actually became psychiatrically better.

Two vivid stories illustrate the point. One elderly nurse remembered a particular patient, Ruth, whom she had nursed before the antibiotic and anti-psychotic era. This young woman had been extremely psychotic in the most bizarre ways, requiring constant observation to prevent self-harm. Yet one day she had seemed astonishingly better. She behaved normally, recalled her life before hospitalization, talked about family and friends in a normal way. The only thing which had changed was that she had developed a high fever. She had no pain and for forty-eight hours no cause could be found until a doctor finally decided, correctly, that the problem might be appendicitis. The inflamed appendix was successfully removed, her temperature returned to normal, and Ruth retreated irrevocably to her state of madness.

John was an exceptional young man, slightly odd but top of his high-school class in most subjects. His first year at university was an intellectual triumph, although his friends and family became increasingly worried about his behaviour. In his second year it all fell apart and he became deeply and uncontrollably mad. For three years he wandered around a major city, homeless and in despair. He accumulated an entourage of dogs. Eventually one of these savaged him and he developed a severe infection with antibiotic-resistant organisms. He was taken to a hospital and cleaned up, but it was two weeks before his infection could be brought under control. During that time his psychosis disappeared, his relations with his family were resumed and he expressed disgust at what had happened over the past few years.

Then an antibiotic was found which cured the infection. His family were delighted that he was now getting better and would be able to return home. But to their horror, as his physical illness improved, so his psychosis returned. John returned to his life on the streets and never spoke to his family again.

HOW CAN THESE OBSERVATIONS
MAKE SENSE?

Schizophrenic patients rarely get arthritis, they feel less than normal pain, and they may improve psychiatrically when they are ill with a feverish illness. How can we put all these findings together?

For me, the moment of inspiration came when I was asked to advise on the management of the schizophrenic brother of a friend. The patient had been found to have high cholesterol levels. What would I suggest?

This was long before the era of modern cholesterol-lowering drugs. At that time by far the best cholesterol-lowering agent was the B-group vitamin nicotinic acid, or niacin. Normally niacin is required only in doses of a few milligrams (thousandths of a gram) per day and in these doses it does not lower cholesterol; but when given in doses of several grams per day it is an effective cholesterol-lowering agent.

The main problem with niacin is that in most people, at these doses, it causes a violent flushing reaction. About fiteen to thirty minutes after taking the niacin, the skin begins to tingle over the upper part of the body and a redness spreads across the face, the chest and the arms. This is due to a great increase in the blood flowing to the skin. If it is not expected, it can be alarming, particularly as it is accompanied by a pounding heart and palpitations. Especially in someone who is schizophrenic, this sort of event can be very worrying. I therefore carefully warned the patient of what might happen.

To my great surprise, as Sherlock Holmes would say, the dog did not bark. Instead of the expected flushing, nothing happened. I was astonished and could not stop thinking about what might be the explanation. I called Abram Hoffer, who had been using high-dose niacin to treat schizophrenic patients. He confirmed that severe flushing reactions were unusual.

I vividly remember the moment when it clicked. It was a wonderfully crisp (which means −20°C) sunny February day in Montreal. I was walking from the place where I worked, the Clinical Research Institute, along to the McGill Medical Library in the McIntyre Building. The road looked over the city and then out to the St Lawrence River, where the ice gleamed in the bright sunlight. I have no idea why things came together at that moment, but they did. I realized what bound together my patient's failure to flush, the failure to feel pain, the resistance to arthritis and the beneficial effect of fever.

They were all linked by arachidonic acid (AA) and its conversion to cell-signalling molecules called prostaglandins. Arachidonic acid is usually locked up at the Sn2 position of membrane phospholipids, but for the body to respond normally to many different situations that arachidonic acid must be released from the phospholipids as free AA. This then regulates the cellular function in appropriate ways. Furthermore, some of the AA is converted to those highly reactive cellular-switching mechanisms called prostaglandins, which do things like opening up blood vessels to allow the blood to flow through them faster.

I suddenly realized that the most likely reason for my patient's failure to flush was a problem with AA and its conversion to prostaglandins. If sufficient AA could not be released, or if it could not be converted to prostaglandins, this would explain why the patient did not go red as expected. It would also explain the other observations.

AA is required in order to enable the body to respond to injury by mounting an inflammatory response. The redness, pain and swelling which occur after an injury or an infection are in large part mediated by the release of AA from phospholipids and the conversion of that AA to prostaglandins. Steroids, like hydrocortisone cream, act as anti-inflammatory agents by blocking the release of AA from phospholipids. Non-steroidal anti-inflammatory drugs, like aspirin and ibuprofen, act to block the conversion of the AA to prostaglandins. So a failure to release AA or to convert it to prostaglandins could explain why schizophrenics are resistant to arthritis. It could also explain why they do not respond to pain in the normal way. AA release, both in the brain and at the site of injury, is a necessary component of the body's reaction to pain.

The fourth clinical observation, the surprising improvement during fever, also fell into place. High fever is one of the strongest known stimulants to the release of AA from phospholipids. During a fever AA pours out from the cell membranes. It helps to defend the body against infections and other noxious agents, but AA and the prostaglandins formed from it also help to make us feel sick. That is why aspirin and related drugs help us to feel better during fever.

Physiologically we need a constant ongoing low level of AA release and prostaglandin formation for all our body systems to work normally. Suppose that in schizophrenic patients this normal low level of release is not occurring. All sorts of bodily systems will not work normally. Brain cells will not communicate properly with each other, the skin will not respond normally to stimulation, the stomach and intestines will contract less than usual, the membranes which normally keep body compartments from communicating too freely will not be quite normal in their function. If these things were true, schizophrenia would be a whole-body disease, with something slightly, but not very, wrong with the way in which cells communicated with each other. Because brain functions require many millions of sequential interactions, even a tiny problem at each interaction would produce a big problem overall. The brain would not function normally. But in other tissues, where only three or four sequential interactions would produce a normal body response, the abnormalities might easily be missed.

What I think happens in fever is that the body is filled with hormones and other agents which stimulate the release of AA and its conversion to prostaglandins. In normal people this is one of the things which makes the body feel sick. Excessive amounts of prostaglandins are formed. These can be partially suppressed by anti-inflammatory drugs like aspirin, which helps to explain why such drugs can make people feel better. But in schizophrenic patients, whose AA release is normally impaired, all these stimuli to AA release would help to create a normal situation. Instead of having too little AA and prostaglandins, the schizophrenic body would now have a normal amount. This is in contrast to the high amounts usually present in the normal individual with a fever. For one of the rare moments in their lives, the AA release allows the schizophrenic brain and body to function normally. Relatives and friends are astonished and delighted, only to fall again into despair once the fever abates, AA and prostaglandin levels revert to their sub-normal level and the psychotic state returns.

I knew at that moment in Montreal that I might be on track to find the cause of and cure for schizophrenia. But could this itself have been a delusion?

I put my ideas together in a paper called 'Schizophrenia as a prostaglandin deficiency disease' and sent it off to one of the world's most prestigious journals, the *Lancet*. To my surprise, they accepted it without much fuss and my paper duly appeared. I expected that people would read it, immediately experience the same insights I had experienced, and change the directions of their research programmes. I thought that within five years we might have major new treatments for this terrifying illness. I did not realize how utterly naïve I was.

The publication and various follow-up reports were greeted with silence. No one was interested in what I had to say. Without a single exception, every application for funding I made to every public and private grant-giving body was rejected. Every time I submitted a paper for presentation at a meeting, it was either rejected or given a graveyard slot right at the end of the meeting when almost everyone had gone home. No one wanted to hear what I had to say. No one wanted to give me any money to fund the research I hoped to do. I became known as someone who was clever but crazy, a maverick who bored everyone with my off-the-wall theories.

What went wrong? I now see, of course, that this sort of behaviour was entirely normal for scientists, doctors and the pharmaceutical industry. As with the initial discovery of the cave art at Altamira, new concepts were not welcomed. Schizophrenia was obviously a disease of the brain, or perhaps of the mind. The idea that it was a whole-body disease was absurd. Most psychiatrists had forgotten or never known of Wagner-Jauregg's work, or the work on pain, or on inflammation. It certainly did not seem relevant to the understanding of what might be going on in a schizophrenic brain.

Besides, the general view was that we had a pretty good idea of what might be going wrong in schizophrenia. We had a paradigm to work with. The anti-schizophrenic drugs we now have were

discovered entirely accidentally as a result of careful clinical observation in the early 1950s. Henri Laborit, a French surgeon, was
using them as post-operative sedatives. But Laborit realized that
the effect on some patients was more than simply sedative. He
persuaded some psychiatrist colleagues to look seriously at the
drug in schizophrenic patients. The results appeared miraculous
and so the anti-psychotic drug era was born. Jean Thullier has
described what happened in his illuminating book *Ten Years that
Changed Psychiatry.*

But neither Laborit nor anyone else had any idea how the drugs
might work. They had an immense range of different effects on
the body, any one of which might have been the crucial one.
Eventually Arvid Carlsson of Sweden proposed the idea that
interference with the action of the neurotransmitter dopamine
was the key effect. Many others found supporting evidence. The
pharmaceutical industry wanted a story to tell and a rational basis
for future discovery. The idea that blocking the effects of dopamine
was the basis for anti-psychotic action became an unstoppable
steamroller. It was then just a short step further to the conclusion
that, if blocking dopamine worked therapeutically, then the
problem in schizophrenia must be an excess of dopamine. The
dopamine theory became the dominant paradigm.

In the enthusiasm and the rush to collect research grants and find
new drugs, three facts were overlooked. First was that the anti-
dopamine drugs were not very effective. They relieved only about
20 per cent of the symptoms of schizophrenia, leaving 80 per cent
unchecked: almost no one taking one of these drugs was employed
doing something relevant to their intellectual performance level
before they became ill. They were not really very well. There must
be something other than dopamine to the story. Second, and related
to the first, there was little persuasive evidence, other than the effect
of the drugs, that there was anything wrong with dopamine in
schizophrenic patients. Third, the dopamine theory treated schizophrenia entirely as a brain disease and had no explanations for the
phenomena which suggested that it might be a whole-body disease.

The phospholipid–AA story progressed depressingly slowly
for over twenty years before it began to be taken seriously.
Quite separately from me, various independent-minded researchers

around the world made observations which led them to conclusions similar to mine. Wagner Gattaz, first in Mannheim and then in São Paulo, became convinced that overactivity of a phospholipase acting on AA was important in schizophrenia. Jeffrey Yao and Dan van Kammen in Pittsburgh demonstrated deficits of AA in both red cells and the brain in schizophrenia. By using the technique of magnetic-resonance spectroscopy, Jay Pettegrew in Pittsburgh and Peter Williamson in London, Ontario, demonstrated in living, unmedicated patients that brain phospholipid metabolism in schizophrenia was abnormal. Sukhdeb Mukherjee and Sahebarao Mahadik in Georgia found increased rates of oxidation of AA in schizophrenia. And my colleagues Iain Glen in Inverness and Malcolm Peet in Sheffield made a series of important discoveries. Glen along with Pauline Ward turned the niacin flushing response into a useful diagnostic test. They found that by applying graded doses of niacin to the inner forearm the test could be made more reliable, accurate, quick and tolerable. There really could be a skin test for a psychiatric disease, something which has now been confirmed by others in the USA, Canada, Poland, China, India and Australia. Schizophrenia is definitely not just a disease of the brain. Malcolm Peet in Sheffield showed that in schizophrenia there was increased oxidation of unsaturated fatty acids, reduced AA in membranes, and reduced levels of n-3 EFAs in the blood. Most important of all, Peet and his colleagues pioneered novel treatments based on these findings.

We are still developing our understanding of the details of the errors in biochemistry. But gradually a consensus is developing that there are two important problems in phospholipid biochemistry in schizophrenia. One relates to a chronic overactivity of one or more of the phospholipase A_2 group of enzymes. This leads to a steady leak of AA and other fatty acids from cell membranes, not leaving sufficient AA behind to mount a normal cell-signalling response to stimulation. The second relates to a failure to incorporate AA and related fatty acids back into phospholipids. The problem may be in one of a group of enzymes called FACL, the absence of one of which can lead to Alport syndrome (see Chapter 6). As a consequence of these two abnormalities, brain HUFAs are readily oxidized, and the breakdown products, which are volatile, are excreted in the breath.

A consequence of this understanding of biochemistry is that it leads to new approaches to treatment. These have the potential of reducing a patient's symptoms without causing the major side-effects of the existing drugs. In principle, what should work is an increased availability of the fatty acids which are required for normal brain phospholipid structure and function and which are found in some abundance in meat, bone marrow and brain, eggs and also in the food chain which is based on water. One fatty acid in particular, eicosapentaenoic acid (EPA), looks promising because it can reduce the activity of phospholipase A_2 and increase the activity of FACL. As will be seen in later chapters, this novel approach works for at least some patients.

At last, over twenty years after it was first proposed, the phospholipid story is now being taken seriously. Reviewers still sometimes describe it as unproven rubbish, but about twenty groups of investigators around the world are now investigating it thoroughly. They are being given better slots at conferences and their abstracts are now rarely rejected. Most important of all, the new approach is leading to a genuine revolution in therapy. And although some of the traditionalists may not like it, patient power is forcing psychiatrists everywhere to take the new therapeutic approach with more than a pinch of salt.

Unexpectedly, these new insights about the role of fat biochemistry in schizophrenia were to lead to a new concept of human evolution.

11

'ONLY CONNECT!'

E. M. FORSTER, 1879–1970

BY ITSELF, BIG IS NOT NECESSARILY BRIGHT, NOR IS SMALL necessarily stupid. Males consistently have slightly larger brains than females. There are some small but important differences in what most males are good at, and what most females are good at. But all attempts to demonstrate that, overall, males are cleverer than females have met with complete failure.

Descartes, one of the cleverest people ever, had an unusually small brain. There are other clear examples that size is not enough. The brain cases of Neanderthals, as revealed by skull size, are consistently larger than those of modern humans, but the evidence from the cultures they left behind strongly suggests that Neanderthals were less imaginative, less technologically skilful and less intellectually able than modern humans or their immediate predecessors. Autistic children also tend to have larger brains than normal children, and they can occasionally demonstrate extreme ability, but that ability is almost always equally extremely narrow. One of the main problems exhibited by autistic children is that they tend to focus intensely on a very limited and often entirely trivial (to the outside world) range of activities. In some respects they behave like computers: they can have extraordinary calculating and information-processing skills, but they are unable to cope sensibly with even minor changes in the instructions they receive. Flexibility and imaginative interpretation of events in the surrounding world are almost completely absent. Their relatively large brains are not particularly helpful when coping with everyday life.

Some of the most memorable evidence about the relationship between brain bulk and intellectual ability comes from children born with the problem known as hydrocephalus. This is an increased pressure of the fluid-filled spaces in the centre of the brain. The increased pressure compresses and destroys brain tissue. Fortunately, now the problem can usually be detected early and treated surgically so that the brain develops normally, but before about thirty years ago this was not possible and the hydrocephalus had to run its natural course.

Hydrocephalus is not an all-or-nothing disease. There were grades of pressure and hence grades of brain destruction. John Lorber, a paediatrician in Sheffield, began to realize that many hydrocephalic patients, who had very little brain tissue left, could function normally. Brain scans demonstrated that in two of the most remarkable patients there was little brain tissue left. The weight of the cerebral cortex was estimated to be about one-third of that in a normal chimpanzee. Yet one of the young men in question had won first-class honours in mathematics at university and the other was of normal or above-normal intelligence.

Ralph Holloway, John Lorber and Joseph Lebeer have all drawn attention to the problem. One of Lebeer's articles is vividly entitled 'How much brain does a mind need?' Severe loss of brain mass, if it occurs early in life, may still be associated with normal or near-normal human types of behaviour and function, even if the remaining amount of the brain's cortex is substantially less than that present in a normal chimpanzee.

What seem to differentiate normal modern humans, even modern humans with hydrocephalus, from Neanderthals, and also from those who suffer from autism, are openness, connectedness and flexibility. We show an extraordinary ability to generalize, to accept instructions or items of information which are not absolutely precise, and to make sense of them. We quickly learn to recognize categories like dogs, cows, books or apples, even though most of the members of these classes differ from each other, often in very substantial ways. We can link quite different classes of object or concept, sometimes in extraordinary ways. Poems, scientific discoveries and jokes all frequently depend on the unexpected conjugation of disparate and normally unconnected events, observations or concepts, and also on the ability of large numbers of people to understand the connection. Functioning in the world depends on being able to select without undue distress what matters and what does not matter from a myriad alternatives. Social skills depend on the ability to receive, process and integrate an almost infinite range of subtle facts about other people. Autistic individuals almost always perform badly in all these areas. Big is certainly not necessarily best for a human brain. As we have seen, even humans with little cerebral cortex left may perform surprisingly well.

Yet these skills must have a physical basis in neuronal organization, and that physical basis is almost certainly related to the degree of functional connectedness between nerve cells. One obvious clue is that our brains are usually about three and a half times bigger than chimpanzees' brains, but we have substantially less than twice as many individual nerve cells. In fact, some counts suggest that the human cerebral cortex has only about 20 per cent more neurons than that in a chimpanzee's brain. If the bigger brain of modern humans is not associated with a proportionate increase in the *number* of nerve cells, something else other than mere number must be taking up the space. And the most likely candidate is that in the modern human brain each nerve cell has many more functional connections with other nerve cells. It is the connections which take up the space and which give us our humanity.

In Chapter 6 we saw how Cajal and Golgi exposed for us the astonishing complexity of each individual nerve cell. Each neuron does not have a single input and a single output, nor even a few dozen inputs and a few dozen outputs. For each neuron the input connections are rarely less than a thousand and may be over a million. There may often be a single exit channel for information, the axon, but that axon may divide ten, a hundred, a thousand or in some cases perhaps even a million times, sending the information to myriads of other cells. But the complexity does not end there. For each of these connections is not a digital 0 or 1 connection. Each connection has an almost infinite range of function so that the complexity of events at even a single neuron exceeds that in most computers. There are 100 billion nerve cells making the connections, and 1000 billion glial cells, about ten for each neuron, provide structural, functional and nutritional support for the nerve cells.

ANATOMICAL AND FUNCTIONAL CONNECTIVITY

The most likely explanation for the extraordinary flexibility of the modern human brain is an enormous increase in the functional connectivity between the individual neurons, as compared to the situation in the great apes and in our pre-human precursors. That functional connectivity between any two neurons has two elements. First, there must be an anatomical connection: the two neurons must come close enough together via their dendrites and axonal branches to allow a connection to take place. Without the anatomical connection there can be no functional connection.

But the anatomical connection by itself is not enough. Anatomical connections may exist, but may not function or may have disturbed function. Full functionality depends on an effective mechanism for releasing a neurotransmitter, an effective mechanism (receptor) for receiving the information conveyed by that neurotransmitter, and finally an effective mechanism for communicating that information to the next neuron and allowing that neuron to modulate its function accordingly. Defects at any of these stages may lead to impaired functional connectivity even in the presence of apparently normal anatomical connectivity.

And as if that were not enough, we are beginning to learn that the brain may be subject to influence by a range of subtle factors which tune in a highly variable way the sensitivity of neurons at each of the three stages. Some neurons, like those of the *locus coeruleus*, a part of the brain which helps to regulate responses to change and stress, do not release their transmitters only at specific nerve endings. They spray their neurotransmitter over the whole brain, changing the activities of many if not most of the connection systems. Both nerve cells and glial cells can release a wide range of chemicals, some acting very locally, some acting more widely, but all of which can modify brain function. The blood can bring to the brain other chemicals, some, like hormones, from within the body itself and some, like alcohol or drugs, from outside, which can change the way much of the brain functions. Finally, mysterious and at present poorly understood waves of electricity can spread over the whole brain, changing its behaviour.

One cannot help but conclude that the differences from a computer are much greater than the similarities. The computer analogy falls far short of describing the complexity of the human brain. It is not just the sheer number of connections, which, even if they were merely on/off, 0/1 switches, would make the brain by far the most complex computer on earth. It is the fact that each of those switches has an almost infinite range of variation, that the consequences of switch opening or closure are almost infinitely variable, and that we can flood the brain with literally thousands of chemicals which can change the way the whole thing works.

The complexity is almost inconceivable and the more one learns about the brain the more complex it appears. Analogies, although almost always misleading to some degree, can be useful in conveying the scale of things. Imagine the largest supercomputer in the world. Imagine that at each switch point, instead of a digital 0 or 1, all open or all closed, about 100,000 variable positions were available. And finally imagine that the whole computer were bathed in a fluid containing well over a thousand different chemicals, each of which could modify the functioning of the switches and each of which could vary with time, with season, with stress and with a myriad other influences. You would then begin to get a feel for the complexity of the brain.

With such complexity, it is obvious that much could go wrong. What is surprising about most brains is that so little does go wrong. Most people, even those regarded as mentally ill, at most times have brains which function in perfectly serviceable and reasonable ways. Yet it is clear that not very much would need to go wrong for the system to be messed up. This is a fact which gives considerable hope for progress. It may be, even with such an apparently serious disease as schizophrenia, that only relatively minor things have gone wrong at a biochemical level and therefore that only relatively minor changes are needed to correct the problems – that is if we can identify the problems correctly in the first place. The best evidence for this is the dramatic improvement in psychosis which can occur with just a small rise in temperature. This change must be producing relatively modest alterations in brain function, yet within hours it can convert someone from madness to near sanity. What we need to do is understand the effect of temperature and then mimic it in an effective, safe and permanent way.

MAKING THE CONNECTIONS

All the connections between all our nerve cells are made up of phospholipid membranes. All dendrites, all axons and all their branches are phospholipid tubes. New connections cannot be made, old connections cannot be broken, the micro-architecture of the brain cannot be modelled or remodelled, except by using phospholipids as the basic building blocks. And, as we saw in Chapter 6, the crucial components of the phospholipids, which cannot be made by the body itself, are the essential fatty acids and their metabolites. If arachidonic acid (AA) is not available, and if it cannot be converted to LTC4, then a tiny brain results: the consequence is death.

It is, of course, true that embedded in the phospholipids are many different proteins which are necessary if neurons are to work properly. Some of these proteins are guidance molecules, ensuring that particular axons and dendrites make connections with other specific axons and dendrites required for normal function. Some of these proteins may well be abnormal in particular psychiatric or neurological disorders. But it is the phospholipids which are universal, which are intimately involved in the neuronal connections.

Micro-anatomists have shown that there are three major periods of life when synapses are organized, reorganized and disorganized.

At these times the enzymes of the phospholipase cycles are extremely active in generating and recycling AA and other fatty acids.

The first period, of course, is in the foetus and young infant, when the micro-architecture of the brain is laid down and when the micro-connections of the neurons first form. The second is around the time of puberty, when the phospholipase cycle enzymes in synaptic endings become extraordinarily active again. Much of the synaptic architecture is broken down and remodelled around this period. Adolescents may well be confused because their brains are truly being reorganized. The third period is during normal ageing and also, unfortunately, in the accelerated brain ageing of dementia. Again the synapses become broken down, again phospholipases are active, but this time normal remodelling does not occur.

At each of these stages phospholipids play a crucial role in establishing micro-connectivity. Phospholipid metabolism is central to the injunction 'only connect'. If one doubts this, the examples of the Dougie mouse and the Mensa mouse provide incontrovertible evidence that this is so (see Chapter 6). The increased amounts of the NMDA receptor protein in the Dougie mouse lead to greater release of AA, which activates GAP-43 and generates new synapses. The greater amounts of GAP-43 in the Mensa mouse have the same end result. Interactions between proteins, phospholipids and essential fatty acids are central to the development of the brain in general and of cognitive, intellectual and creative functions in particular.

12

'THE EVER-WHIRLING WHEEL OF CHANGE, THE WHICH ALL MORTAL THINGS DOTH SWAY'

EDMUND SPENSER, 1552–1599

THE ORGY OF MILLENNIUM REVIEWS TOWARDS THE END OF 1999 HAD one overarching theme: the rapidity of change, and the acceleration of that rate of change. It does not take a profound social commentator to recognize that over the past 10,000 years, and especially over the past 200 years, the rate of change has been extraordinary. That change has been apparent in virtually every aspect of human life, from the mundane to the most intellectually high flown. Transport, food production, engineering, health, entertainment, art and science have all expanded and will continue to expand at an amazing rate. And that rate of change, as acknowledged by everyone, has its origins in that restless, creative object, the human brain.

Contrast the last two centuries with all that went before, or contrast the last 10,000 years with all that went before that. The outstanding feature of our culture, whether expressed in art, in technology, or in social organizations, has been the ephemeral nature of all structures and all fields of knowledge. Ways of knowing, of organization, of dressing and of eating are constantly being replaced by the new and the supposedly better. Often, but not always, the changes can be reasonably characterized as progress. Sometimes, however, the change is early on recognized as a regression. Often it is difficult to know, early in its development, whether a particular change is helpful. What one can know with certainty is that for the last 10,000 years, the one constant feature of modern humans has been divine discontent. We, as a species, have felt an inordinate pressure always to do things differently. Sometimes the change may be relatively large, such as the new way of looking at nature and art forced on the world by the Impressionists and their successors, or the new way of getting around the world created by the mass-transit aeroplane, or the new ways of treating disease opened up by penicillin. But whether the change be large or small, humans are characterized by an inability to keep still. It is almost as though a condition of our survival was the need to change.

It was not always like this. From the time when pre-human brains began to grow, around 2.5–3 million years ago, the main features of pre-humans for most of the period until about 100,000 years ago were cultural unity and a glacial rate of change. If one lays out a sequence of stone tools from a particular geographical area, such as East Africa, originating from between 3 million and 1.5 million years ago, or a series of hand-axes from about 1.5 million to 0.5 million years ago, what is impressive is how little appeared to happen and how slow were the changes over 100,000 generations, as compared to how much happens within one or two generations now. The designs of the tools and axes change, but they do so to a very limited degree given the aeons of time available.

And it is not only a glacial rate of change with time; it is a glacial rate of change across geographical areas. Stone-tool and hand-axe design did not just persist almost unchanged in one place for half a million years at a time; they showed little variation from place to place. Tools from Europe can easily be confused with tools from Africa or Asia if one does not know the exact context in which they were found. Again, what a contrast this is to the last 10,000 years. From about 10,000 years ago, each tiny geographical area has its own characteristic cultural artefacts of many different types: the expert can identify to within a few miles and a few years where and when a particular artefact was made. The sheer variety across time and place quickly becomes astounding.

Another obvious feature is the absence of any evidence of religion for most of the last 3 million years, in contrast to the central role played by religion in almost all cultures in certainly the last 10,000 years, and probably in the last 100,000. Similarly there is a huge difference in art, with painting, music and crafts of many different types being important in the last 50,000 years at least, and probably for the last 100,000 years, but not for the 2.5 million years before that.

WHEN DID THE SHIFT TO RAPID CHANGE OCCUR?

At some time, pre-humans, with their inability to change and innovate, were transformed into modern humans who are dominated by their desire and indeed their need to change quickly. When did the transition occur? We do not know with certainty but we can begin to guess within reasonable limits.

Something did happen about half a million years ago when brain size grew rapidly, when human bodies became substantially modern in form and when stone tools became more crafted, differentiated geographically and complex. But even then, until about 150,000 years ago at least, life definitely proceeded in the slow lane.

About 150,000 years ago, we can still be fairly confident that the shift to rapidly changing humanity had not occurred. All the evidence we have, even though that evidence remains fragmentary, is that 150,000 years ago our ancestors had no religion, no art and only minimal technology. They made stone tools and wooden tools, but not tools which combined both elements. They did not use bone, ivory or antlers. They did not bury their dead, did not decorate themselves or their environment and had no religion. Therefore, 150,000 years ago is a reasonable upper time limit before which the transformation is unlikely to have occurred.

On the other hand, by 35,000 years ago, at the time of what John Pfeiffer called the Creative Explosion, it is clear that the shift to new ways of thinking has already taken place. Cave art is already sophisticated. Technology has improved dramatically, as is shown by weapon design. Religion and symbols are well established, as is suggested by the cave art, by the numerous carved symbolic artefacts and by the way people bury their dead. Music has probably begun to develop, as is indicated by findings of fragmentary flutes and other instruments. Diversity is clearly apparent, as these cultural features differ sharply from one geographical area to another. No longer is there any serious possibility of an informed person being unable to distinguish between an African artefact, an Asian artefact and a European artefact. The truly knowledgeable person, on being shown an object, can make reasonable guesses both as to the date when it was made and the precise geographical location where it was found.

So we can now with reasonable confidence date the emergence of the transition from an almost changeless to a rapidly changing society to somewhere between 35,000 and 150,000 years before the present (BP). When one considers that the transition almost certainly began in a single band of pre-humans, that the statistical likelihood of finding any artefacts from small numbers of people is very low, and that it would take many years for such knowledge and practices to develop, spread and become as diverse as the degree seen by 35,000 BP, it seems unlikely that the change took place much later than about 100,000 BP. A reasonable guess – and that is all it can be at this stage – is that the change took place some 100,000–150,000 years ago. But that guess is based upon several diverse lines of evidence, most of which are converging.

THE ADAM AND EVE CONJECTURE

Both biblical and genetic/evolutionary accounts of the origins of modern humans agree in their insistence that there was a founding couple. The critical changes that made us human took place at first in a single offspring of a particular couple. And we can make a pretty good stab at guessing exactly when, using the technologies discussed in Chapter 2.

This is because spontaneous mutations in DNA occur at a

relatively consistent rate depending on the precise nature of the DNA and its location. By looking at a particular stretch of DNA in a large number of individuals, and by identifying the points at which individuals are different from each other, it is possible to identify the degree of diversity between modern humans. We can also compare the diversity between humans and the great apes. We can do this for any section of DNA we choose to look at. However, particular interest has been paid to mitochondrial DNA, which is inherited only through the female line, to Y-chromosome DNA, which is inherited only via the male line, and to DNA on certain well-known stretches of other chromosomes which are transmitted by both sexes.

Remarkably, all three methods yield broadly similar results. Each suggests that we are all descended from a single ancestor who lived somewhere between about 60,000 and 160,000 years ago. The mitochondrial and autosomal DNA evidence point to an earlier date and the Y-chromosome DNA to a later date, discrepancies which are still being actively discussed. The last common male ancestor may possibly have been later than the last common female one.

The DNA evidence fits nicely with the evidence from conventional archaeology. As we have already seen, two remarkable finds from two widely separated parts of Africa – Ethiopia and the eastern Cape – show that structurally modern humans had developed a sophisticated maritime culture by the period 100,000–125,000 years ago. Beautifully carved ivory fish hooks and other objects which must have been the products of modern minds have been found in the eastern Congo region dating to about 90,000–100,000 years ago. Allowing for the time needed to spread from a point of origin, this evidence also points to an African origin 120,000–140,000 years ago.

The implications of these parallel DNA and archaeological findings are considerable.

First, all the evidence, from all three types of DNA, points to an African origin because there is more DNA variation in Africans than in other races. This and the archaeological evidence provide almost overwhelmingly strong evidence that the original modern humans came from Africa. Second, this means that from an African origin some 120,000–140,000 years ago, the ancestors of modern humans spread across the whole globe. Third, since there is plenty of evidence of large populations of other pre-humans, such as *Homo erectus* and *Homo neanderthalensis*, being alive in the period from 30,000 to 150,000 years ago, the spread of modern *Homo sapiens* must have been associated with the complete elimination of all other species or varieties of *Homo*. Fourth, the elimination of our close relatives raises serious questions about how that elimination was achieved. Did our evolutionary cousins simply die out because they could not take the heat, or did we kill them?

These cultural pointers on the one hand and molecular genetics on the other suggest that modern humans are intellectually very different from pre-humans, and that the first modern humans probably arose between about 120,000 and 140,000 years ago. Ian Tattersall has emphasized that this change was not a minor event. Something literally world shattering happened. There is a clear break when human culture took a huge leap forward. How can we explain it on the basis of standard evolutionary mechanisms, which emphasize gradual change in response to environmental pressures? Or is the event so different that, as many have argued, we must invoke something different to explain it? Even Alfred Wallace, who, with Darwin, was the originator of the concept of evolution by natural selection, felt that some special and different explanation might be required.

WHEN DID SCHIZOPHRENIA START?

The near-uniform racial distribution of schizophrenia provides strong evidence that the disease originated prior to the separation of the races. Otherwise it is difficult to explain why schizophrenia is present in approximately 1 per cent of all races, including Australian Aborigines. Australian Aborigines are a particularly important example, as they show that groups who have had no genetic interaction with Europeans still suffer from schizophrenia.

Schizophrenia must therefore have entered humanity prior to the separation of the Australian Aboriginal line from all the rest of the human race. The date of that separation is uncertain, but it is possible to make reasonable guesses. The first date to settle is the date when Australians first entered Australia and became separated from their near neighbours. This is a controversial subject, clouded by uncertainties about the dating of bones, of artefacts and of pigments associated with cave art. It is also associated with the equally controversial discussion about the dating of the extinction of most of Australia's large mammals and birds, which many now attribute to the arrival of humans. Similar extinctions seem to have occurred in most other places, like the Americas, when modern humans arrived.

What seems to be happening is that, as more research is carried out, the date is progressively being put backwards. Initially people thought that Aboriginals may have arrived as recently as 10,000 years ago, but as evidence has accumulated the consensus date is now perhaps 50,000 years ago, with a few experts pushing for a date as early as 80,000 years ago.

If we are looking for a date for the origin of schizophrenia, we must add to the date for human entry to Australia the time elapsed between the separation of the races in Africa, or possibly in the Near East. Again there can be no certain knowledge of this time frame, but an interval of less than 20,000 years seems unlikely and one of 50,000 is perfectly possible.

Thus, on this basis, an origin of schizophrenia less than 80,000 years ago is unlikely, and one of 140,000 years ago is perfectly reasonable.

So we can say with confidence that something very interesting seems to have happened somewhere between 80,000 and 140,000 years ago. On the basis of DNA analysis, we can fix a date of between 60,000 and 160,000 years ago. On the basis of cultural change and the emergence of art and religion, a date of between 80,000 and 150,000 years ago seems reasonable. On the basis of the separation of the races, and the origins of schizophrenia, we can fix a date of somewhere between 80,000 and 140,000 years ago.

Could these events be related?

13

'WHOM GOD WOULD DESTROY - OR CREATE - HE FIRST SENDS MAD'

JAMES DUPORT, 1606–1679 [AUTHOR'S UNDERLINING]

IF WE WERE ASKED TO DRAW UP A LIST OF THE FEATURES WHICH characterize modern human culture and behaviour, each of us would produce our own idiosyncratic collection. But high among the characteristics on most people's lists would be a religious sense, the creation of art in all its forms, the ability to make scientific and technological advances, and the lust for change and progress. All these things seem to have been substantially, if not totally, missing from our last pre-human ancestors, as exemplified by Neanderthals and by the many variations on the *Homo erectus* theme. Religion and art seem to have been largely absent, technological skills were limited, and change was almost infinitesimally slow, leading to cultures persisting largely unchanged over long eras of time and vast spatial distances. Something happened between 160,000 and 60,000 years ago which transformed our minds and made religion, art, technology, rapid change with time and differentiation from our neighbours of immense interest to us.

We can be less certain about exactly what were the behavioural characteristics which separated us from our immediate ancestors; we will never be able to know with any real assurance how they behaved. We can, though, be confident about the features, summarized above, which characterize our species today. But to them we must add a darker side. Suspicion of others, doubts about their motives and a sense that others are trying to take advantage of us are present in us all, shading from what most would call common-sense concerns into the most vicious and senseless paranoia and xenophobia. The desire to take advantage of others, to struggle to come out on top and sometimes to use violent or non-violent ruthlessness to achieve our ends are also all too human.

Some might reasonably argue that suspicion, shading into paranoia and xenophobia, is merely based on a realistic assessment of the likely behaviour of others. Sometimes others are indeed trying to take advantage in many different ways. And a disturbing proportion of those others seem to seek to gain such advantage in a way which is unrestrained by any sense of fairness, common humanity or fellow feeling for those being exploited or damaged. Individuals who behave in this way are technically known as sociopaths or psychopaths. It is unfortunate that in the public mind these words have become associated with physical violence. This is not surprising, given the frequent use of such phrases as 'psychopathic killer' and the fact that those who use gratuitous violence to pursue an end are indeed frequently psychopaths. But the core concept of psychopathy (or sociopathy, for the two words are essentially interchangeable) does not relate to violence, but to complete disdain for the feelings and concerns of others. Disdain may even be the wrong word because it implies that the psychopath may understand the feelings of others and dismiss them. The true psychopath often behaves as though he (or, less commonly, she) does not even understand that others have feelings and concerns or, if he does understand them, uses that understanding for exploitation rather than empathy.

Psychopaths are therefore found not just in prisons, but in any situation where at some stage it may be helpful to personal progression to be able to ignore or even to utilize the feelings of others. Leaders in business, in government and in any organization may sometimes be psychopaths. Paradoxically, charitable, academic and intellectual organizations are particularly likely to generate psychopathic leaders, because the decent, honourable, rank-and-file members of such groups, working for what seems to be a transparently good cause, often cannot bring themselves to believe that they are being so manipulated.

Interestingly, in any structure where there is some form of genuine democratic control, an ability to 'throw the rascals out', psychopaths rarely survive very long at the top. This is because their absence of empathy with the needs and aspirations of others and their naked self-interest usually lead to an overreaching which arouses such a sense of disgust that the psychopath cannot survive. But he, and it is usually a he, can do a great deal of damage in a relatively short period of time.

In organizations where democratic control is weak, and that includes most businesses and many charities, psychopaths can not only readily reach the top, but can survive for long periods, sometimes doing immense damage in the process. That is the real argument in favour of democracy: psychopathic leaders are eventually seen to be so and are thrown out. In the absence of democratic control, where power is unrestrained and can be enforced ruthlessly by legal or illegal dismissal or even murder, then it is the norm for psychopaths to become leaders and for the worst of them to remain in power for many years. That, of course, was the historic norm. Psychopathic families seized power and by utterly ruthless behaviour kept it. One cannot read any history without recognizing the truth of that fact.

Of course, we cannot be certain that some early modern humans were psychopathic, but, unfortunately, such evidence as we have is relatively persuasive. The best-known evidence for the behaviour of early human societies comes from the Bible, but the early stories from all cultures, from Babylon, Egypt, India, give the same picture. Leaders gained power by ruthless behaviour, they kept it by systematically destroying their rivals, and they organized their societies in a paranoid, xenophobic way which allowed people of other societies who were not chosen or identified in some way to be treated as less than human and to be quite reasonably 'hacked to pieces before the Lord'.

We do not know whether this behaviour was also characteristic of our immediate pre-human ancestors, but there are some clues to suggest that it might not have been. Chimpanzees can be violent, and can conduct apparent warfare, but they do not seem to be capable of the totally ruthless and planned lethal campaigns so characteristic of modern humans – although it must be admitted that the behaviour of one of the chimpanzee bands described by Jane Goodall at Gombe in Tanzania came close to what might be called ethnic cleansing. There is also a distressingly convincing case to be made that modern humans eliminated both the large mammals with which they came into contact and their immediate predecessors, the various forms of *Homo erectus*, who had spread across most of Africa, Europe and Asia.

One hundred and fifty thousand years ago, *Homo erectus* and its variants and successors, such as the Neanderthals, covered the contiguous continents and the nearby reasonably accessible islands. From northern Europe to the Cape of Good Hope, from West Africa and Iberia to Java, their remains are relatively common. By 30,000 years ago they have all gone, replaced by our own species, *Homo sapiens*, a creature with perhaps a slightly smaller, but immensely more powerful brain. What caused the disappearance? Could it be related to the fact that the large mammals in every area but Africa also disappeared?

There are many relatively benign explanations for the elimination of *Homo erectus*, of Neanderthals and of the giant mammals and birds. Perhaps climate changed to a degree which meant that people who had lived for a million years through other more severe climatic changes this time simply could not cope. Perhaps *Homo sapiens* was so effective in its exploitation of the world's resources that nothing was left for *Homo erectus* or for the large mammals, and they died out because of starvation and inadequate resources. But perhaps they were killed by us. Perhaps we behaved towards them as the ancient Israelites did to their enemies, as Genghis Khan did to his enemies, and as twentieth-century Europeans, Africans and Asians have done to theirs. Regrettably, to me, the simple answer is the most likely. We killed them. Only thus is it possible to explain the apparently complete absence of their DNA in us.

FAMILIES WITH SCHIZOPHRENIC AND
BIPOLAR MEMBERS

In Chapter 9 we saw some of the characteristics of the families of patients with schizophrenia and bipolar disorder. Many of these family members are decent people, undistinguished from their fellow humans by either high ability or infamy, but a disproportionate number of them are exceptional. They are intensely interested in music, an interest which is matched by ability. They are fascinated by religion and spend a high proportion of their lives thinking about it. They are highly imaginative and do interesting things with their lives. They are artistically, technically, scientifically, politically and commercially creative, contributing enormous achievements to almost every field of intellectual, political and commercial endeavour. If one includes with schizophrenia the constellation of related disorders which runs in the same families, including bipolar disorder, dyslexia and depression, the degree of achievement in such families as compared to those without any disabling mental illness can be even more striking.

But there is also a darker side which it has been professionally fashionable to ignore, except perhaps in the more lurid columns of the popular press. All the family studies which have considered the issue are consistent in describing more criminality, more paranoia and more psychopathy in the families of schizophrenic patients than in families where schizophrenia is absent. And while it is untrue that schizophrenic patients are substantially more violent than non-schizophrenic individuals, it is true that there is some increased risk, and also that when schizophrenic people are violent they may be so in exceptionally bizarre ways – hence the popular press headlines. Schizophrenic patients are also particularly likely to be paranoid about family as opposed to non-family members, and violent to those family members. As already noted, when someone kills their mother, it is not unreasonable to make the initial assumption of a diagnosis of schizophrenia in the murderer.

Put these characteristics of schizophrenic patients and their families side by side with the characteristics of modern humans as compared to their immediate ancestors and the parallels are obvious. Religion, art, scientific and technical creativity, violence and psychopathy are all present in modern humans but possibly not in their ancestors. They are also present to highly developed degrees in families which have schizophrenic members. Could the genetic changes which produced schizophrenia also be the changes which produced modern humanity?

We will never know the answer with certainty, but it is possible to create an interesting scenario. And, when creating that scenario, it is important to remember that schizophrenia 100,000 years ago was probably a much milder disease than it is now. As the Christensens argued, even today schizophrenia is a milder disease in those supposedly less-developed populations which have a low intake of saturated fats and a high intake of the essential fatty acids which are needed for the brain. As we have seen, 100,000 years ago saturated fat intake was undoubtedly very low. Much of the fat in the diet from meat, organs, marrow, brain, insects and grubs, especially when the organisms eaten came from marine and freshwater sources, was in the form of essential fatty acids. This diet would have greatly attenuated the impact of the biochemical changes which characterize schizophrenia. People with the genetic basis for schizophrenia would have perhaps had a touch of the disease, possibly without the more extreme and disturbing features. They may have been more like schizotypal people today, or like the non-psychotic identical twins of schizophrenic patients, often odd, often strange, often eccentric, but not psychotic.

Imagine what might have happened somewhere between 80,000 and 140,000 years ago when the first family to possess the genetic changes characteristic of schizophrenia came into existence. That family would have been members of a band of perhaps thirty to a hundred individuals living somewhere in East Africa, probably by a watercourse surrounded by open savanna. The band's territory would have bordered on the territories of other pre-humans with whom the first band might occasionally have interacted. These bands might have come together sometimes for social or commercial purposes. It was a society which had changed little for hundreds of thousands of years.

But something was about to happen which would set the course for the dramatic history of the next 100,000 years. A mother and a father each had some of the genes which, when combined, were necessary for the development of schizophrenia. And in one of their children there was an additional mutation – a genetic change which, against the background of the parental genome, created the first person with a schizophrenic genome. Given the diet based on food from the adjacent watercourse, which would have greatly attenuated the severity of the disorder, the person was probably not very strange. But there was something unusual about him or her, a remoteness, an awareness of the environment, a divine discontent with the way things were. Perhaps that unusual nature generated reproductive success, or at least did not block it, and within three or four generations the first schizophrenic person had ten or twenty descendants.

By that time it was apparent that there was something special about that family. One member liked to be alone and apart, and while wandering in the bush began to hear voices. Pondering on the significance of what he heard, he began to develop the ideas of invisible others, of beings present in other living things, and eventually, perhaps, of a being above all who was able to direct the lives of both humans and other living creatures and who had chosen to speak through him. So began the story of the first shaman, who gave rise to the first priest and the beginnings of the first structured religion.

Another member of the same family, while walking in the savanna or by the riverside, noted that some grasses or reeds were tougher than others. Idly one day, while playing with those grasses or reeds, she noticed that they could be woven together to produce either a fabric or a rope. Thus began the use of vegetable fibres to create baskets, ropes, clothes and other useful items.

Or another, using a gourd to carry water, decided that the natural gourd could be made more attractive by scratching on to it various patterns. She began to decorate all the family gourds in this way, and then to draw representations of living things. She and her dreamy brother began to work together to create the beginnings of symbolic religion.

And another, technologically inclined, noticed how poorly the throwing sticks penetrated the hide of large animals. The sticks might be hardened in the fire, but to do real damage they had to make a lucky hit in a vulnerable spot like an eye, or had to be thrown from up close. Perhaps the weapons could be improved if the cutting edges, which were so successful in slicing hides when held in the hand, could somehow be fixed to the end of what would become a spear? The brother interested in weapons talked to the sister interested in weaving fibre and together they devised a way of binding the sharp, shaped cutting stone to the spear end. Hunts became much more successful and safer. Food supply increased and the band size grew.

Eventually there emerged a man – because this one was almost certainly male – who resented the other bands of humans nearby. They were taking game which was needed by his growing band. He saw that what was required was the elimination of the next band and realized that the new weapons provided the technical superiority to do this safely. He began to talk, to build support for what he was going to do. One of his brothers and his mother stood up to him and argued for friendship and collaboration rather than elimination. In a rage he killed them both, so removing the possibility of internal dissent because everyone in his own band was now afraid. He sent out scouts to find out where the next band was. He planned a dawn assault, in which all the men of his band were armed with the new weapons. Just as the neighbouring band was beginning to wake, they were devastated by a shower of spears which disabled many of the males. The rest of the victim band could put up little resistance and were all killed. The attacking band had gained a large new territory in which they could hunt.

This is, of course, the merest skeleton of a fantasy. But it is a plausible fantasy and it suggests how families with schizophrenic members might become the dominant aristocrats of their band, providing shamanic priests for religious guidance, artists to encapsulate the aspirations of the band and to provide music for celebration, technologists to make better weapons and other tools and artefacts for living, and psychopathic males to dominate their own band and to destroy others. They were embryonic Medicis, prototypes of the many ruling families that have produced political and religious leaders or people with artistic and technical skills. Thus was our world won for *Homo sapiens*. All the glory and all the horror may have sprung from the same fundamental source – a small change in phospholipid metabolism which altered

THE MADNESS OF ADAM AND EVE

brain connectivity and which, depending on the background brain function, led to artists, priests, technologists and kings.

CAN WE PROVE THIS?

The short answer is not yet, but we are well on the way to demonstrating whether it is fantasy or has a solid basis in fact. The details of how it happened in a social sense will forever remain a mystery, but within a few years we will know the structure of the genome of normal individuals, of schizophrenic patients and of their family members, and of chimpanzees and the other great apes. We will also have a much better understanding of the biochemical features of the relatives of schizophrenic patients which can be so valuable. We will thus be able to know precisely which genes differentiate us from the great apes, and what relationship there is between these genes and the genes which have the potential to make us mad.

Within twenty years at most, then, we will know which genes made us human, and also whether or not those human genes are related to the genes which make some of us schizophrenic. We are likely to find that it was the presence of the genes for schizophrenia which made us human and which gave us both the glory and the horror, the joy and the despair.

14

'HIS SNUG LITTLE FARM THE EARTH'

SAMUEL TAYLOR COLERIDGE, 1772–1834

IF THE PHOSPHOLIPID CONCEPT OF SCHIZOPHRENIA IS CORRECT, for Stone Age people living on the diet we think they consumed the impact of the illness may have been relatively mild. The problem, as described in Chapter 10, is a slight increase in the normal rate of loss of the key brain fatty acids from membranes, coupled with a slight reduction in their normal rate of incorporation. The abnormality at each nerve cell is small, but because anything the brain does involves sequential and parallel interactions of millions of neurons, the impact on this finely balanced, extraordinarily complex machine can be considerable.

These biochemical abnormalities can be at least partially counteracted by diet. A good supply from food of those fatty acids specifically needed by the brain will reduce the impact of both enzyme abnormalities and so allow the brain membranes to function almost, but not quite, normally. So when schizophrenia first emerged, prior to the separation of the races and while we remained hunter-gatherers, it is possible that what became apparent for the most part were the desirable rather than the adverse features. The imagination, the creativity, the technical and artistic skills, the new religious sense, and even mild psychopathy, might all have been apparent without the disabling descent into madness.

But this attenuation of the consequences of biological change would have depended upon the direct dietary supply of the key fatty acids such as EPA, DHA and AA. These fatty acids, as discussed earlier, would have come from water-based foods, fish, animals, birds, eggs and grubs; from animal organs, including marrow and brains; and from meat. So long as the new humans ate a diet of this sort, it may well have been possible to have some of the creativity of schizophrenia without too much of the dark downside. As emphasized in earlier chapters, almost all the findings of fossils of the genus *Homo* and its various members have been made along watercourses, by lakesides and, more recently, along the seashore. The foods available in these environments would have been rich in these brain fatty acids and would have limited the adverse consequences of the genetic biochemical changes which produced schizophrenia.

The agricultural revolution, occurring in different places between 5000 and 15,000 years ago, changed things. Instead of being predominantly dependent on truly wild food, humans began to eat increasing amounts of foods which had been grown deliberately, and domesticated rather than wild animals. Initially crops were probably used to supplement wild-food gathering, but gradually arable crops became the food staples of the majority of the population. Much has been written about the consequences of this. The presence of potential food surpluses, and hence the availability of time to spend other than on food procurement, allowed hierarchical structures to emerge, allowed the emergence of people with special skills in the arts and technologies, allowed the development of a priesthood which could devote itself entirely to religion, and allowed political and military classes to establish themselves.

It is, of course, true that the development of leisure and of surpluses was necessary for these features of society to develop. But what was also required was a supply of people – people who had the artistic, religious, military and political skills needed to take advantage of these new conditions. Leisure alone is not enough. And it is my contention that the people required to fill the new emerging niches were those who either had the full or a partial schizophrenic genome, or a related genome such as one which provides the basis for bipolar disorder or dyslexia.

What is certainly true is that the establishment of stable towns and cities, drawing sustenance from the surpluses of an agricultural hinterland, allowed the emergence of a truly extraordinary diversity of culture. No longer do we see similar cultures being established across whole continents or even groups of continents. No longer are similar cultures spread over thousands of miles of land. No longer are cultures even along the course of a single river similar. Instead, what we see is the emergence of thousands of microcultures, each based on a single city-state. Each population group of around 5000 or more developed a culture all of its own, with different architecture, different domestic artefacts, different crafts, different art, different religion, different political organiz-ation and even different languages. Instead of uniformity, we have a situation where the only consistency is in diversity. The glacial changes of the previous 2.5 million years, and the stupefying consistency of culture across the world, have been replaced by a situation where every unit of a few thousand, or perhaps even a few hundred, individuals has its own culture.

What we also see is the emergence of violence and terror as the main bases for political organization. If you doubt this, take the time to read through Genesis, or any of the equivalent early accounts of world history. It is irrelevant whether each individual story is literally true. What matters is the overall impression given by the accounts – accounts which must have reflected what was happening on the political ground. What comes through repeatedly is that the political leaders were psychopathic killers who used religion to justify their political control, art to glorify their political success and murder to quell all opposition. The leaders in all fields, both the good and the bad, were those same sorts of people who are over-represented in the families of schizophrenic and bipolar people. It is my contention that the emergence and explosion of this diversity of political, social and artistic culture would have been quite impossible without the schizophrenic genome. The sheer exuberance of what happened is almost unbelievable – except that it happened. Every community of a few hundred people or more produced an array of talent which generated the diversity which contrasts so starkly with what went before.

THE IMPACT OF NUTRITION

I suspect, however, that this frenzy of creativity, religious fever, power lust and atrocity was not solely attributable to the presence of food surpluses and the creation of classes who did not need to spend most of their lives searching for food. I think that the switch in nutrition, from a hunting and gathering diet based on wild foods, particularly water-based foods, to a diet based primarily on grains, had a major impact on those carrying all or component parts of the schizophrenic genome.

The concept that nutrition changed in major ways is fact, not hypothesis. It is also fact that the agricultural foods were less healthy for humans than the traditional diet. We know this because, in study after study, examination of the remains of hunter-gatherers and of the agriculture-based peoples who succeeded them in the same location has shown that health declined rather abruptly. People became several inches shorter and their skeletons showed evidence of degenerative diseases which were either absent or much milder in hunter-gatherers. We can therefore be certain that, as compared to a hunter-gatherer diet, an early agricultural diet was bad for our bodies.

My contention also is that the change in diet had serious implications for brain function, especially in those individuals carrying some or all of the elements of the schizophrenic genome. The main reason for this is that an agriculture-based diet contains much smaller amounts of the EPA, DHA and AA required for normal brain function than are found in the hunter-gatherer diet. Meat in general became much less important as a component of diet, and water-based foods probably declined or disappeared. The fat in domesticated animals changed and became much less rich in the important fats. Only eggs might possibly have remained as an important source of the brain fatty acids. Instead of EPA, DHA and AA, the main fats in grains are linoleic acid (LA) and, usually, much smaller amounts of alpha-linolenic acid (ALA). These fatty acids cannot be used by the brain directly. Instead they must be converted within the body. ALA must be converted to EPA and DHA, while LA must be converted to AA. The brain must therefore get its EPA, DHA and AA indirectly and not directly from the food. Unfortunately, these necessary conversion steps are relatively slow in humans. While a normal brain may be able to acquire all the EPA, DHA and AA it needs by this route, brains carrying all or part of the schizophrenic genome may not receive sufficient quantities. As a result, the impact on brain function in people with schizophrenia or bipolar disorder may be increased.

A further factor which may have contributed to a worsening of schizophrenia and related disorders at the time of the agricultural revolution is a directly damaging effect in some susceptible individuals of certain proteins found in grains. F. C. Dohan first drew attention to the adverse effects of grain consumption in some patients with schizophrenia and there has been a steady accumulation of evidence over the past thirty years, although this concept has never attracted mainstream research interest. It appears that some fragments of partially digested grain proteins may seriously damage the gastrointestinal tract and interfere with normal brain function, possibly by changing the metabolism of AA, EPA and DHA. Gwynneth Hemmings advises members of the Schizophrenia Association to avoid certain grains and has obtained excellent results in some individuals.

The impact of changed nutrition may have led to complex effects. Some people may have been made more creative, imaginative and religious. As a result, the sheer exuberant variety of art and of religion may have been enhanced. On the other hand, the paranoid, violent and psychopathic tendencies may also have become worse, leading to ever more ruthless leaders who would stop at nothing to gain, maintain and retain power. Alliances between political, military and religious leaders may well have been alliances between siblings or various types of cousin. One does not need to read much of the Bible, early history of other cultures, medieval history or the history of the twentieth century to see the frequent family alliances and their often internecine quarrels between related political, business, military and religious leaders in the ruthless quest for domination.

My contention, therefore, is that the first cultural and political revolution, when pre-humans became modern humans, was triggered by the development of the group of mutations required for schizophrenia. The second cultural and political revolution, following the introduction of agriculture, when diversity of culture becomes florid, was triggered not only by the availability of leisure, but also by a change in diet which dramatically enhanced the impact of these schizophrenia- and bipolar-associated mutations, and provided the class of people who could fully exploit such leisure. Leisure alone, without the creative and psychopathic people to take advantage of it in good or bad ways, would have had a much smaller impact.

15

'DARK SATANIC MILLS'

WILLIAM BLAKE, 1757–1827

THERE HAVE BEEN SERIOUS ACADEMIC ARGUMENTS OVER WHETHER schizophrenia existed prior to the Industrial Revolution. The Bible is full of stories of people who heard voices, now regarded as one of the key features of schizophrenia. These same people are clearly passionately religious, another characteristic of many schizophrenic patients and their relatives. Julian Jaynes, in his extraordinary book *The Origins of Consciousness in the Breakdown of the Bicameral Mind*, emphasizes the importance of hearing voices in the early history of religion. However, it has been argued that these historical characters do not exhibit the frank madness and disintegration of personality which are characteristic of the modern schizophrenic.

The balance of evidence suggests that schizophrenia did exist in ancient and medieval times, but that it may have been a somewhat, or even much, milder illness than we have recognized in the past 150 years. Schizotypy, rather than schizophrenia, may be a better description. Almost all writers, Greek, Roman, medieval, Chinese or Indian, who have attempted to portray the full range of the human condition have described people who are recognizably schizotypal if not frankly schizophrenic. Shakespeare described psychosis and its association with creativity: 'the lunatic, the lover and the poet are of imagination all compact'. As so often, he was a remarkable observer of the fine detail of humanity. One of the features which people who know schizophrenic patients have long recognized is the 'layered clothing sign'. Severely ill schizophrenics quite commonly wear several layers of inappropriately matched clothing. This is something which is diagnostic of schizophrenia, since it is rarely if ever shown by people with other types of psychiatric disorder. An article in the *British Medical Journal* recently pointed out that Poor Tom (Edgar) in *King Lear* is portrayed as wearing layers of clothes. Shakespeare clearly knew the layered clothing of the madman and described it well. It is therefore a near certainty that schizophrenia is an old disease, not something which has developed recently.

But the doubters do have a point. It is likely to be their interpretation of the evidence rather than the evidence itself which is wrong. They claim that schizophrenia is a disease of industrialization, that it became a severe illness only in those societies which are heavily industrialized. Schizophrenia may have existed earlier, but the numbers affected were much smaller and/or the disease was much milder.

The major study by the World Health Organization, one of the largest schizophrenia studies ever organized, does provide evidence for the association of severe schizophrenia with industrialization. We have seen that this study demonstrated that schizophrenia is present in all the world's races to approximately the same extent. But the study asked two major questions, not just one. The first was whether or not schizophrenia was present. The second was, 'If schizophrenia is present, how severe an illness is it over a patient's lifetime?' The WHO team devised an elaborate scoring system covering many aspects of life. Their aim was to try to estimate over a lifetime just how damaging to a person schizophrenia might be.

Again, the answer was clear-cut. Although all the countries examined had just about the same proportions of people with schizophrenia, the lifetime severity of the illness was very different in different societies. The lifetime severity was less severe in non-industrialized countries than in industrialized ones.

These findings are very important because they suggest that

there are things which can modify the impact of this often appalling disease. Not surprisingly, initial attempts to explain these differences focused on drug use and the health-care system. Could a better long-term outcome be produced by medical care? If anything, embarrassingly, the outcome of schizophrenia seemed to be better in countries where, according to the latest and supposedly best Western standards, medical care was worse. This seemed to suggest that supposedly good-quality drugs and Western treatment methods might actually be harming schizophrenic patients. This, on the whole, was not thought to be a productive line of research and so little was done to explore the implications.

Other approaches taken were studies of family, social and economic structures. Might it be that certain types of society provided more support than others, so allowing a better long-term course of the illness? There is some modest evidence that this may be true, with relatively rural societies with extensive support systems beyond the nuclear family being associated with a better outcome. Even so, the concept that this could explain the large national differences observed is not particularly persuasive.

To my mind, the most convincing explanation has come from the two Danish investigators, the Christensens, who took a quite different and apparently less sophisticated approach. They simply asked whether what people eat might make the difference. They used the outcome scores for each country from the WHO study, and then obtained from the Food and Agricultural Organization (FAO) of the United Nations the figures for each country's consumption of various types of food. Most foods seemed to have little relation to outcome. However, fat consumption seemed strongly associated in two contrasting ways. First, the consumption of solid, saturated fat, mostly from domesticated animal sources, was associated with a bad outcome: the higher the consumption, the worse was the long-term outcome of schizophrenia.

In contrast, the consumption of fat from fish and vegetables had the opposite effect. This fat is rich in the unsaturated fatty acids important for the brain. The more fish and vegetable fat that was consumed, the better was the outcome. The strongest effect was found when the ratio of saturated fats on the one hand to vegetable and fish fats on the other was plotted against outcome.

The higher this ratio, the worse the outcome. The relationship was very strong statistically and accounted for about 80 per cent of the outcome differences between countries.

Such a strong statistical relationship indicates that there may be a true causal interaction between the two factors. But it does not *prove* such a causal relationship and it does not demonstrate which way the chain of causation operates. Could schizophrenia outcome be *causing* the differences in fat intake, or could the differences in fat intake be *causing* the differences in schizophrenia outcome? The first is inherently implausible since it is difficult to see how differences in schizophrenia outcome could change the pattern of fat consumption of a whole country. It makes more sense that a fat-consumption pattern could change the outcome of schizophrenia. Phospholipid biochemistry provides a mechanism whereby this might happen.

INDIVIDUAL STUDIES

Country-by-country studies of health and disease which attempt to demonstrate causation can be seriously misleading. If a factor appears to cause disease when comparing one country with another, it is important to verify the results by looking at that factor in individuals *within* the same country. All too often some factor which appears to exert a strong effect on a national level disappears when comparing individuals within that country. Breast cancer is a good example of this. In countries which consume a lot of saturated fat the risk of breast cancer in women is higher. Because of this, for years it was thought that a high-fat diet caused breast cancer. But when looking at fat intake within a country, the results have been universally negative. Women who eat more saturated fat do not have a higher risk of breast cancer. The connection between countries with a high fat intake and those with a high risk of breast cancer must have another explanation.

Malcolm Peet, working at Sheffield University in England, decided to try to test the fat effect in individual schizophrenic patients. He and his research student, Jan Mellor, studied a very restricted group of individuals, chronic schizophrenic patients ill enough to be in a long-stay hospital. They were therefore all in the same environment, all looked after by the same doctors, all exposed to the same food choices in the hospital meals, and all able to supplement their food intake by purchases at the hospital shop or with food brought in by relatives and friends.

Even among those patients there were substantial differences in illness severity. Although they were all ill enough to be hospitalized, some were more seriously affected than others. The severity of their illness was monitored by rating them on the Positive and Negative Symptom Scale for Schizophrenia (PANSS). This is a standard way of measuring schizophrenia severity, widely used in research studies. Then, for a week in each case, Jan Mellor obsessively rated every item of food actually consumed by the patient, making estimates of food ordered but left on the plate and food brought in from outside sources.

The first surprise was that, in spite of such an apparently restricted environment, patients often consumed rather different diets. They exercised a good deal of choice. The second finding was that most foods seemed to be unrelated to the severity of the schizophrenia. The third finding, however, which was very clear, was that the severity of schizophrenia was inversely related to the consumption of omega-3 fatty acids from fish. These are the fatty acids, notably EPA and DHA, which are so important in the brain.

This dietary factor, the consumption of oily fish, had also showed up in the country-by-country analysis carried out by the Christensens. So the conclusion from the national studies holds up on an individual basis. It really does look as though fish fatty acids in particular, and essential fatty acids in general, may be protective against schizophrenia. It also looks as though a high consumption of solid saturated fats may be harmful. The only way of finally proving this is to do a test of treatment. We will come to this in Chapter 17, but in the meantime we will look at how Peet and Mellor's discovery relates to what happened during the Industrial Revolution.

THE INDUSTRIAL REVOLUTION, NUTRITION
AND SCHIZOPHRENIA

As the Industrial Revolution and consequent urbanization gathered
pace, first in Britain and then in other countries, similar patterns
of psychiatric illness developed. Schizophrenia was not then
called schizophrenia, but the illness which acquired that label over
a hundred years later was clearly apparent. The hallucinations,
delusions, paranoia, thought disorders and inexorable downhill
course, in many patients requiring prolonged hospitalization, were
all well recognized. It seemed as though more and more of these
patients were coming to the attention of doctors, who, along with
the political authorities, did not know what to do. The only thing
seemed to be to incarcerate patients, partly for their own good and
partly to keep them away from the rest of society. The more
humane institutions truly deserved the term 'asylum', in its old
sense of a place of refuge. Patients were housed in reasonable
conditions, where they were freed of stress as far as possible, and
employed in constructive and useful work, often on the hospital
farm or in the hospital workshops. But in many cases, where the
management was poor, the institution short of money, or the flow
of patients simply overwhelming, the asylum concept degenerated
into warehousing and control. The illusion of order and peace was
often maintained by siting the institution in beautiful parkland
away from a town or city, but the internal reality was all too often
appalling. In every industrialized country in the world these vast
asylums were established. The public soon acquired a sense of what
really went on in these places, calling them 'loony bins' or similar
pejorative terms.

What was going on? What was causing this immense and un-
precedented flow of obviously mad people? The short answer is
that we simply do not know. Many explanations have been put
forward. One is that there was no real increase at all in the
proportion of people affected, but rather as the population of each
country rose so did the total number of mad people. A second
explanation is also that there were no changes in the proportions
affected, but that in a rural society mad people can be much more
readily tolerated than in an urban society of nuclear families. Thus,

although the proportions may not have increased, the numbers rejected by family and community informal care systems increased dramatically, so forcing the authorities to take notice and do something about it.

A third explanation is that schizophrenia may not have existed prior to the Industrial Revolution and is truly, as Fuller Torrey has suggested, a disease of civilization, or at least of urbanization. The most immediately obvious explanation if this were true would be that schizophrenia is an infectious disease, able to spread in crowded urban conditions in a way which would be more difficult in a rural environment with a dispersed population. Among the infectious diseases, bacterial and protozoal causes can now with moderate confidence be ruled out, although, by analogy with cerebral syphilis, the possibility of a bacterial origin was taken seriously for many years. What cannot be ruled out is a viral infection. Indeed, work funded by the Stanley Foundation at Johns Hopkins University has provided good evidence that schizo-phrenic patients are prone to more and different brain viral infections than normal people. However, whether these infections are cause or consequence remains to be determined. No specific single virus has yet been isolated, and in my view it is difficult to explain the uniform distribution of schizophrenia across the world on the basis of a viral infection. More likely, in my opinion, is the concept that the abnormalities of biochemistry in schizophrenia make patients more likely to suffer from viral infections. This would explain the increased presence of viruses, the presence of different viruses in different patients, and the uniform distribution of schizophrenia better than the idea that schizophrenia itself is primarily due to a viral infection.

The idea that schizophrenia is a disease of the Industrial Revolu-tion is in part based on the apparent absence of severe schizophrenia in some rural societies. However, the more carefully a study is done, and the more intensively patients are sought, the more certain does it appear that schizophrenia is indeed present in all racial groups and in all societies. Nevertheless, it seems possible that, although the total proportions affected may be the same, the disease might have been a much milder condition in pre-industrialized society.

What I think happened with industrialization was that patients whose schizophrenia might have caused only modest and reasonably tolerated disturbance in a rural society became much more seriously ill and at the same time less well tolerated. People who in a pre-industrial society might have been described as schizotypal emerged as the frankly mad. Therefore, the apparent numbers rose. But what was really happening was that all the patients with schizophrenia who might not previously have been recognized as mad, but rather as merely odd, now were seen to be truly and seriously mad.

I think that this process can at least partially be understood on the basis of nutrition, as hinted at by the work of the Christensens and of Mellor and Peet. Both the type of food consumed and the processing and preservation of food changed with industrialization. In a rural society there is a relatively direct relationship between food production and consumption. There is no major need to prevent food deterioration on a large scale because the chain is relatively short. On the other hand, the supply of food to an industrialized population presented problems not previously encountered on a large scale.

Three of these problems were solved in ways which could have had a negative impact on schizophrenia. First, it was important to increase the supply of calories and the easiest way to do this was with saturated fat rather than with protein or even carbohydrates. The use of lard and of hydrogenated fat rocketed: these are the fats which make incorporation of essential fatty acids into the brain more difficult and so make schizophrenia worse. Second, natural grains do contain a modest amount of vegetable fat which supplies some essential fatty acids. These are linoleic and alpha-linolenic acids – not the EFAs directly required by the brain, but EFAs which can be converted to the brain fatty acids, albeit inefficiently and slowly. But the EFAs, especially if not kept under perfect conditions, become oxidized and rancid, leading to the spoilage of large amounts of stored food. This was unacceptable to the food suppliers and so the fats were extracted and the residual flour was bleached, an oxidizing process which destroyed any remaining EFAs. This process made the flour more stable, but destroyed its nutrient value at least as far as schizophrenia is concerned. Third, there are a number of vitamins which are important in the normal metabolism of EFAs within the body and particularly in the conversion of LA and ALA to the EPA, DHA and AA required by the brain. For example, vitamin E is required to preserve the EPA, DHA and AA, while pyridoxine is required for the conversion of ALA to EPA and DHA. Both of these vitamins and others were removed by the new methods of processing the food.

The overall effect of industrialization, therefore, was to reduce drastically the supply of brain EFAs, and to increase the supply of saturated fats which could replace the EFAs in the brain structure, but which were not capable of performing the same brain function. Nothing could be worse for the brain of a schizophrenic patient. The adverse consequences of the relatively minor genetic changes in phospholipid metabolism will be greatly exaggerated. The EFAs lost from brain phospholipids because of the changes in phospholipases and FACL described in earlier chapters will not be replaced by a high-quality EFA-rich diet such as might occur in a river, lake or marine environment. In short, the abnormal brain function of someone with schizophrenia will deteriorate further and the symptoms will become more florid.

Thus, in my view, the increases in the numbers of obviously mad people in association with industrialization had three origins. First, population growth simply meant that there were more mad people. Second, changes in society meant that mad people were less easily tolerated. Third, and possibly most important, the madness, which had previously been relatively mild in most patients, became much more severe because of the changes in nutrition.

OVERVIEW OF DIET CHANGE AND SCHIZOPHRENIA

The impact of schizophrenia on society occurred in three broad phases. First, the development of the mutations necessary for schizophrenia and bipolar disorder produced abnormalities in phospholipid metabolism which were relatively mild. These mild abnormalities had only a modest impact because they were alleviated by the high intake of brain-type EFAs in the hunter-gatherer diet. They were, however, responsible for the generation of highly creative individuals who founded religions, created art and invented technology, and for the highly destructive individuals who invented warfare and genocide and eliminated all our near relatives.

In the second stage, at the time of the agricultural revolution, the impact of the mutations became more severe. This was because the brain-type EFAs in the diet were replaced by their precursors, LA and ALA, which required metabolic effort to convert them to the EFAs required specifically by the brain. Creativity, but also psychopathology, became more exuberant.

In the third stage, at the time of the Industrial Revolution, there was a drastic fall in the intake of EFAs and of the co-factors required for their preservation and metabolism. At the same time, there was an increase in potentially harmful saturated fats. The disaster of the nineteenth-century asylums was generated.

These three stages produced increasing severities of schizo-phrenic illness, at the same time increasing the manifestations of bizarre and creative behaviour among schizophrenics and their relatives, and, unfortunately, also increasing amounts of violent, destructive and psychopathic behaviour.

In some ways it is a depressing story, but, on the other hand, it is also an exciting one. If true, and if we can reasonably conclude that schizophrenia is exacerbated or attenuated by diet, it offers new approaches to the control of the symptoms of the disease. It may even offer approaches which could leave much of the creativity intact, yet allow it to be exploited effectively because the personality and the capacity for constructive action are not so destructively damaged.

16

'GREAT WITS ARE SURE TO MADNESS NEAR ALLIED'

JOHN DRYDEN, 1631–1700

I BEGAN WRITING A FIRST DRAFT OF THIS CHAPTER OVER THE Christmas holiday of 1999. The papers and TV broadcasts were full of reports of a man who had invaded the home of former Beatle George Harrison and tried to kill him with a knife. The lurid articles in even some of the supposedly quality British papers were full of pejorative statements like 'madman', 'crazed', 'loonie' and so on. The descriptions of the man made it clear that he was a paranoid schizophrenic patient, who often refused medication, who had been capable of great charm and of being a useful member of society, but who had gone seriously off the rails. Naturally and correctly, there was lots of sympathy for George Harrison, who had narrowly escaped being killed. But there was little sympathy for the patient, who was clearly acting in a way which was quite outside his control, having been driven to this bizarre act by the insistent nature of his delusions and compulsive voices.

Sympathetic and informed news coverage of schizophrenia is very rare. As I have emphasized earlier, the great majority of schizophrenic patients are peaceful people, and the proportion of the schizophrenic population which is violent is not much greater than the proportion of the so-called normal population. But unfortunately, when schizophrenics are violent, they are sometimes violent in bizarre and headline-grabbing ways. They kill their mothers, they kill complete strangers, they try to kill public figures with whom they have become obsessed, people like George Harrison or Ronald Reagan. The pattern of violence is therefore quite different from that exhibited by 'normal' violent people. As a result, schizophrenic patients have gained a reputation for being much more violent than normal. For the great majority of schizophrenic patients this reputation is completely undeserved.

The second common type of story featuring schizophrenia centres on homelessness. Since many of the great psychiatric hospitals have closed, many people who really do need asylum in the best sense of that word have been forced on to the streets. In theory, they are supposed to be looked after by some version of what has been called 'care in the community'. Depressingly, all too often either the 'care' is inadequate or, even when adequate, is rejected by the patient. The 'community' may also be less than enthusiastic about welcoming someone who is patently odd even if not frankly mad. As a result, schizophrenic patients make up a substantial proportion of homeless people, leading to the frequent press stories.

Even the most sympathetic media coverage of schizophrenia treats the illness as a major problem with no redeeming features. It is portrayed as a condition which should be managed more appropriately and often more humanely by the relevant professionals, but no one suggests that it is something for which we should be thanking Providence.

THE NATURE OF SCHIZOPHRENIA

It would be foolish to deny that schizophrenia is a problem. Some schizophrenic patients are very seriously ill. Some are violent, often to themselves in the form of self-mutilation or suicide, and occasionally to others in the form of violent attack, murder or attempted murder. Most schizophrenic patients are unemployed and are living on some form of welfare. Of those who are employed, only a minuscule proportion work at a level compatible with their school achievements before they became ill. Few schizophrenic patients have a good or normal relationship with the rest of their family. Paranoia and delusions take their toll and patients are frequently disproportionately hostile to those closest to them.

But this apparently uniformly gloomy picture has another side. As we have seen, sometimes schizophrenic patients do achieve what is expected of them according to their ability: John Nash and at least one other well-known recent Nobel prize-winner fall into that category. Many bipolar patients have achieved great things during the non-psychotic phases of their illness.

Many patients, however, while not high achievers themselves, come from families where achievements are extraordinary and have parents, grandparents, siblings, children or cousins of various degrees of relationship who have been extremely successful. Clearly something about being a close relative of a schizophrenic or bipolar patient may be able to generate ability and creativity of a high order. As the Maudsley and McLean hospital researchers realized, the elimination of such genetic characteristics by a process of eugenic control could have disastrous consequences for humanity. If we really were successful, we might eliminate most of the highly creative, imaginative and energetic people in many fields of endeavour.

Fortunately, as well as being off the political agenda in most societies, eugenic control of a genetically based illness which requires the simultaneous presence of more than one gene is almost impossible. This is because the majority of people who carry one of the genes will not be ill, and also because the genes are likely to be very common.

We do not yet know whether schizophrenia is a disease requiring the simultaneous presence of two, three, four or more genes. We can be pretty confident that more than one is required because none of the family studies of whatever design support a single-gene concept. It is instructive to do some simple calculations of the numbers of people in the population who will be carrying one or more genes for schizophrenia, if the simultaneous presence of two, three or four genes is required for the illness to become apparent. We do not yet know what these genes are, but it is already reasonable to propose that one will be found to be involved in dyslexia, another in bipolar disorder, another in schizotypy and another in high intelligence. These are all commonly found in the first- and second-degree relatives of schizophrenic patients. But the simultaneous presence of two, three or four of them will be required for a full schizophrenic illness to emerge.

We can start off with the reasonable assumption that in a given population around 1 per cent of people will exhibit the illness during their lifetime. But we know from the studies of identical twins that if 1 per cent of people have the illness, two to three times as many will have the necessary genome without being psychiatrically ill. This is because, if one identical twin is schizophrenic, there is only about a 30–50 per cent chance of the other twin being schizophrenic, even though they have the same genome. So a conservative estimate is that around 2 per cent of the population must carry *all* the genes which are necessary for schizophrenia to develop. I will call the sum of all the necessary genes 'the schizophrenic genome'. In order to provide the fully sufficient conditions for the genome to emerge as a schizophrenic illness, some other environmental factors, whether social, stress-related, nutrition-related or others must be present.

If 2 per cent of the population carry a schizophrenic genome, and if two different genes are required to provide that genome, how many of the population must carry one of these genes? The answer, of course, is the sum of any two numbers which when multiplied together will give 2 per cent. Some examples are as follows:

- If 20 per cent of the population carry one gene, and 10 per cent carry the other, then 2 per cent will have both (20 per cent × 10 per cent = 2 per cent). The total percentage of the population carrying one, or other, or both genes will be 30 per cent, with 28 per cent of those not being at risk of schizophrenia. However, that 28 per cent may be unusual in ways which fall well short of psychosis, and they may be particularly talented.

- If 40 per cent of the population carry one gene, and 5 per cent carry the other, then 2 per cent of the population will carry both (40 per cent × 5 per cent = 2 per cent). The total percentage of the population carrying one, or other, or both genes will be 45 per cent, with 43 per cent of those not being at risk of schizophrenia.

The principles are obvious. If three genes must be simultaneously present for a full schizophrenic genome to occur, then well over 50 per cent of the population is likely to carry one or two of these genes without the third, and so not be at risk of schizophrenia. If four genes must be simultaneously present, then almost everyone in the population may well be carrying one, two or three of the necessary genes.

The clear conclusion is that the genes which are necessary for the development of schizophrenia are likely to be exceedingly common, but that only a small proportion of people will carry them all simultaneously. Of those who do carry them all, as with identical twins, only between a third and a half will actually develop the disease.

THE VALUE OF THE GENES FOR SCHIZOPHRENIA

What I have suggested in this book is that the genes for schizophrenia, which are likely to include genes for bipolar disorder, dyslexia, high intelligence and schizotypy, are responsible for most of the religious sense, most of the technical and artistic creativity, and most of the leadership qualities in modern humans. Sometimes these exceptional abilities may be exhibited by people who carry all the genes required for the schizophrenic genome. More often, they are apparent in people who lack one of the genes required for the full expression of that genome but who have the other (if there are two main genes) or the others (if there are more than two genes of major effect). Without the genes which in combination cause schizophrenia we would be like Neanderthals or *Homo erectus* – large brained, cleverer than most other species, but lacking that creative spark and lust for change which have so dramatically distinguished our species from our immediate predecessors.

People who lack one of the genes required for schizophrenia, but who have the other or others, may well not be fully normal as perceived by most people, even though they are clearly not psychotic. Depending on which genes they have and which they do not, they may well be dyslexic, schizotypal, borderline, bipolar or psychopathic, exhibiting in partial form some of the skills and the disabilities which, when fully expressed in the schizophrenic individual, can be so distressing.

While the dark side is not all there is to schizophrenia, it would be as unrealistic and inappropriate to ignore it as it would be to ignore the creativity and the achievements. Schizophrenic patients themselves, and those who carry a partial schizophrenic genome, can be violent, psychopathic and criminally inclined. These qualities, if restrained and controlled by superior intelligence, can be of immense value in the struggles for position, recognition and money. This is particularly true in societies or in parts of society where there is no truly democratic possibility of 'throwing the rascals out'. So in all societies until very recently, in many societies even today, and in many parts of societies which are democratic overall, these characteristics offer unscrupulous individuals the opportunity to gain and retain power over their fellows.

What is required is a clear-eyed recognition of both problems and opportunities, of both the good and the bad. One of the most exciting observations in the whole of schizophrenia research is the fact that only about one-third to one-half of people carrying a full schizophrenic genome actually become schizophrenic. In the others who do not develop the illness some environmental factor must be controlling its emergence. Perhaps it is possible, by manipulating the environment, to prevent the expression of the illness even in those who have a 100 per cent genetic risk.

The idea that environment may be able to influence the emergence and development of schizophrenia is not new. It is inherent in the earliest concepts of the asylum, a place where the stresses of the world can be attenuated, where time can be spent constructively in some form of education, employment or leisure, and where the course of the disease may thereby be changed for the better. More recently, the idea has been developed in the process of social and familial studies of schizophrenia, where it has been argued that particular sorts of society, or particular types of immediate family environment, may increase or reduce the likelihood of the emergence of schizophrenia in those who are at risk. There is therefore nothing intellectually implausible in the fundamental concept that environment may influence the development of a disease which seems so serious and so 'hard-wired' as schizophrenia.

But the problems with the explanations and procedures put forward in the previous paragraph are of two main types. First, the explanations are exceedingly complex. It is possible to tell plausible just-so stories about the familial and social factors which precipitated or avoided the emergence of schizophrenia in any particular patient, but the details of the just-so stories seem to be constrained only by the imagination of the investigator and not by any consistently observable facts. All individual cases of patients are so complex that selecting the key social or familial factors, and expressing them in a way which allows them to be generalized to all or most other patients, is an almost impossible task. The field offers wonderful opportunities for those with fertile imaginations but a weak grasp of reality.

The second major problem with the approach is that it is almost always therapeutically useless or, when therapeutically valuable, is inordinately resource-consuming and expensive, so that it cannot be practically applied to the majority of patients. If a particular family environment precipitates schizophrenia, and another environment prevents it, how is it possible to use that information in a useful preventive or therapeutic mode? Almost all attempts to change family structures by outside intervention, short of physically removing one or more members of the family, have failed miserably. Providing a true asylum may also work, but it is a solution which is impossibly expensive for the generality of patients, and is in itself almost an admission of failure, for it accepts that the patient cannot live in a normal society.

The idea that the most important environmental factor may be something which is as simple and as generalizable as nutrition is one which is inherently offensive to a high proportion of the professionals in the field. The experts in social and familial environments are much more interested in the complications of the social dynamics than they are in the idea that a rather simple biological factor may explain most of the impact of the environment.

The experts in biological aspects of psychiatry like the idea of a biochemical explanation but sometimes seem to hate the idea that the biochemistry may relate to nutrition rather than to some ultra-modern, and what they see as sophisticated, molecular biology. They have forgotten the relatively recent history of bio-medical science. Some of the most sophisticated researchers of all time have unravelled the impact of nutrition on health brilliantly, and by doing so have eliminated most of the scourges which cut life short as recently as a hundred years ago, or even more recently in the case of pellagra in the USA. Pellagra, a deficiency of vitamin B_3, caused the four Ds – dermatitis, diarrhoea, dementia and death – in large areas of the US South as recently as the 1930s. Its elimination as the result of nutritional research had one of the largest of all impacts on US health in the past two centuries. There is a tendency among modern molecular biologists to believe that work on nutrition is all old hat and has no role to play in modifying the expression of those illnesses, like schizophrenia, which still so trouble us today. But the fact is that the drugs of which the biological psychiatrists are so proud were all discovered almost fifty years ago by observant clinicians making serendipitous discoveries. Since that first wonderful therapeutic dawn of the 1950s, progress has been trivial in relation to the amount of brain power and money fired at the problem.

Perhaps it is time to get back to first principles and give nutritional biochemistry and clinical observation a chance.

17

'ONE SHOULD EAT TO LIVE'

MOLIÈRE, 1622–1673

SCHIZOPHRENIA IN ITS FULLY EXPRESSED FORM IS ONE OF THE MOST serious afflictions that can strike an individual. And for the family it can be, as one mother described it to me, an almost infinitely prolonged living death. This boy or girl who seemed so promising and so close to their family gradually drifted away to become someone else. The body is the same, and there are not infrequent but all too brief moments of near-normal behaviour. But something elusive has gone, the thread has been broken and there seems to be nothing that can bring it all back.

While in familial and personality terms the problem is devastating, in biochemical terms the problem *cannot* be very serious. After all, the young person functioned near normally for fifteen, twenty-five or thirty-five years before becoming ill. More-over, all schizophrenic patients vary in the severity of their illness, often, as documented earlier, becoming near normal while the body temperature is elevated. The fundamental biochemical problem therefore cannot be too serious and must be reversible. If only one could find out how to tip the balance in the right direction, a substantial improvement might be possible.

The drugs currently available do have some good effects and it would be inappropriate to downplay their impact in controlling the more florid features of psychosis. The state of psychiatry immediately prior to the introduction of the neuroleptic drugs, as they were called, has been sympathetically described by John Cawte and Jean Thullier. Cawte writes in his recent book *The Last of the Lunatics* how truly, deeply, madly mad were many schizophrenic patients before the availability of drug therapy. The new neuroleptic drugs dramatically took the edge off that distress, allowing patients to live out of hospital because their behaviour was no longer so wildly and obviously outrageous.

But in their enthusiasm for these dramatic outcomes, many psychiatrists failed to be good clinical observers. They downplayed the Parkinson's disease-like abnormal movements, the weight gain, the sedation and the dysphoria which patients experienced. They trivialized the concerns of families who had first lost a son or daughter to madness, and then had seen that son or daughter lose the more florid aspects of their madness but turn into a fat, slothful, withdrawn, shaking shadow of their former self. They forgot that study after study has shown that the average improvement on drug treatment is only 15–25 per cent, an improvement which means that 75–85 per cent of the symptoms remain. Doctors minimized the fact that most schizophrenic patients remained unemployed, and that those who were employed were almost always in work which would normally have seemed far below what they should have been capable of on the basis of their school achievements before they became ill. The literature is drowned in excessively optimistic reports of drug effects, which over-emphasize the therapeutic improvement and underestimate the side-effects. As one psychiatrist I know put it, his colleagues forgot that the real evidence of improvement is that the patient is paying tax, preferably at more than the minimal rate. Very few schizophrenic patients are paying taxes, a situation which has not changed substantially with the availability of the newer drugs.

The Parkinson's disease-type tremors which commonly occurred as side-effects of treatment with the old drugs were regarded as inevitable consequences of the therapeutic action of the drug. The dogma was that, in order to be an effective anti-schizophrenic agent, a drug had to induce Parkinsonian symptoms. Too few people asked whether inducing symptoms of another illness really could be the best treatment. There was little major concern because the patients were so seriously ill anyway, and if this was the price of some improvement, so be it. In any case, if the drug dose was lowered, the Parkinsonian symptoms usually went away, so no permanent harm was being done.

Then, particularly by the 1970s, it began to be noticed that some patients were developing a different sort of movement disorder. This consisted of uncontrollable twitches and writhing movements, often most apparent in the face but also affecting other parts of the body. These movements could sometimes be seen in patients who had never received neuroleptic drugs, but they were distressingly more common in patients who did receive such drugs. What was worse, the movements did not stop if the drugs were stopped. If anything, they became more marked and seemed to be caused by a permanent drug-induced change to a susceptible brain. This quite different type of abnormal movement became known as tardive dyskinesia or TD.

TD terrified doctors and drug companies even more than it did patients and their families. It opened up the possibility of legal claims for compensation, especially when, as was commonly the case, the drugs had been used in inappropriately high dosage for long periods of time. The patient and family complaints about this side-effect, which, unlike the Parkinsonian symptoms, did not seem to be readily reversible, gained force. As a result, the search was on for drugs which might help schizophrenic patients without causing TD.

Attention focused on a drug called clozapine. Like the prototypes of all the major drugs used in psychiatry, clozapine had been discovered accidentally in the 1950s. Clinical studies in the 1960s suggested that it might be a very effective anti-schizophrenic drug, able to improve symptoms without causing either Parkinsonian symptoms or TD. It was introduced into a few European markets, but then disaster struck. Several patients died because of agranulocytosis, a complete failure of the production of the white cells required to fight infection. The drug was largely withdrawn and even where it remained on sale was used only as a very last resort.

Then in the 1980s, as concerns about TD grew, attention turned back to clozapine as the only effective anti-schizophrenic drug which did not seem to cause TD or Parkinsonian symptoms. With extremely careful monitoring of white-cell counts it was reintroduced into some of the markets from which it had been withdrawn, and introduced for the first time into others, such as the USA. It was evident that for some patients clozapine was much better than any other available drug. The risk of agranulocytosis was substantially reduced by the careful monitoring. It did have important side-effects, particularly sedation, weight gain and massively excessive hypersalivation. But to many these did not seem as worrying as TD.

The search was therefore started for drugs which, like clozapine, would cause neither TD nor Parkinsonian symptoms, but which, unlike clozapine, would not produce agranulocytosis. Thousands of variants of the clozapine molecule were produced to try to find the ideal one. Several companies succeeded, at least in part. In the late 1990s the so-called new 'atypical' neuroleptics were brought to market. They had a low risk of causing Parkinsonian symptoms or TD, and also a low risk of producing agranulocytosis. Unfortunately, they still often produced weight gain and sedation, they could cause cardiac side-effects in some patients, and, in longer-term use, with some drugs a significant proportion of patients became diabetic. Some of this group of new drugs are safer than others, but unfortunately these are also less effective, often even less effective than the old neuroleptic drugs.

And that is the situation today. Almost fifty years after the first anti-schizophrenic drug, chlorpromazine, was produced we have made virtually no further progress in controlling schizophrenic symptoms. Drugs, on average, still improve symptoms by only 15–25 per cent, leaving 75–85 per cent of symptoms unresolved. The side-effects of Parkinsonism, TD and agranulocytosis have been drastically reduced, but new side-effects of weight gain, sedation, diabetes and cardiac problems are still there and may have worsened. There has not been much change in tax paying, nor in employment at levels commensurate with the underlying abilities of the patient. Despite billions of dollars of expenditure, we have not made that much progress. A different approach may be worth trying.

TREATING SCHIZOPHRENIA WITH FAT

The elements which are leading to a new understanding of schizophrenia have been documented in this book. The problem is not primarily in the neurotransmitters which send signals between nerve cells, but in the phospholipid cell-signalling mechanisms which translate the neurotransmitter signals into action. Hence the problem is only a small one at each individual cell, which is only marginally impaired, but the consequences affect the whole body. The impact is minimal outside the brain, where physiological effects in the normal body are produced by only a relatively small number of sequential stages. A minor defect occurring at each of three or four sequential steps in a physiological response system is unlikely to be enough to damage the overall system severely. The defects are, however, large enough to be picked up by the niacin skin test. But in the brain, where any action depends on the co-ordinated behaviour of millions of cells, even a small abnormality at each one will produce a disastrous overall impact on the whole system. Conversely, a small shift towards normal in the functioning of each small step may produce a dramatic improvement in overall performance.

The early work in this field suggested that the main problems might relate to defective availability of essential fatty acids and particularly of AA. This could explain the resistance to pain and arthritis, the improvement in response to fever and the biochemical changes noted in the red blood cells and the brain. My collaboration with Krishna Vaddadi, then a research fellow at the University of Leeds and now a Professor of Psychiatry at Monash University in Melbourne, was the first to attempt to exploit this. AA was not available at the time, but its precursor, gamma-linolenic acid (GLA) was. GLA is converted to AA in the body and we hoped that this might have a therapeutic effect in schizophrenia. We conducted a placebo-controlled trial. There were effects both on schizophrenic symptoms and on TD, but they were modest and so the research stalled. No funds were available because all the grant-giving bodies felt that such an unconventional approach was a waste of time. Krishna moved to Australia and needed time to get established in his new environment.

But neither Krishna nor I was ready to give up. We collected new evidence that omega-3 as well as omega-6 fatty acids were deficient in schizophrenic patients. Wagner Gattaz, the Christensens, Jeffrey Yao, Jay Pettegrew, Sukhdeb Mukherjee, Iain Glen and many others all collected further evidence which suggested that phospholipid metabolism might be important in schizophrenia. In particular, Malcolm Peet in Sheffield began to start thinking about fatty acids, their oxidation products and schizophrenia. We did a joint study which confirmed that red blood cells from schizophrenic patients were deficient in both omega-6 and omega-3 fatty acids. Malcolm and Jan Mellor then did the nutritional study mentioned in Chapter 5. This confirmed on an individual basis the Christensens' work on the potential importance of omega-3 fatty acids.

The time seemed ripe for a further therapeutic trial, this time concentrating on omega-3 fatty acids. Malcolm Peet and Jan Mellor decided to see what fish oil might do to help schizophrenic patients. In a small pilot study they showed that a high dose of fish oil (10g/day) produced a small improvement of around 15 per cent in a group of chronic patients resistant to treatment with conventional drugs.

The effect was modest, but it was significant in that it was produced in patients who were unresponsive to existing drugs. More important, it was achieved without any side-effects. Malcolm Peet was encouraged to go further. We decided to try to dissect out the effects of the individual components of the fish oil. Fish oil contains a lot of different fatty acids, some which have no particularly obvious relationship to brain function, some which might be beneficial and some which might be harmful. However, two fatty acids, both of which were present in the fish oil used in the first study, do have potential effects on the brain. One of these is DHA, which is present in the brain in large amounts and in reduced amounts in both brain and red cells of schizophrenic patients. The other is EPA, which is present in the brain in only very small amounts. However, it also is reduced in red blood cells from schizophrenic patients and is potentially important for a number of reasons. It can give rise to a large number of very active cell-signalling molecules. It can reduce the activity of phospholipase A_2, the enzyme which is overactive in schizophrenia, and it can regulate the functions of FACL, one of the enzymes in the phospholipase cycle which is underactive in schizophrenia.

We wanted to do a placebo-controlled study to check that any improvements were not simply due to the patients feeling that someone was taking an interest in them. We were not able to make pure EPA or DHA at that time, but we did the next best thing. We prepared one oil which contained 25 per cent of EPA and little DHA (Kirunal) and a second oil which contained 25 per cent of DHA and little EPA (Docanol). We did not know which, if either, would work, but our prediction was that DHA would be the effective fatty acid. This was because it is so important in the brain and also because levels in schizophrenic patients were so reduced.

Malcolm Peet then set up another study in forty-five chronic, partially treatment-resistant patients. Placebo, Kirunal or Docanol were given to the patients for twelve weeks in addition to their standard treatment. The treatments appeared identical and were given on a double-blind basis, which means that neither doctor nor patients knew who was on what treatment. During the study some patients improved and some were unchanged. We were eager to know who was on what treatment and could hardly wait to break the code on completion of the last patient. When the code was broken we found it difficult to believe the results. Both the placebo group and the DHA group had shown small improvements but there were no major differences between the two. If anything, DHA was rather less good than placebo. Our hypothesis was wrong and we reluctantly concluded that DHA was not an effective part of the fish oil. But something very exciting had happened in the EPA Kirunal group. Most of the patients in this group had improved. The average improvement was around 22 per cent, substantially and significantly greater than in either of the other two groups. It was comparable to what can be achieved in patients by standard anti-schizophrenic drugs, with all their side-effects. But this effect was apparent in patients who had already improved as much as they could on standard drugs but were still ill. It was also achieved with no sedation, no weight gain, no Parkinsonian movements, no TD and no hypersalivation. In fact, in some patients the TD actually improved. We knew we were on to something important. Never before had any drug been able to produce such an improvement without side-effects. But this group of patients had been ill for a very long time. They had also been treated for many years with standard drugs and we had no idea what EPA might do in a patient who had not received conventional drug therapy.

ENTER JONATHAN

At about this time I made contact with two researchers who were to have a major impact on the subsequent course of events. Alex Richardson is a psychologist who has specialized in studying the relationship between schizophrenia, schizotypy and dyslexia; her work on schizotypy has been referred to in Chapter 8. She had found that many dyslexic individuals have schizotypical personalities. Many relatives of schizophrenic patients are also dyslexic, a connection which was immediately interesting to me. Alex was working at Charing Cross Hospital Medical School in London and some of her research involved a collaboration with Basant Puri, a psychiatrist working at the Magnetic Resonance Imaging (MRI) Unit at the Royal Postgraduate Medical School at the Hammersmith Hospital which is run by Professor Graeme Bydder. MRI is a tool which enables the imaging of the living brain in exquisite detail, in a way which is non-invasive. Alex and Basant were collaborating on an imaging study of the brains of people with dyslexia and schizophrenia, with the strong support of Graeme and of Joe Hajnal, who had developed a particularly accurate way of doing comparative sequential imaging.

Alex and Basant were looking after a patient called Jonathan. He was thirty-one years old and had had a schizophrenic breakdown at the age of nineteen which caused him to drop out of college. He had received a single dose of an anti-schizophrenic drug but had experienced such a severe adverse reaction that he vowed never again to take such a drug. For ten years he drifted around London, leading the all-too-typical life of an unemployed schizophrenic patient. Then he had come into contact with a long-term evaluation programme at Charing Cross Hospital and had been seen regularly by Alex and Basant over the past two years. During that time his schizophrenia scores on standard rating scales had been unchanged, in spite of the fact that he had learned to trust Alex and Basant. During the second of the two years he had allowed himself to be evaluated by MRI at the Hammersmith Hospital at six-month intervals. The three scans showed a pattern which is disturbingly common in young schizophrenic patients: the ventricles, the fluid-filled spaces within the brain, were slowly, but without doubt, becoming larger. This indicated a progressive loss of brain tissue, a process which may underline the steady deterioration which can occur over a lifetime in schizophrenia. This loss does not occur in all patients, but does so in a substantial sub-group.

Alex and Basant heard Malcolm Peet talk about his results with EPA-rich Kirunal. They wondered whether Jonathan might be persuaded to try Kirunal, in spite of his hostility to standard anti-psychotic drugs. They carefully explained to him that Kirunal was an extract from fish which contained a material normally present in the human brain but which might be required in larger than normal amounts in schizophrenia. Jonathan considered the situation carefully. Because of his trust in Alex and Basant he agreed.

Jonathan took 8g a day of Kirunal, providing about 2g a day of pure EPA, and agreed to return at four-weekly intervals for evaluation. After four weeks there was no effect on his psychiatric state detectable by the standard rating scales. His delusions, his auditory hallucinations and his general apathy were unchanged. But Alex felt that there was some improvement which was difficult to define. She felt that he looked healthier, that his skin and hair condition had improved. She was not yet ready to write off Kirunal as useless.

By eight weeks, Jonathan, Alex and Basant all knew that something important had happened. Jonathan was clearly better, with reduced scores on all the rating scales. His appearance was transformed. He was more alert, more interested in life and had experienced a dramatic reduction in his delusions and hallucinations. One of the reasons why Alex was so interested in Jonathan was that he was dyslexic as well as schizophrenic. She noted that on her tests for dyslexia his performance was improving. It was now not difficult to persuade Jonathan to continue with the Kirunal.

Over the following twelve months Jonathan progressively improved with regard to all aspects of his condition. After twelve years of illness, his scores on the schizophrenia rating scales were somewhat above the normal mean but not much. People meeting him for the first time thought him somewhat quirky and unusual but certainly not schizophrenic. His dyslexia also improved substantially and he began to contemplate the idea of going back to university. Now, three years after starting EPA, he has returned to his studies.

But perhaps the most exciting aspect of Jonathan's EPA treatment from the point of view of the biological psychiatrist is that his brain changes, as seen on the MRI scans, have gone into reverse. His ventricles have reduced in size and he has regained some of the brain tissue which everyone thought had been irrevocably lost. The brain is structurally much more open to change than anyone previously had thought. EPA is an agent which can change not only function, but the underlying structure as well, possibly by changing the ways in which dendritic and axonal endings proliferate. Jonathan's previous psychiatric state has gone: anyone trying to evaluate it has to take on trust the clinical descriptions and rating-scale scores recorded by Alex, Basant and others. But the MRI scans provide an objective and permanent record of what happened to Jonathan's brain. They are available for any interested doctor or scientist to evaluate for themselves.

A STUDY IN NEWLY DIAGNOSED SCHIZOPHRENIC PATIENTS

Malcolm Peet's work was in chronic, difficult-to-treat schizophrenic patients, all of whom had been on long-term treatment with standard psychiatric drugs and who continued treatment with these drugs during the Kirunal trials. Jonathan's case made us wonder what would happen if we were to treat newly diagnosed patients with EPA. In industrialized countries such studies are difficult to set up and perform quickly. Most patients with schizophrenia are quickly put on to standard anti-schizophrenic drugs and doctors are often unwilling to test entirely new treatments.

However, Malcolm Peet had established a close working relationship with C. N. Ramchand, a scientist from the University of Baroda in India working as a research fellow with Gwynneth Hemmings, the Director of the Schizophrenia Association of Great Britain based in Bangor, north Wales. On completion of his fellowship, Ramchand, as he prefers to be known, went to work with Malcolm in Sheffield. From that connection grew a series of collaborative research projects with Sandeep Shah at the University of Baroda. Sandeep did a pilot study of Kirunal in his patients and was so pleased by the results that he decided to establish a study in newly diagnosed patients coming to see him for the first time.

The study was designed in the following way. Identical-appearing capsules of Kirunal and placebo were packed and coded in the UK and supplied to Baroda. Sandeep did not know which capsules were which. On seeing a new patient who was appropriate for the study, Sandeep immediately assigned him or her to the Kirunal or placebo treatment without knowing who was getting what. He tried to hold off giving standard anti-schizophrenic drugs for one week, but after that gave the patients standard drugs as required. The patients were evaluated at twelve weeks in two main ways. Were they using standard anti-schizophrenic drugs? How much had they changed on the standard schizophrenia rating scale, the PANSS? The results of these evaluations were then sent back to Malcolm Peet in Sheffield and after sixty-three patients had completed the trial the code was broken.

Malcolm could hardly contain his excitement. I knew by the tone of his voice on the phone that something very dramatic had happened. Only four patients had dropped out, three on placebo and one on Kirunal: this in itself was surprising. Drop-out rates in schizophrenia trials are usually much greater, often over 50 per cent in twelve-week studies, partly due to drug side-effects. On breaking the code, it was found that everyone who had been assigned to placebo and who had completed the trial had required full doses of standard drug therapy (29/29). They had achieved an average improvement on the PANSS of 28 per cent, a result entirely consistent with all other trials. But in the group assigned to EPA, at twelve weeks 10 of 31 patients did not require any standard drug treatment: they were being controlled by Kirunal alone. In the EPA group as a whole, the average improvement in score was 43 per cent – much better than the placebo group, all of whom were receiving standard therapy. Thus EPA alone was able to treat a substantial proportion of newly diagnosed patients and to do so without causing any of the standard side-effects. Moreover, the overall improvement in the EPA group was substantially better than in the standard treatment group.

A very great deal of work must be done before we can be sure exactly what role Kirunal or other forms of EPA will play in the management of schizophrenia. It is unlikely that EPA alone will produce the optimum results. It is also unlikely to be helpful in all patients. The dose must be correct; both too little and too much will fail to generate good results. Combinations with other fatty acids and other micro-nutrients are likely to be required to produce the optimal effects on the disordered phospholipid metabolism. But we can be confident already that this is the beginning of a revolution – a true paradigm shift in our understanding and management of the condition. At least some patients can achieve near normality without the often disabling side-effects of standard drugs.

ADDITIONAL SPIN-OFFS: BIPOLAR DISORDER AND PRISON VIOLENCE

The clinical picture of schizophrenia and the family studies suggest that schizophrenia should not be seen in isolation. Some components of the schizophrenic genome may also be involved in bipolar disorder, in depression and in criminal and violent behaviour. Might the new understanding of schizophrenia also be relevant to other disorders?

In a development quite independent of ours, Emanuel Severus from the Free University of Berlin and Andy Stoll from Harvard were trying to understand what might go wrong in bipolar disorder. They too came to the conclusion that the problem lay not in the neurotransmitter mechanisms, but rather in the signal transduction processes. They thought that omega-3 fatty acids might influence those in an appropriate way.

They therefore decided to set up a study. They used a mixed preparation of EPA and DHA and gave almost 10g of it, or a matching placebo, per day to thirty patients with treatment-resistant bipolar disorder. All patients were still experiencing cyclic behavioural changes despite adequate treatment trials with lithium, or valproate or both, the two drugs approved in the USA for the management of bipolar disorder. Twenty-two were continuing on standard drugs, but eight had discontinued these because of either side-effects or lack of efficacy. All thirty patients were randomized to omega-3 or placebo and followed for four months on a double-blind basis.

By the end of the study nine of the sixteen patients on placebo had experienced a major relapse of their bipolar disorder, as compared to only three of the fourteen on EPA and DHA. Among the eight patients not receiving any other drugs, three of four on placebo had experienced a severe relapse, as compared to none of four on omega-3. Nine of the fourteen on omega-3 had not only not relapsed, but had shown a substantial improvement from their baseline state, including an improvement in depression. Only three of the sixteen on placebo had shown a similar improvement.

Thus in bipolar disorder, as well as in schizophrenia, omega-3 fatty acids have a substantial therapeutic effect. As in schizophrenia, the patients like the treatment much better than the standard drugs. It seems a real possibility that the psychiatric disorder can be controlled without producing the sedation and stalling of the intellect which many patients complain of on standard drug therapy. In bipolar disorder no studies have yet been completed on EPA and DHA separately, although several are in progress. It is therefore uncertain whether it is the EPA, the DHA or a combination of the two which is effective. My own clinical impression of the responses of the patients who have been treated with EPA-rich or DHA-rich oils on an open-label basis is that, as in schizophrenia, and somewhat surprisingly, it is the EPA which is the more effective. Whether this clinical impression will be borne out by formal trials will become apparent in the near future.

The family studies of schizophrenia and bipolar disorder indicate that substantial numbers of people from such families have criminal records. Prison violence is an appalling problem to which there seem to be few answers. Stephen Schoenthaler, working in the USA, has pointed out that most prisoners eat diets which have inadequately low levels of several micro-nutrients. The prison food may theoretically be adequate, but many prisoners do not consume it and obtain much of their calorie intake from junk food and drink. Since the brain consumes 20 per cent of the calories used by the body, in spite of being only 2 per cent of the body's weight, and since micro-nutrients are required for the normal functioning of the brain, Schoenthaler has argued that some violent behaviour may relate to nutritionally based brain malfunction.

To say the least, this view has not been warmly received by experts in criminal violence. The field is dominated by criminologists, sociologists and psychologists who all tend to see violence as being related to social structure and education at levels ranging from the family right up to the state. They are undoubtedly partially right, but their refusal to consider the possibility that violence may have some biological basis resulting from brain malfunction is near complete and borders on the wilfully bizarre. These people have no difficulty in understanding that the proper function of their motor car requires it to be supplied with oil and water as well as petrol or gasoline, yet they seem unable to grasp that normal functioning of the brain may require at least an equivalent level of care and maintenance.

Schoenthaler's ideas have been taken up and developed with very great persistence by a UK organization called Natural Justice which is run by Bernard Gesch. He realized a number of things. First, the sceptics would be convinced only by a double-blind, placebo-controlled trial of nutritional intervention in which people were randomly allocated to a nutrient supplement or placebo without either the prisoner or the assessor knowing which was which. Second, whatever the dieticians might say, prisoners were highly unlikely to change their diet to something more nutritious: the only way to ensure that prisoners took the micro-nutrients would be to provide them in a capsule or tablet. Third, any trial must be kept as simple as possible because complex trials in a prison environment are just not feasible.

After an enormous amount of persistent effort, Bernard finally persuaded the UK government's Home Office, the ministry responsible for prisons, to allow a trial in a prison for young offenders. Like all prisons, this one kept a daily record of acts of violence, ranging from the relatively trivial to the most severe. The Home Office would permit this record to be used as an outcome measure but would not permit any other evaluation. In addition, all prisoners had to be given the opportunity to take part: there was to be no selection.

As can be imagined, the processes of obtaining ethical and administrative approval for the study, and of obtaining informed consent from each prisoner, were administrative nightmares. However, eventually all these difficulties were resolved by Bernard's persistence and the trial could begin. Half the prisoners were randomized on a double-blind basis to receive placebos. The other half were randomized to receive a multivitamin capsule, plus two capsules containing a mixture of omega-6 and omega-3 fatty acids from evening primrose oil and fish oil.

The results were difficult to believe, but nevertheless unequivocal. In all the prisoners who received nutritional treatment, as compared to all those who received matching placebos, there was about a 30 per cent reduction in the number of violent events. When the analysis was confined only to those prisoners who had been violent in the previous six months, the reduction in violence on active treatment was over 50 per cent.

It is hard to overestimate the importance of these findings. They have implications not just for prison violence, but for violence in our society as a whole, and for our understanding of our violent history. The brain is a delicate machine which requires a wide range of micro-nutrients, including essential fatty acids, for its normal function. Provide these nutrients in inadequate amounts and the brain will cease to function normally. No amount of education or socialization is likely to be effective with a biochemically malfunctioning brain. People with certain genetic traits, especially including some or all of the components of the schizophrenic genome, will be more susceptible than others to harm. Conversely, they will also be more likely to benefit from proper nutrition.

18

A JUST-SO STORY FOR THE TWENTY-FIRST CENTURY: HOW THE SCHIZOPHRENIC GENOME MADE US HUMAN

EARLIER IN THIS BOOK I DISCUSSED OTHER PEOPLE'S JUST-SO stories of human evolution in a way which might be seen as inappropriately pejorative. I think, however, that my argument is fair: the available just-so stories discuss the selective pressures in great detail but completely fail to specify the precise nature of the resulting responses or to propose a genetic mechanism by which such responses might have occurred and become fixed. Evolution involves an interaction between selective pressure and spontaneous genetic change: both must be precisely specified if evolution is to be properly explained.

I believe that progress can come only out of clarity in hypothesis-making and not out of confusion: only then can specific concepts be rejected, accepted or subjected to the Scottish legal judgement of 'not-proven'. So I also believe I have a responsibility to set out a clear process whereby I think we made the transition from the last common ancestor of humans and chimpanzees to our modern selves. The just-so story which follows is a hypothesis which may well prove to be wrong: but, unlike most other evolutionary just-so stories, it makes specific predictions which are experimentally falsifiable.

THE ESTABLISHED FACTS

Successful hypotheses must use established facts but transcend them and make predictions about possible new facts which may emerge in the future. The most important hypotheses go well beyond the facts, because only in this way can major advances be made. But there must be some firm ground on which most people of open-minded good will can agree. The most important items of that firm ground, which I think will be accepted by most experts in the various fields, have been discussed earlier in the book and may be summarized as follows:

1.   We and the chimpanzees shared a common ancestor, probably about 5–7 million years ago. That common ancestor lived at the forest edge, was partly arboreal and partly terrestrial, with an ability to stand upright occasionally as do all the remaining great apes today. Almost certainly the common ancestor, like all other great apes, had little subcutaneous fat and a thick pelt of fur. The diet was predominantly vegetarian but, like that of modern chimpanzees, regularly included termites and sometimes small animals. Language was absent but, as with most other primates, communication could occur by means of calls which had various fixed meanings but which were not usually linked together in sequences capable of more complex interpretation.

2.   Virtually all the remains of hominids on or near the pre-human line have been found at sites which, at the time their death occurred, would have been within easy reach of water, either riverine, lacustrine or marine.

3.   Humans are well adapted to heat but their heat-loss system works well only if there is an abundant water supply. Their kidneys conserve water poorly and their skins pour water out by sweating. Their naked bodies allow efficient cooling by sweat but absolutely

require a near-immediate availability of large amounts of water: without water the human cooling system leads to early death.

4. Many of the most obvious differences between chimpanzees and other great apes and humans relate to fat. The size of the brain, the subcutaneous fat storage and the sculpted body shape all depend on fat.

5. The most difficult step in evolution to explain is the last, whereby a sophisticated but highly conservative hominid with modern body structure, without any increase in brain size, became a human with symbolic culture, technical skill and a hunger for constant change. That step took place not less than 60,000 and not more than 140,000 years ago.

6. Many of the features which distinguish families with and without schizophrenic members are similar to the features which distinguish modern humans from our immediately pre-human ancestors. Because schizophrenia is common to all races, it must have entered humanity prior to the separation of those races.

These facts are incorporated into the following just-so story. The order in which the proposed events occurred may well not be correct, but there is reasonable evidence that each of the major steps did take place.

THE LAST COMMON ANCESTOR
TO 2.5 MILLION YEARS AGO

We do not know what the last common ancestor looked like but it is a reasonable assumption that it was an ape which lived on the edge of the forest, that it was covered with fur, that it usually walked on all fours but occasionally stood upright like any primate, and also that it was able to use its hands to perform relatively simple manipulations. It was mainly vegetarian but not infrequently ate insects and grubs, and relatively rarely, like modern baboons and chimpanzees, caught weak or helpless animal prey and ate them. Its teeth had only a thin layer of enamel.

Somewhere around 5–6 million years ago a group of these apes settled near a river which entered a lake with marshy margins. As apes do, they began to experiment with the available food and soon recognized that it was rather abundant. There were many grubs and other invertebrates which could easily be caught. There were many birds' nests and reptile nests in the lake margins which could provide an abundance of eggs at certain times of the year. And there were small reptiles, such as turtles, and amphibians which could also be caught with relative ease. At certain times of the year some fish came into shallow water to spawn and provided another easily captured source of food.

At about this time, one of the group generated the first of three or four key mutations which I believe gave our ancestors the edge in survival. A mutation in one of the fatty acid binding proteins (FABP), or fatty acid transport proteins (FATP), or apoliopoproteins, or lipoprotein lipase, or acylation stimulating proteins (ASP) allowed fat to be taken up by tissues more efficiently. This certainly applied to the subcutaneous tissues and possibly also to the brain. During seasons of abundance, the descendants of this individual became fat with extensive sub-cutaneous deposits. During relatively brief periods of shortage, the descendants of this individual used their fat stores to survive.

The Rift Valley lake and river food chains are today, and prob-ably always have been, exceptionally rich in micro-nutrients, as has been pointed out by Leigh Broadhurst and her colleagues. The consequence of this is that micro-algae often grow in abundance in the lakes and watercourses. These algae even today provide the food for the spectacular flamingos of Lake Nakuru and some of the other Rift Valley lakes. The micro-algae are rich in minerals, vitamins and the key essential fatty acids (EFAs) such as AA, DHA and EPA which are so important in brain function. The micro-algae are at the bottom of the food chain. They are eaten by tiny fish, insects, larvae, molluscs and crustaceans, which in turn are eaten by larger creatures, so passing the micro-nutrients and EFAs up the food chain. At the top, bird, mammal and reptile predators benefit.

One important piece of evidence which suggests that our

Australopithecine ancestors ate EFA-rich aqueous foods is the change in their tooth enamel. The enamel coating of the teeth becomes much thicker than in most primates. To date there is no obvious explanation, although everyone suspects it must be something to do with diet. Surprisingly, tooth enamel contains EFAs, and its thickness, and its ability to resist dental caries, is dependent on a supply of the EFAs important in brain function. Animals deprived of these EFAs develop extensive tooth decay. Animals treated with EFAs, in contrast, are resistant to cavities. In the Island of Lewis, in the Outer Hebrides of Scotland, in the 1920s dental caries was relatively unusual even though sugar consumption was high. In the 1960s, with no major change in sugar consumption, cavities were rampant. Between the two dates there had, however, been a major change in diet. The inhabitants of the island had drastically reduced their consumption of herrings and other seafood which had been rich in the brain EFAs. An increase in EFA intake from a watery environment could thus explain why in the *Australopithecines* tooth enamel became suddenly thicker. The EFA intake could have come from grubs, insects, small creatures like turtles, and eggs, without any need for predation or scavenging of large animals.

A water-based food chain would also help to explain why our ancestors became increasingly bipedal and, by the time of Lucy and Laetoli, 3.6–3.2 million years ago, were completely bipedal. Bipedality confers advantages but it also has disadvantages. The most obvious advantages are that bipedalism frees the hands to manipulate and carry things, gives one a broader view of the world and, as Peter Wheeler has pointed out, in a hot environment presents a smaller surface area to the sun's rays. These advantages have usually been presented in the context of humans becoming adapted to the open savanna. Bipedalism has been thought to result from savanna-related selective pressure. It has also been suggested that loss of body hair and the development of sweating as the main cooling mechanism of the body, a major difference from other primates, is also a savanna adaptation.

There is one major flaw in this whole argument about the savanna. This is that we humans are totally profligate with water. Unlike all other animals which truly are adapted to dry savanna conditions, our kidneys are not very efficient. We can produce urine which is only modestly concentrated and in comparison to true savanna animals we must pour out large amounts of water to get rid of our waste solids. Moreover, while sweating from a naked body is certainly an efficient way of cooling off, it requires large amounts of drinkable water. Running or working in the equatorial sun requires as much as 2 litres per hour in sweat to achieve efficient cooling. We cannot have moved far away from generous water supplies because otherwise we would have died. Our thrifty fat genes enabled us to do without food for as much as a couple of months, but a day's exercising without water in a hot East African climate would have killed us. This physiological fact, coupled with the palaeontological fact that most fossils of our ancestors are found near ancient lake or river margins, clinches the story for me. We are a water-edge species, in plant terms a 'marginal'. We thrived on the marginal interface between water and land. We may well have made excursions into the hot, dry savanna, but they cannot have lasted for long.

Alister Hardy, an Oxford University Professor of Zoology, first proposed that humans had an aquatic phase in evolution. This idea was taken up, developed and vigorously promoted by Elaine Morgan, a feminist journalist. For various reasons, few of which have weight, this concept has been completely ignored by palaeontologists while they have steadily been accumulating solid evidence that our ancestors were at least 'marginal' apes, if not 'aquatic' apes. Part of the reason for rejection may also relate to the fact that both Hardy and Morgan emphasized the sea rather than fresh water as the probable environment in which we were aquatic. Another reason may be that they postulate a phase when our ancestors were almost wholly aquatic. But at least some of their arguments make considerable sense, especially when considered in the context of a 'marginal' as compared to a wholly aquatic existence.

For a marginal ape, bipedalism would have many obvious advantages. Anyone who has ever tried to gather plants, shellfish or anything else from a marsh or shallow water can instantly recognize what an advantage it is to be bipedal. One can go in much more deeply, and so cover much more food-bearing ground, if one can comfortably stand upright. With spare hands to collect items from the water or mud, one can gather food much more effectively. It is not difficult to see how large numbers of small mutations would lead to the natural selection of better and better upright walkers if the pre-human population were taking food from marginal environments.

A marginal phase could also have led to other changes characteristic of humans. Wet fur is a potential nuisance, and so progressive hairlessness would likely be favoured by selection, especially when combined with subcutaneous fat to provide insulation, which would be an alternative to fur. The fat would also give buoyancy and make it easier to swim. For a swimming primate, loss of fur, as with many aquatic mammals, would be an advantage. Swimming would further expand the area of food collection and would be a behaviour subject to powerful selection because there would be many opportunities for non-swimmers or weak swimmers to drown. Most important of all, swimming and searching for food under water would be facilitated by effective control of breathing. For the first time in the primate line, the development of breathing control might acquire a function other than the simple supply of air.

So, in this scenario, by about 3 million years ago our ancestors walked upright, had developed subcutaneous fat, had begun to lose their body hair, lived in a marginal aqueous environment with excursions out to the adjacent savanna, and had learned to exploit the enormously rich marginal landscape. They had begun a major shift from a vegetarian lifestyle, not because they killed or scavenged many large animals, but because they exploited the easy-to-obtain insects, grubs, turtles, bird and reptile eggs and other small creatures of marsh, riverside and lakeside.

3 TO 1.8 MILLION YEARS AGO

Somewhere in the period between 3 and 2.5 million years ago three things happened. Our predecessors' brains grew, we began to make tools and we began to hunt. As shown by the wonderful Ethiopian sites, where the bones smashed by stone tools were found, we still lived in waterside, marshy areas and we were keen to ensure we extracted fat from the bones of the animals we killed. We used our stone tools to smash open the marrow-containing bones.

I propose that all these things happened because some of us acquired the genetic change which in modern times predisposes to dyslexia. This is related to an as yet ill-defined abnormality in phospholipid metabolism which may stimulate the growth of certain synapses. Alex Richardson and others are currently building the evidence for this. The change allowed some people to see the shapes within stones, to understand the precise movements required to knap stones skilfully, and to use that information to make large amounts of stone tools. In order to make these tools, and in order to use them effectively, we had to develop more sophisticated control of our breathing. We had to hold our breath when making the crucial strokes, so reinforcing and expanding the breathing skills needed for putting our heads beneath the water in search of food.

I propose that the change in synaptic organization of neurons involved in dyslexia generated some growth in our brains but, much more importantly, allowed those brains to remember things and to organize large amounts of information, skills essential both for the hunt and for group organization. These are similar skills to those which help to make some dyslexic people brilliant financiers. And in order to allow the brain to grow to its optimal level, we needed fat. Marrow is one of the richest sources of fat and even today is eagerly sought by hunter-gatherers as the most prized part of any carcass. So we started breaking open bones to supplement the supply of EFAs from the aquatic environment.

Some of the personality characteristics associated with modern dyslexia had another effect. As Alex Richardson has found, schizo-typy and dyslexia are commonly associated. John Price has pointed out that schizotypy is a feature of human behaviour which is associated with group splitting. Dyslexic and schizotypal people can be highly curious. Some are unusually open to new experiences, hence their tendency to be interested in paranormal events and magical phenomena. Their idiosyncratic thinking can make them impatient with the social structures of the group in which they find themselves. They can become the focus of dissident factions who want to break away from existing organizations. As a result schizo-typal and/or dyslexic individuals can become the catalysts of group splitting. And one thing we can be sure about the various types of *Homo* 1.5 to 2 million years ago is that they split, split and split again, dispersing in small groups across the mass of connected continents. Schizotypy, coupled with our new abilities to make tools and exploit the environment, could have provided part of the basis for our extraordinary dispersal.

1.8 TO 0.6–0.4 MILLION YEARS AGO

During this long period, apart from our dispersal across the world, only one major cultural event seems to have happened. This was the development of the shaped, so-called Acheulian types of hand-axe and cleaver. This change in tool-making was not accompanied by any obvious development of skeletal anatomy. During this period we continued to live by rivers, lakes and the seashores, with the seashore routes and great rivers possibly providing the major channels for dispersal. Environmental pressures probably led to minor but progressive changes in our soft tissues, including better sweating, less hair and better control of breathing. We needed breathing control while throwing objects, making tools and putting our heads under water in the search for food. But these changes did not produce anything dramatic in terms of either our skeleton or our behaviour. Nevertheless, our search for aquatic-based foods, and our tool-making and tool-throwing, probably helped us to hone the complexity of our control of breathing.

0.6 TO 0.15 MILLION YEARS AGO

Important things happened in this period. Brain size grew rather rapidly. There begins to be evidence of larger groups of people, of the controlled use of fire, of the manufacture of wooden weapons, of the emergence of some geographical cultural diversity and possibly even of simple symbolic objects.

I propose that at this time there occurred a mutation similar to the ones generated in the Mensa mouse and the Dougie mouse. This change in phospholipid metabolism led to an enormous increase in synaptic complexity. Hence there was a large rise in brain size because of the increased complexity of the connections, but without any great increase in the numbers of nerve cells involved. This produced an abrupt improvement in cognitive function and memory. We could immediately understand and remember more, and this led to an increased efficiency in almost everything we did. In particular, an increased effectiveness of short-term memory began to make sophisticated communication more possible. In my view, not enough attention has been paid to William Calvin's idea that short-term memory is a key limiting factor in language development. If we cannot hold in memory a relatively long sequential string of codes, then language is effectively impossible. In almost all languages we need to remember the beginning of the sentence if we are correctly to interpret the end. It is also an enormous advantage to be able to remember the previous sentence and the one before that, if we are to understand and respond effectively.

Language involves both the receipt and the dispatch of information. Our breathing adaptations, resulting from our need to hold breath for throwing, tool-knapping and water immersion, had provided the necessary pre-adaptations to enable us to generate more complex streams of sounds. Our abrupt increase in cognitive ability gave us the necessary skill to interpret and respond to meaningful strings of sound. We began to communicate with each other in much more complex ways. And, as Geoffrey Miller has pointed out, such communication probably became a driving force for sexual selection, leading to some of our modern sexual features.

But we were still relatively dull and boring.

0.15 MILLION YEARS AGO TO THE PRESENT

The final major mutation which made us human took place perhaps between 150,000 and 130,000 years ago. This was, I think, the mutation which in one context, when combined with other biochemical characteristics, gives a cyclothymic personality, in another genetic context gives us bipolar disorder and in another gives us schizophrenia. The interactions between the 'bipolar' mutation and the 'schizotypy/dyslexia' mutation probably proved of particular significance. This mutation was, I believe, one of those related to the phospholipase A_2 cycle. It greatly amplified our neuronal responses and made our reactions much more variable and flexible.

What happened then has already been documented in this book. Some of us became schizophrenic, some bipolar and some psychopathic. In each case the pathological behaviour was relatively mild because the biochemical changes were compensated for and attenuated by our water-based diet, rich in the fatty acids needed by the brain. But the change was sufficient to unleash the extraordinary surge of creativity which characterized the past 100,000 years. Instead of being uniform, we became diverse; instead of being relatively stable, we created constant change; instead of being egalitarian, we began more and more to differentiate from the rest those with special skills in technology, art, religion and psychopathic leadership. We became human.

These trends became exaggerated and both more productive and more destructive when the agricultural revolution took us irrevocably away from our water-based hunter-gatherer food chain. And finally, the Industrial Revolution, with its dramatic increase in saturated-fat consumption and reduction in the range and amounts of essential fatty acids and other micro-nutrients found in fresh food, created our present frantic, enormously creative yet enormously destructive society, with its large numbers of people who have fallen over the edge into psychosis.

THE FUTURE

This is, of course, simply a just-so story, perhaps fed by my own personal delusions. But it is a story with at least some testable elements. We will know with certainty in the next twenty years, and perhaps much earlier than that, whether the key mutations that differentiate us from the great apes are in the genes coding for proteins which regulate fat metabolism, and particularly the phospholipid metabolism of the synapses of the brain. This is therefore a just-so story where the fantasy will be limited by hard evidence.

Of perhaps greater practical and humanitarian importance is the fantasy that in the past schizophrenia and bipolar disorder were illnesses where the balance between the good and the bad, the creativity and the destructiveness, was much more positive than it is now. This fantasy is based on the idea that some of the components of the water-based food chain were specifically beneficial to people with those disorders. This also is a testable proposition which will soon have firm answers. If the story continues to be as encouraging as it is now, we may be able to return to a situation where schizophrenia and bipolar disorder become controllable 'creative maladies' rather than the destructive forces they are at present.

EPILOGUE

SCHIZOPHRENIC PATIENTS AND THEIR FAMILIES EXHIBIT, WRIT
large, all the best and worst of the features which seem most
characteristic of us as human beings. Schizophrenia, because it
affects almost the whole span of life, and because it affects
the mind, the central component of our being as humans, causes
more distress than any other single condition. There is reasonable
evidence that the timing of the emergence of schizophrenia as
an illness was simultaneous with our emergence as a species.
Schizophrenia may indeed have been the cause of that speciation
event.

Schizophrenic patients have been ill served by the narrow ultra-
specializations of the second half of the twentieth century. Each has
seen the illness from its own very limited perspective. Those
inclined to psychological and psychoanalytical levels of explanation
have blamed dysfunctional families for the disease. Those interested
in a broader sociological picture have blamed society as a whole.
Those interested in drug action have blamed neurotransmitter
malfunction. Almost no one has taken any interest at all in the
whole-body manifestations of the illness, which careful clinicians
in the first half of the century had noted. Almost no one has

attempted to integrate what we know in a coherent and integrated fashion.

We seem to be approaching a situation where schizophrenia is a soluble problem, and one which may even be soluble without producing the appalling side-effects of so many of the drugs which have been used to treat the condition. The solutions are not coming from within any of the narrow specializations, but from attempts to integrate all aspects of the illness, from the broadest evolutionary interpretations down to the molecular biology of the neuron.

The solution of schizophrenia has implications for many other diseases and also for many malfunctions of society. In many of these conditions, as in schizophrenia, narrow specialization has failed to produce solutions. Our obsession with genomics and molecular biology may prove a partial blind alley, since a narrow reductionist approach will cause us to miss many clues which may help to provide answers. Only the open minded, who are willing to consider observations and explanations at many different levels, are likely to make much impact on the problems that face us. We have not solved schizophrenia yet, but the progress made can provide guidelines for all.

BIBLIOGRAPHY

This Bibliography provides references for most of the factual statements made in this book. It is divided into several major sections, each covering a different field. Web sites which discuss some of the recent work on nutrition and mental illness are available at: *www.mhnj.com* and *www.fincastle.com*. The Schizophrenia Association of Great Britain can be contacted at www.btinternet.com/~SAGB/.

HUMAN EVOLUTION, PALAEONTOLOGY AND ARCHAEOLOGY

Andrews, P., 'Evolution and environment in the Hominoidea'. *Nature* 1992; 360: 641–6.

Ardrey, R., *African Genesis*. Collins: London, 1961.

—, *The Territorial Imperative*. Dell Publishing: New York, 1966.

—, *The Social Contract*. Collins: London, 1970.

—, *The Hunting Hypothesis*. Collins: London, 1976.

Balter, M., Gibbons, A., 'Paleoanthropology. A glimpse of humans' first journey out of Africa'. *Science* 2000; 288: 948–50.

Behrensmeyer, A. K., 'Taphonomy and paleocology in the hominid fossil record'. *Yearbook Phys Anthropol* 1975; 16: 36–50.

Binford, L. R., *In Pursuit of the Past: Decoding the Archaeological Record*. Thames and Hudson: New York, 1983.

Blumenschine, R. J., 'Characteristics of an early homonid scavenging niche'. *Current Anthropol* 1987; 28: 383–406.

—, Masao, F. T., 'Living sites at Olduvai Gorge, Tanzania? Preliminary results in the basal Bed II lake margin zone'. *J Human Evolution* 1991; 21: 451–62.

Brauer, G., Singer, R., 'The Klasies zygomatic bone: archaic or modern?' *J Human Evolution* 1996; 30: 161–5.

Brooks, A. S., Helgren, D. M., Cramer, J. S., et al., 'Dating and context of three middle stone age sites with bone points in the Upper Semliki Valley, Zaire'. *Science* 1995; 268: 548–53.

Brown, F., Harris, J., Leakey, R., Walker, A., 'Early *Homo erectus* skeleton from west Lake Turkana, Kenya'. *Nature* 1985; 316: 788–92.

Brunet, M., Beauvilain, A., Coppens, Y., Heintz, E., Moutaye, A. H., Pilbeam, D., 'The first australopithecine 2,500 kilometres west of the Rift Valley (Chad)'. *Nature* 1995; 378: 273–5.

Churchill, S. E., Pearson, O. M., Grine, F. E., Trinkaus, E., Holliday, T. W., 'Morphological affinities of the proximal ulna from Klasies River main site: archaic or modern?' *J Human Evolution* 1996; 31: 213–37.

Clark, J. D., 'The middle stone age of E. Africa and the beginnings of regional identity'. *J World Prehistory* 1988; 2: 235–305.

Coffing, K., Feibel, C., Leakey, M., Walker, A., 'Four-million-year-old hominids from East Lake Turkana, Kenya'. *Am J Phys Anthropol* 1994; 93: 55–65.

Cole, S. M., *Leakey's Luck: The Life of Louis Seymour Bazett Leakey, 1903–1972*. Collins: London, 1975.

Coppens, Y., 'East side story: the origin of humankind'. *Sci Am* 1994; 270: 62–9.

Cutler, R. G., 'Evolution of human longevity: a critical overview'. *Mech Ageing Dev* 1979; 9: 337–54.

Dayton, L., 'Ageing fast'. *New Scientist* 1999; 29 May: 13.

de Heinzelin, J., Clark, J. D., White, T., et al., 'Environment and behavior of 2.5-million-year-old Bouri hominids'. *Science* 1999; 284: 625–9.

Deacon, H. J., 'Southern Africa and modern human origins'. *Philos Trans R Soc Lond B Biol Sci* 1992; 337: 177–83.

Delson, E., Tattersall, I., Van Couvering, J. A., Brooks, A., *Encyclopedia of Human Evolution and Prehistory*. 2nd edn. Garland: New York, 1999.

Eaton, S. B., Konner, M., Shostak, M., 'Stone agers in the fast lane: chronic degenerative diseases in evolutionary perspective'. *Am J Med* 1988; 84: 739–49.

Gabunia, L., Vekua, A., Lordkipanidze, D., et al., 'Earliest Pleistocene hominid cranial remains from Dmanisi, Republic of Georgia: taxonomy, geological setting, and age'. *Science* 2000; 288: 1019–25.

Gardner, H., *Intelligence Reframed: Multiple Intelligences for the 21st Century*. Basic Books: New York, 1999.

Gibbons, A., 'Chinese stone tools reveal high-tech *Homo erectus*'. *Science* 2000; 287: 1566.

Howell, F. C., 'Isimila: A paleolithic site in Africa'. *Sci Am* 1961; 205: 118–29.

Isaac, G. L., Isaac, B., *Olorgesailie Archaeological Studies of a Middle Pleistocene Lake Basin in Kenya*. University of Chicago Press: Chicago, 1977.

Johanson, D. C., Edey, M. A., *Lucy: The Beginnings of Humankind*. Simon and Schuster: New York, 1981.

Johanson, D. C., Edgar, B., *From Lucy to Language*. Simon and Schuster: New York, 1996.

Kingdon, J., *Self Made Man and His Undoing*. Simon and Schuster: London, 1993.

Kleindienst, M. R., Keller, C. M., 'Towards a functional analysis of handaxes and cleavers: the evidence from eastern Africa.' *Man* 1976; 11: 176–87.

Lahr, M. M., Foley, R. A., 'Towards a theory of modern human origins: geography, demography, and diversity in recent human evolution'. *Yearbook Phys Anthropol* 1998; 41: 137–76.

Larick, R., Ciochon, R. L., 'The African emergence and early Asian dispersals of the genus *Homo*'. *Sci Am* 1996; 84: 538–51.

Leakey, M., Walker, A., 'Early hominid fossils from Africa'. *Sci Am* 1997; 276: 74–9.

Leakey, M. G., Feibel, C. S., McDougall, I., Walker, A., 'New four-million-year-old hominid species from Kanapoi and Allia Bay, Kenya'. *Nature* 1995; 376: 565–71.

Leakey, M. D., Harris, J. M., *Laetoli: A Pliocene Site in Northern Tanzania*. Clarendon Press: Oxford, 1987.

Leakey, R. E., Roger, L., *Origins Reconsidered: In Search of What Makes Us Human*. Little, Brown: New York, 1992.

Lewin, R., *Bones of Contention: Controversies in the Search for Human Origins*. Simon and Schuster: New York, 1987.

Mellars, P., *The Neanderthal Legacy: An Archaeological Perspective from Western Europe*. Princeton University Press: Princeton, NJ, 1996.

Morrell, V., *Ancestral Passions. The Leakey Family and the Quest for Humankind's Beginnings*. Simon and Schuster: New York, 1995.

Morwood, M. J., 'Fission-track ages of stone tools and fossils on the east Indonesian island of Flores'. *Nature* 1998; 392: 173–6.

O'Brien, E. M., 'What was the Acheulean hand ax?' *Natural History* 1984; 93: 20–3.

Pfeiffer, S., Zehr, M. K., 'A morphological and histological study of the human humerus from Border Cave'. *J Human Evolution* 1996; 31: 49–59.

Phillipson, D. W., *African Archaeology*. 2nd edn. Cambridge University Press: Cambridge, 1993.

Pickford, M., Lewis, S. B., *Leakey. Beyond the Evidence*. Janus: London, 1997.

Pitts, M., Roberts, M., *Fairweather Eden: Life in Britain Half a Million Years Ago as Revealed by the Excavations at Boxgrove*. Century: London, 1997.

Rightmire, G. P., Deacon, H. J., 'Comparative studies of late Pleistocene human remains from Klaisies River Mouth, South Africa'. *J Human Evol* 1991; 20: 131–56.

Ruff, C. B., 'Climate and body shape in hominid evolution'. *J Human Evolution* 1991; 21: 81–105.

—, 'Morpholigical adaption to climate in modern and fossil hominids'. *Yearbook Phys Anthropol* 1994; 37: 65–107.

—, 'Biomechanics of the hip and birth in early *Homo*'. *Am J Phys Anthropol* 1995; 98: 527–74.

Schick, K. D., Toth, N., *Making Silent Stones Speak: Human Evolution and the Dawn of Technology*. Phoenix Press: London, 1995.

Shreeve, J., *The Neandertal Enigma*. William Morrow: New York, 1995.

Steele, J., 'Stone legacy of skilled hands'. *Nature* 1999; 399: 24–5.

Stringer, C., 'Palaeoanthropology – coasting out of Africa'. *Nature* 2000; 405: 24–7.

—, McKie, R., *African Exodus: The Origins of Modern Humanity*. Random House: London, 1996.

Stringer, C. B., 'The evolution of regionality in humans'. *Proc Intl Congress Systematic Evolutionary Biol* 1990; 1: 466–70.

Tattersall, I., *The Human Odyssey: Four Million Years of Human Evolution.* Prentice-Hall: New York, 1993.

—, *The Fossil Trail: How We Know What We Think We Know About Human Evolution.* Oxford University Press: Oxford, 1995.

—, Schwartz, J. H., *Extinct Humans.* Westview Press: Boulder, Col., 2000.

Tudge, C., *The Day Before Yesterday: Five Million Years of Human History.* Jonathan Cape: London, 1995.

Walker, A., Leakey, R. E., 'The hominids of East Turkana'. *Sci Am* 1978; 239: 44–61.

—, —, *The Nariokotome Homo Erectus Skeleton.* Harvard University Press: Cambridge, Mass, 1993.

Walker, A., Shipman, P., *The Wisdom of Bones: In Search of Human Origins.* Weidenfeld and Nicolson: London, 1996.

White, T. D., Suwa, G., Asfaw, B., '*Australopithecus ramidus*, a new species of early hominid from Aramis, Ethiopia'. *Nature* 1994; 371: 306–12.

Wood, B., 'Early-hominid species and speciation'. *J Human Evolution* 1992; 22: 351–65.

—, Collard, M., 'Anthropology – the human genus'. *Science* 1999; 284: 65–71.

Yamei, H., Potts, R., Baoyin, Y., *et al.*, 'Mid-Pleistocene Acheulean-like stone technology of the Bose basin, south China'. *Science* 2000; 287: 1622–6.

EVOLUTIONARY MECHANISMS AND DNA ANALYSIS

Bohossian, H. B., Skaletsky, H., Page, D. C., 'Unexpectedly similar rates of nucleotide substitution found in male and female hominids'. *Nature* 2000; 406: 622–5.

Bowles, J. T., 'Sex, kings and serial killers and other group-selected human traits'. *Med Hypotheses* 2000; 54: 864–95.

Brookfield, J. F. Y., 'Human evolution: how recent were the Y chromosome ancestors?' *Curr Biol* 2000; 10: R722–R723.

Brown, M. H., *The Search for Eve.* Harper and Row: New York, 1990.

Cavalli-Sforza, L. L., *Genes, Peoples and Languages.* Allen Lane: New York, 2000.

—, Cavalli-Sforza, F., Thorne, S., *The Great Human Diasporas: The History of Diversity and Evolution.* Addison-Wesley: Reading, Mass, 1995.

Clark, G. A., 'Modern human origins – highly visible, curiously intangible'. *Science* 1999; 283: 2029ff.

Destro-Bisol, G., Boschi, I., Caglia, A., *et al.*, 'Microsatellite variation in Central Africa: an analysis of intrapopulational and interpopulational genetic diversity'. *Am J Phys Anthropol* 2000; 112: 319–37.

Dicks, L., 'All for one'. *New Scientist* 2000; 8 July: 31–5.

Disotell, T. R., 'Human evolution: origins of modern humans still look recent'. *Curr Biol* 1999; 9: R647–R650.

—, 'Human evolution: the southern route to Asia'. *Curr Biol* 1999; 9: R925–R928.

Gagneux, P., Wills, C., Gerloff, U., *et al.*, 'Mitochondrial sequences show diverse evolutionary histories of African hominoids'. *Proc Natl Acad Sci USA* 1999; 96: 5077–82.

Gibbons, A., 'Which of our genes make us human?' *Science* 1998; 281: 1432–4.

Goldstein, D. B., Ruiz Linares, A., Cavalli-Sforza, L. L., Feldman, M. W., 'Genetic absolute dating based on microsatellites and the origin of modern humans'. *Proc Natl Acad Sci USA* 1995; 92: 6723–7.

Holden, C., 'Random samples: southern African "Eve" '. *Science* 1999; 286: 229.

Hopkin, K., 'The greatest apes'. *New Scientist* 1999; 15 May: 26–30.

Horai, S., Hayasaka, K., Kondo, R., Tsugane, K., Takahata, N., 'Recent African origin of modern humans revealed by complete sequences of hominoid mitochondrial DNAs'. *Proc Natl Acad Sci USA* 1995; 92: 532–6.

Hoss, M., 'Ancient DNA – Neanderthal population genetics'. *Nature* 2000; 404: 453–4.

Jorde, L. B., Watkins, W. S., Bamshad, M. J., *et al.*, 'The distribution of human genetic diversity: a comparison of mitochondrial, autosomal, and Y-chromosome data'. *Am J Hum Genet* 2000; 66: 979–88.

Krings, M., Stone, A., Paabo, S., 'Neandertal DNA sequences and the origin of modern humans'. *Cell* 1997; 90: 19–30.

Labuda, D., Zietkiewicz, E., Yotova, V., 'Archaic lineages in the history of modern humans'. *Genetics* 2000; 156: 799–808.

Mace, R., 'Human behaviour – fair game'. *Nature* 2000; 406: 248–9.

McKee, J. K., *The Riddled Chain: Chance, Coincidence and Chaos in Human Evolution*. Rutgers University Press: New Brunswick, NJ, 2000.

Norris, S., 'Family Secrets'. *New Scientist* 1999; 19 June: 42–6.

Ovchinnikov, I. V., Gotherstrom, A., Romanova, G. P., Kharitonov, V. M., Liden, K., Goodwin, W., 'Molecular analysis of Neanderthal DNA from the northern Caucasus'. *Nature* 2000; 404: 490–3.

Paabo, S., 'Human evolution'. *Trends Biochem Sci* 1999; 24: M13–M16.

Smith, J. M., Szathmary, E., *The Origins of Life: From the Birth of Life to the Origin of Language*. Oxford University Press: Oxford, 1999.

Strachan, T., Read, A. P., *Human Molecular Genetics*. Bios: Oxford, 1996.

Thomson, R., Pritchard, J. K., Shen, P. D., Oefner, P. J., Feldman, M. W., 'Recent common ancestry of human Y chromosomes: evidence from DNA sequence data'. *Proc Natl Acad Sci USA* 2000; 97: 7360–5.

Vigilant, L., Stoneking, M., Harpending, H., Hawkes, K., Wilson, A. C., 'African populations and the evolution of human mitochondrial DNA'. *Science* 1991; 253: 1503–7.

Wallace, D. C., Brown, M. D., Lott, M. T., 'Mitochondrial DNA variation in human evolution and disease'. *Gene* 1999; 238: 211–30.

Wiegand, P., Meyer, E., Brinkmann, B., 'Microsatellite structures in the context of human evolution'. *Electrophoresis* 2000; 21: 889–95.

Zhao, Z. M., Jin, L., Fu, Y. X., *et al.*, 'Worldwide DNA sequence variation in a 10-kilobase noncoding region on human chromosome 22'. *Proc Natl Acad Sci USA* 2000; 97: 11354–8.

EVOLUTION OF BRAIN AND MIND

Alvarez-Maubecin, V., Garcia-Hernandez, F., Williams, J. T., Van Bocksaele, E. J., 'Functional coupling between neurons and glia'. *J Neurosci* 2000; 20: 4091–8.

Corballis, M. C., Lea, S. E. G. (eds), *The Descent of Mind: Psychological Perspectives on Hominid Evolution*. Oxford University Press: Oxford, 1999.

Falk, D., 'Hominid brain evolution: looks can be deceiving'. *Science* 1998; 280: 1714–31.

Foley, R. A., Lee, P. C., 'Ecology and energetics of encephalization in hominid evolution'. *Philos Trans R Soc Lond B Biol Sci* 1991; 334: 223–32.

Garey, L. J., Ong, W. Y., Patel, T. S., *et al.*, 'Reduced dendritic spine density on cerebral cortical pyramidal neurons in schizophrenia'. *J Neurol Neurosurg Psychiatry* 1998; 65: 446–53.

Glynn, I., *An Anatomy of Thought: The Origin and Machinery of the Mind.* Weidenfeld and Nicolson: London, 1999.

Holloway, R. L., 'The evolution of the primate brain: some aspects of quantitative relations'. *Brain Res* 1968; 7: 121–72.

Kaufmann, W. E., Yamagata, K., Andreasson, K. I., Worley, P. F., 'Rapid response genes as markers of cellular signaling during cortical histogenesis: their potential in understanding mental retardation'. *Int J Dev Neurosci* 1994; 12: 263–71.

Lebeer, J., 'How much brain does a mind need? Scientific, clinical, and educational implications of ecological plasticity'. *Dev Med Child Neurol* 1998; 40: 352–7.

Leigh, S. R., 'Cranial capacity evolution in *Homo erectus* and early *Homo sapiens*'. *American J Phys Anthropology* 1992; 87: 1–13.

Mayatepek, E., Zelezny, R., Lehmann, W. D., Hammond, J. W., Hoffmann, G. F., 'Defects in the synthesis of cysteinyl leukotrienes: a new group of inborn errors of metabolism'. *J Inherit Metab Dis* 2000; 23: 404–8.

McHenry, H. M., 'Behavioral ecological implications of early hominid body size'. *J Human Evolution* 1994; 27: 77–87.

Nimchinsky, E. A., Gilissen, E., Allman, J. M., Perl, D. P., Erwin, J. M., Hof, P. R., 'A neuronal morphologic type unique to humans and great apes'. *Proc Natl Acad Sci USA* 1999; 96: 5268–73.

Previc, F. H., 'Dopamine and the origins of human intelligence'. *Brain Cogn* 1999; 41: 299–350.

Shariff, G. A., 'Cell counts in the primate cerebral cortex'. *J Comparative Neurology* 1953; 98: 381–400.

Tomasello, M., *The Cultural Origins of Human Cognition.* Harvard University Press: Cambridge, Mass., 2000.

Vesce, S., Bezzi, P., Volterra, A., 'The active role of astrocytes in synaptic transmission'. *Cell Mol Life Sci* 1999; 56: 991–1000.

THE DOUGIE MOUSE AND THE MENSA MOUSE

Benowitz, L. I., Routtenberg, A., 'GAP-43: an intrinsic determinant of neuronal development and plasticity'. *Trends Neurosci* 1997; 20: 84–91.

Bliss, T. V. P., 'Neurobiology – young receptors make smart mice'. *Nature* 1999; 401: 25–7.

Routtenberg, A., Cantallops, I., Zaffuto, S., Serrano, P., Namgung, U., 'Enhanced learning after genetic overexpression of a brain growth protein'. *Proc Natl Acad Sci USA* 2000; 97: 7657–62.

Tang, Y. P., Shimizu, E., Dube, G. R., *et al.*, 'Genetic enhancement of learning and memory in mice'. *Nature* 1999; 401: 63–9.

EVOLUTION OF BEHAVIOUR

Allman, J. M., 'Evolving brains'. Scientific American: New York, 1999.

Barkow, J. H., Cosmides, L., Tooby, J. (eds), *The Adapted Mind: Evolutionary Psychology and the Generation of Culture*. Oxford University Press: Oxford, 1995.

Brookes, M., 'Apocalypse then'. *New Scientist* 1999; 14 August: 32–5.

Byrne, R., *The Thinking Ape*. Oxford University Press: Oxford, 1995.

Cartmill, M., *A View to a Death in the Morning: Hunting and Nature through History*. Harvard University Press: Cambridge, Mass, 1993.

Changeux, J.-P., Chavaillon, J., *Origins of the Human Brain*. Clarendon Press: Oxford, 1996.

Clark, G., *The Identity of Man as Seen by an Archaeologist*. Methuen: London, New York, 1983.

Corballis, M. C., *The Lopsided Ape: Evolution of the Generative Mind*. Oxford University Press: Oxford, 1991.

Cummins, D. D., Allen, C. (eds), *The Evolution of Mind*. Oxford University Press: Oxford, 1998.

Diamond, J. M., *Guns, Germs, and Steel: The Fates of Human Societies*. W. W. Norton: New York, 1997.

Fisher, H. E., *The Sex Contract: The Evolution of Human Behavior*. Quill: New York, 1982.

Fodor, J., *The Modularity of Mind*. MIT Press: Cambridge, Mass., 1985.

Foley, R., *Humans before Humanity*. Blackwell: Oxford, 1995.

Foley, R. A., 'Ecological and social variance and the evolution of increased neocortical size'. *Behav Brain Sci* 1993; 16: 702.

—, 'An evolutionary and chronological framework for human social behaviour'. *Proc British Acad* 1996; 88: 95–118.

—, 'Multiple dispersals and the environment in hominid evolution'. *Hum Evol* 1997; 12: 9–15.

—, 'Hominid behavioural evolution: missing links in comparative primate socioecology'. *Camb Stud Biol Anthropol* 1999; 22: 363–86.

— (ed), *The Origins of Human Behaviour*. Unwin Hyman: London, 1991.

—, Lahr, M. M., 'Mode 3 technologies and the evolution of modern humans'. *Camb Archaeol J* 1997; 7: 3–32.

—, Lee, P. C., 'Finite social space, evolutionary pathways and reconstructing hominid behaviour'. *Science* 1989; 243: 901–6.

Gamble, C., *Timewalkers: The Prehistory of Global Colonization*. Harvard University Press: Cambridge, Mass., 1993.

Humphrey, N., *A History of the Mind*. Vintage: London, 1993.

Ingersoll, D., Yellen, J. E., Macdonald, W. L. (eds), *Experimental Archaeology*. Columbia University Press: New York, 1977.

Jaynes, J., *The Origin of Consciousness in the Breakdown of the Bicameral Mind*. Houghton Mifflin: Boston, Mass., 1976.

Jochim, M. A., *Strategies for Survival: Cultural Behavior in an Ecological Context*. Academic Press: New York, 1981.

Jolly, A., 'Lemur social behavior and primate intelligence'. *Science* 1966; 153: 501–6.

—, *Lucy's Legacy: Sex and Intelligence in Human Evolution*. Harvard University Press: Cambridge, Mass., 1999.

Knight, C., *Blood Relations: Menstruation and the Origins of Culture*. Yale University Press: New Haven, Conn., 1995.

Kohn, M., *As We Know It: Coming to Terms with an Evolving Mind*. Granta Books: London, 1999.

LeDoux, J., *The Emotional Brain: The Mysterious Underpinnings of Emotional Life*. Simon and Schuster: New York, 1996.

Lumsden, C., Wilson, E. O., *Promethean Fire: Reflections on the Origin of the Mind*. Harvard University Press: Cambridge, Mass., 1999.

McCrone, J., 'Fired up'. *New Scientist* 2000; 20 May: 30–4.

Mellars, P., Gibson, K. (eds), *Modelling the Early Human Mind*. MacDonald Institute for Archaeological Research: Cambridge, 1996.

Miller, G., *The Mating Mind: How Sexual Choice Shaped the Evolution of Human Nature*. Heinemann: London, 2000.

Mithen, S., *The Prehistory of the Mind: A Search for the Origins of Art, Religion and Science*. Thames and Hudson: London, 1996.

O'Hear, A., *Beyond Evolution: Human Nature and the Limits of Evolutionary Explanation*. Clarendon Press: Oxford, 1998.

Pawlowski, B., Dunbar, R. I. M., 'Withholding age as putative deception in mate search tactics'. *Evol Hum Behav* 2000; 20: 53–69.

Plotkin, H., *Evolution in Mind*. Allen Lane: London, 1997.

Redman, C. L., *Human Impact on Ancient Environments*. University of Arizona Press: Tucson, 1999.

Ridley, M., *The Origins of Virtue*. Viking Press: London, 1996.

Rose, H., Rose, S. (eds), *Alas, Poor Darwin*. Jonathan Cape: London, 2000.

Ruse, M., *Mystery of Mysteries – Is Evolution a Social Construction?* Havard University Press: Cambridge, Mass., 1999.

Segal, N. L., Hershberger, S. L., 'Cooperation and competition between twins: findings from a prisoner's dilemma game'. *Evol Hum Behav* 2000; 20: 29–51.

Shackelford, T. K., Larsen, R. J., 'Facial attractiveness and physical health'. *Evol Hum Behav* 2000; 20: 71–6.

Storr, A., *Music and the Mind*. HarperCollins: London, 1992.

Tanner, N. M., *On Becoming Human*. Cambridge University Press: Cambridge, 1981.

Trefil, J., *Are We Unique?* Wiley: New York, 1997.

Waal, F. D., *Good Natured. The Origins of Right and Wrong in Humans and Other Animals*. Harvard University Press: Cambridge, Mass., 1996.

Zahavi, A., Zahavi, A., *The Handicap Principle*. Oxford University Press: New York, 1999.

THE CREATIVE EXPLOSION

Appenzeller, T., Clery, D., Culotta, E., 'Archaeology: transitions in prehistory'. *Science* 1998; 282: 1441–58.

Balter, M., 'New light on the oldest art'. *Science* 1999; 283: 920–2.

Dunbar, R., Knight, C., Power, C. (eds), *The Evolution of Culture*. Edinburgh University Press: Edinburgh, 1999.

Hayden, B., 'The cultural capacities of the Neanderthals'. *J Human Evolution* 1993; 24: 113–46.

Humphrey, N., 'Cave art, autism, and the evolution of the human mind'. *Camb Archaeol J* 1998; 8: 165–91.

Knight, C., Power, C., Watts, I., 'The human symbolic revolution: a Darwinian account'. *Camb Archaeol J* 1995; 5: 75–114.

Lock, A., Peters, C. R., *Handbook of Human Symbolic Evolution*. Clarendon Press: Oxford, 1996.

Marshack, A., 'Evolution of the human capacity: the symbolic evidence'. *Yearbook Phys Anthropol* 1989; 21: 1–334.

Mellars, P., Stringer, C., *The Human Revolution: Behavioural and Biological Perspectives on the Origins of Modern Humans*. Princeton University Press: Princeton, NJ, 1989.

Pfeiffer, J. E., *The Creative Explosion: An Inquiry into the Origins of Art and Religion*. Harper and Row: London, 1982.

Randall, P. L., 'Schizophrenia as a consequence of brain evolution'. *Schizophr Res* 1998; 30: 143–8.

Saura Ramos, P. A., Mzquiz Prez-Seoane, M., Beltr n Martnez, A., *The Cave of Altamira*. Harry Abrams: New York, 1999.

Tattersall, I., *Becoming Human: Evolution and Human Uniqueness*. Harcourt Brace: New York, 1997.

—, *The Origin of the Human Capacity*. American Museum of Natural History: New York, 1998.

Tomasello, M., *The Cultural Origins of Human Cognition*. Harvard University Press: Cambridge, Mass., 2000.

Turk, I., Dirjec, J., Kavur, B., 'The oldest musical instrument in Europe discovered in Slovenia?' Zrc Sazu: Ljubljana, 1996; 1–3.

Wallin, N. L., *Biomusicology: Neurophysiological, Neuropsychological and Evolutionary Perspectives on the Origins and Purposes of Music*. Pendragon Press: Stuyvesant, NY, 1991.

NUTRITION DURING THE COURSE OF EVOLUTION

Ackman, R. G., Hooper, S. N., Frair, W., 'Comparison of the the fatty acid compositions of depot fats from fresh-water and marine turtles'. *Comp Biochem Physiol* [B] 1971; 40: 931–44.

Aiello, L. C., Wheeler, P., 'The expensive tissue hypothesis: the brain and digestive system in human and primate evolution'. *Curr Anthropol* 1995; 36: 199–221.

Atkinson, T. G., Barker, H. J., Meckling-Gill, K. A., 'Incorporation of long-chain n-3 fatty acids in tissues and enhanced bone marrow cellularity with docosahexaenoic acid feeding in post-weanling Fischer 344 rats'. *Lipids* 1997; 32: 293–302.

Basalingappa, S., Kudari, S. M., Badami, R. C., Gandhi, M. R., Tharabai, P., 'Fatty acid compostion of body fat from the queens of the termite *Odontotermes (Assmuthi) Obesus* (Termitidae: Isoptfra)'. *Indian J Comp Anim Physiol* 1985; 3: 12–16.

Blumenschine, R. J., Cavallo, J. A., 'Scavenging and human evolution'. *Sci Am* 1992; 267: 90–6.

Bortz, W. M., 'Physical exercise as an evolutionary force'. *J Human Evolution* 1985; 14: 145–55.

Brian, B. L., Gaffney, F. C., Fitzpatrick, L. C., Scholes, V. E., 'Fatty acid distribution of lipids from carcass, liver and fat bodies of the lizard, *Cnemidophorus tigris*, prior to hibernation'. *Comp Biochem Physiol* [B] 1972; 41: 661–4.

Brink, J., Deacon, H. J., 'A study of a last interglacial shell midden and bone accumulation at Herolds Bay, Cape Province, S. Africa'. *Paleoecol Africa* 1982; 15: 31–9.

Broadhurst, C. L., Cunnane, S. C., Crawford, M. A., 'Rift valley lake fish and shellfish provided brain specific nutrition for early *Homo*'. *Br J Nutr* 1997; 79: 3–21.

Bunn, H. T., Bartram, L. E., Kroll, E. M., 'Variability in bone assemblage formation from Hadza hunting, scavenging and carcass processing'. *J Anthropol Arch* 1988; 7: 412–57.

Bunn, H. T., Ezzo, J. A., 'Hunting and scavenging by plio-pleistocene hominids: nutritional constraints, archaeological patterns and behavioral implications'. *Archaeol Sci* 1993; 20: 365–98.

Burley, R. W., Back, J. F., Wellington, J. E., Grigg, G. C., 'Proteins and lipoproteins in yolk from eggs of the estuarine crocodile (*Crocodylus porosus*): a comparison with egg yolk of the hen (*Gallus domesticus*)'. *Comp Biochem Physiol* [B] 1988; 91: 39–44.

Carrier, D. R., 'The energetic paradox of human running and hominid evolution'. *Curr Anthropol* 1984; 25: 483–95.

Carter, F. L., Dinus, L. A., Smythe, R. V., 'Fatty acids of the eastern subterranean termite *Reticulitermes P Flavipes Isopters Rhinotermitidae*'. *Ann Entomol Soc Am* 1972; 65: 655–8.

Chamberlain, J. G., 'The possible role of long-chain, omega-3 fatty acids in human brain phylogeny'. *Perspect Biol Med* 1996; 39: 436–45.

Cordain, L., Miller, J. B., Eaton, S. B., Mann, N., Holt, S. H. A., Speth, J. D., 'Plant–animal subsistence ratios and macronutrient energy estimations in worldwide hunter-gatherer diets'. *Am J Clin Nutr* 2000; 71: 682–92.

Crawford, M. A., Bloom, M., Broadhurst, C. L., *et al.*, 'Evidence for the unique function of docosahexaenoic acid during the evolution of the modern hominid brain'. *Lipids* 1999; 34 Suppl: S39–47.

Cuthbertson, W. F. J., 'Evolution of infant nutrition'. *Br J Nutr* 1999; 81: 359–71.

Das, S. K., Scott, M. T., Adhikary, P. K., 'Effect of the nature and amount of dietary energy on lipid composition of rat bone marrow'. *Lipids* 1975; 10: 584–90.

Dunstan, G. A., Sincair, A. J., O'Dea, K., Naughton, J. M., 'The lipid content and fatty acid composition of various marine species from southern Australian coastal waters'. *Comp Biochem Physiol* [B] 1988; 91: 165–9.

Gibbons, A., 'Solving the brain's energy crisis'. *Science* 1998; 280: 1345–7.

Goodall, J., *Through a Window: My Thirty Years with the Chimpanzees of Gombe*. Houghton Mifflin: Boston, Mass., 1990.

Gordon, K. D., 'Evolutionary perspectives on human diet'. In *Nutritional Anthropology*, Johnston, F. E. (ed), A.R. Liss: New York 1987; 3–39.

Guitart, R., Martinez Silvestre, A., Guerrero, X., Mateo, R., 'Comparative study on the fatty acid composition of two marine vertebrates: striped dolphins and loggerhead turtles'. *Comp Biochem Physiol* [B] 1999; 124: 439–43.

Harris, M., Ross, E. B. (eds), *Food and Evolution: Towards a Theory of Human Food Habits*. Temple University Press: Philadelphia, 1987.

Jenkins, N. K., 'Chemical compositions of the eggs of the crocodile (*Crocodylus novaeguineae*)'. *Comp Biochem Physiol* [A] 1975; 51: 891–5.

Klein, R. G., Cruz-Uribe, K., 'Exploitation of large bovids and seals at middle and late stone age sites in South Africa'. *J Human Evolution* 1996; 31: 315–34.

Kozlova, T. A., Khotimchenko, S. V., 'Lipids and fatty acids of two pelagic cottoid fishes (*Comephorus spp.*) endemic to Lake Baikal'. *Comp Biochem Physiol* 2000; 126: 477–85.

Larsen, C. S., *Skeletons in Our Closet: Revealing the Past Through BioArchaeology*. Princeton University Press: Princeton, NJ, 2000.

Lawick-Goodall, J. V., Jones, L., *In the Shadow of Man*. Collins: London, 1978.

Lee, R. B., 'Mongongo: the ethnography of a major wild food resource'. *Ecol Food Nutr* 1973; 2: 307–21.

—, 'Subsistence: foraging for a living'. In *The Dobe Ju/'Hoansi*, Lee, R. B., Harcourt Brace College Publishers: Fort Worth 1993; 39–60.

—, *The !Kung San Men, Women, and Work in a Foraging Society*. Cambridge University Press: Cambridge 1979.

Lee, Y. Y., Ha, J. K., Ahn, B. H., Kang, D. H., Ki, W. K., Kim, J. K., 'Lipids and fatty acids composition of Korean native goat's bone marrow'. *J Korean Agric Chem Soc* 1988; 31: 177–81.

Leonard, W. R., Robertson, M. L., 'Comparative primate energetics and hominid evolution'. *Am J Phys Anthropol* 1997; 102: 265–81.

Lev-Yadun, S., Gopher, A., Abbo, S., 'Archaeology – the cradle of agriculture'. *Science* 2000; 288: 1602–1603.

Lu, Y., Wang, D., Han, D., Zhang, Z., Zhang, C., '[Analysis of the patterns and contents of amino acids and fatty acids from *Macrotermes annandalei (Silvestri)* and *Macrotermes barneyi Light*.]'. *Acta Nutrimenta Sinica* 1992; 14: 103–6.

Mann, A. E., 'Diet and Human Evolution'. In *Omnivorous Primates: Gathering and Hunting in Human Evolution*. Harding, R. S. O., Teleki, G. (eds), Columbia University Press: New York, 1981; 10–36.

Mann, F. D., 'Animal fat and cholesterol may have helped primitive man evolve a large brain'. *Perspect Biol Med* 1998; 41: 417–25.

Marshall, L., *The !Kung of Nyae Nyae*. Harvard University Press: Cambridge, Mass., 1976.

Meng, M. S., West, G. C., Irving, L., 'Fatty acid composition of caribou bone marrow'. *Comp Biochem Physiol* 1969; 30: 187–91.

Miller, G. J., Frey, M. R., Kunsman, J. E., Field, R. A., 'Bovine bone marrow lipids'. *J Food Sci* 1982; 47: 657–60.

Milton, K., 'Distribution patterns of tropical plant food as an evolutionary stimulus to primate mental development'. *American Anthropologist* 1981; 83: 534–48.

—, 'Nutritional characteristics of wild primate foods: do the diets of our closest living relatives have lessons for us?' *Nutrition* 1999; 15: 488–98.

—, 'Hunter-gatherer diets – a different perspective'. *Am J Clin Nutr* 2000; 71: 665–7.

Naughton, J. M., O'Dea, K., Sinclair, A. J., 'Animal foods in traditional Australian Aboriginal diets: polyunsaturated and low in fat'. *Lipids* 1986; 21: 684–90.

Noble, R. C., Deeming, D. C., Ferguson, M. W. J., McCartney, R., 'Changes in the lipid and fatty acid composition of the yolk during embryonic development of the alligator (*Alligator mississippiensis*)'. *Comp Biochem Physiol* [B] 1990; 96: 183–7.

Noble, R. C., McCartney, R., Ferguson, M. W. J., 'Lipid and fatty acid compositional differences between eggs of wild and captive-breeding alligators (*Alligator mississippiensis*): an association with reduced hatchability?' *J Zool* 1993; 230: 639–49.

Onigbinde, A. O., Adamolekun, B., 'The nutrient value of *Imbrasia belina Lepidoptera: Saturnidae (madora)*'. *Cent Afr J Med* 1998; 44: 125–7.

Oyarzun, S. E., Crawshaw, G. J., Valdes, E. V., 'Nutrition of the Tamandua: 1. Nutrient composition of termites (*Nasutitermes spp*) and stomach contents from wild Tamanduas (*Tamandua tetradactyla*)'. *Zoo Biology* 1996; 15: 509–24.

Pauletto, P., Puato, M., Caroli, M. G., et al., 'Blood pressure and atherogenic lipoprotein profiles of fish-diet and vegetarian villagers in Tanzania: the Lugalawa study'. *Lancet* 1996; 348: 784–8.

Pauling, L., 'Orthomolecular psychiatry: varying the concentrations of substances normally present in the human body may control mental disease'. *Science* 1968; 160: 265–71.

Randall, P. L., 'Schizophrenia as a consequence of brain evolution'. *Schizophr Res* 1998; 30: 143–8.

Richards, M. P., Pettitt, P. B., Trinkaus, E., Smith, F. H., Paunovic, M., Karavanic, I., 'Neanderthal diet at Vindija and Neanderthal predation: the evidence from stable isotopes'. *Proc Natl Acad Sci USA* 2000; 97: 7663–6.

Roberts, C., Manchester, K., *The Archaeology of Disease*. 2nd edn. Alan Sutton: Stroud, 1995.

Rowe, J. W., Holy, L., Ballinger, R. E., Stanley-Samuelson, D., 'Lipid provisioning of turtle eggs and hatchlings: total lipid, phospholipid, triacylglycerol and triacylglycerol fatty acids'. *Comp Biochem Physiol* [B] 1995; 112: 323–30.

Silberbauer, G. B., *Hunter and Habitat in the Central Kalahari Desert*. Cambridge University Press: Cambridge, 1981.

Skinner, M., 'Bee brood consumption: an alternative explanation for hypervitaminosis A in KNM-ER 1808 (*Homo Erectus*) from Koobi Fora, Kenya'. *J Human Evolution* 1991; 20: 493–503.

Speth, J. D., 'Seasonality, resource stress and food sharing in so-called "Egalitarian" foraging societies'. *J Anthropol Archaeol* 1990; 9: 148–88.

—, 'Early hominid hunting and scavenging: the role of meat as an energy source'. *J Human Evolution* 1994; 18: 329–43.

Sponheimer, M., Lee-Thorp, J. A., 'Isotopic evidence for the diet of an early hominid, *Australopithecus africanus*'. *Science* 1999; 283: 368–70.

Stanford, C., *The Hunting Apes*. Princeton University Press: Princeton, NJ, 1999.

Stanford, C. B., 'The influence of chimpanzee predation on group size and anti-predator behaviour in red colobus monkeys'. *Anim Behav* 1995; 49: 577–87.

—, Wallis, J., Mpongo, E., Goodall, J., 'Hunting decisions in wild chimpanzees'. *Behaviour* 1994; 131: 1–20.

Stewart, K. M., 'Early hominid utilisation of fish resources and implications for seasonality and behaviour'. *J Human Evolution* 1994; 27: 229–45.

Strum, S. C., 'Processes and products of change: baboon predatory behavior at Gilgil, Kenya'. In *Omnivorous Primates: Gathering and Hunting in Human Evolution*, Harding, R. S. O., Teleki, G. (eds), Columbia University Press: New York, 1981; 10–36.

—, 'Baboon cues for eating meat'. *J Human Evolution* 1983; 12: 327–36.

Sumida, T., 'Clinical and experimental study on fatty acid composition of bone marrow lipid in hematologic disorders'. *Acta Med Nagasaki* 1965; 9: 222–41.

Tavassoli, M., Houchin, D. N., Jacobs, P., 'Fatty acid composition of adipose cells in red and yellow marrow: a possible determinant of haematopoietic potential'. *Scand J Haematol* 1977; 18: 47–53.

Vogel, G., 'Did early African hominids eat meat?' *Science* 1999; 283: 303.

Walker, A., Zimmerman, M. R., Leakey, R. E., 'A possible case of hyper-vitaminosis A in *Homo erectus*'. *Nature* 1982; 296: 248–50.

West, G. C., Shaw, D. L., 'Fatty acid composition of Dall sheep bone marrow'. *Comp Biochem Physiol* [B] 1975; 50: 599–601.

Zaheer, K., 'Fatty acid composition of total lipids and effects of some insecticides upon them in termite *Odontotermes obesus* (Rambur)'. *Biologia* 1986; 32: 29–38.

—, 'Fatty acid analysis of total lipids in the soldier caste of termite, *Odontotermes obesus* (Rambur)'. *Pakistan J Zoology* 1994; 26: 86–9.

—, Iqbal, Q. J., Athar, F., Iqbal, H., 'Fatty acid composition of phospholipids and effect of insecticides on them in the termite *Odontotermes obesus* (Rambur)'. *Pakistan J Zoology* 1985; 17: 349–56.

Zomborszky, Z., Husveth, F., 'Liver total lipids and fatty acid composition of shot red and fallow deer males in various reproduction periods'. *Comp Biochem Physiol* [A] 2000; 126: 107–14.

TEETH AND THE IMPORTANCE OF FAT

Alam, S. Q., Alvarez, C. J., Harris, R. S., 'Effects of nutrition on the composition of tooth lipids and fatty acids in rats. 2. Effects of restriction of a cariogenic diet on caries and lipid composition of molars and incisors'. *J Dent Res* 1973; 52: 229–35.

—, —, —, 'Effects of nutrition on the composition of tooth lipids and fatty acids in rats. 3. Effects of feeding different oils and fats on caries and on fatty acid composition of teeth'. *J Dent Res* 1973; 52: 236–41.

Bavetta, L. A., Alfin-Slater, R. B., Bernick, S., Ershoff, B. H., 'Effects of a fat free diet on bones, periodontium and the incidence and severity of caries in immature rat'. *J Dent Res* 1959; 38: 686–7.

Das, S. K., Adhikary, P. K., Bhattacharyya, D. K., 'Effects of dietary fats on the fatty acid composition of enamel and dentinal lipids of rabbit molars'. *J Dent Res* 1976; 55: 1061–6.

Das, S. K., Harris, R. S., 'Fatty acids in the tooth lipids of 16 animal species'. *J Dent Res* 1970; 49: 119–25.

—, —, 'Lipids and fatty acids in fossil teeth'. *J Dent Res* 1970; 49: 126–30.

Friedlander, A. A., Brill, N. Q., 'The dental management of patients with bipolar disorder'. *Oral Surg Oral Med Oral Pathol* 1986; 61: 579–81.

Goldberg, M., LeColle, S., Bissila Mapahou, P., Septier, D., Carreau, J. P., 'Radioautographic study of the incorporation of (3H)-choline into the phospholipids of secretory ameloblasts and enamel of normal and essential-fatty-acid-deficient rats'. *Adv Dent Res* 1996; 10: 126–34.

Granados, H., Glavind, J., Dam, H., 'Observations on experimental dental caries. The effect of purified rations with and without dietary fat'. *Acta Pathol Microbiol Scand* 1948; 25: 453–9.

Griess, M., Reilmann, B., Chanavaz, M., 'Telescopic retained overdentures in mentally handicapped and schizophrenic patients – a retrospective study'. *Eur J Prosthodont Restor Dent* 1998; 6: 91–5.

Gupta, O. P., Tiwarri, O. S., Salimeno, T. Jr, Allen, D. R., 'Neuropsychiatric disorders and periodontal disease'. *Ann Dent* 1993; 52: 28–33.

Gustafson, G., Stelling, E. M., Brunius, E., 'Experimental dental caries in golden hamsters. Experiments with dietary fats having different contents of un-saturated fatty acids'. *Br Dent J* 1953; 95: 124–5.

—, —, —, 'Experiments with various fats in a cariogenic diet. IV. Experimental dental caries in golden hamsters'. *Acta Odontol Scand* 1955; 13: 75–84.

Heiferman, A., Gedalia, I., Brayer, L., Rajstein, J., 'Absorption of milk fat on tooth enamel and the effect on debris accumulation'. *Isr J Dent Med* 1981; 29: 61–3.

Kabara, J. J., 'Dietary lipids as anticariogenic agents'. *J Environ Pathol Toxicol Oncol* 1986; 6: 87–113.

Kappelman, J., Swisher, C. C., Fleagle, J. G., Yirga, S., Bown, T. M., Feseha, M., 'Age of *Australopithecus afarensis* from Fejej, Ethiopia'. *J Human Evolution* 1996; 30: 139–46.

Kay, R. F., 'Dental evidence for the diet of *Austalopithecus*'. *Ann Rev Anthropol* 1985; 14: 315–42.

Kennedy, G. E., 'Bone thickness in *Homo erectus*'. *J Human Evolution* 1985; 14: 699–708.

Mester, R., 'The psychodynamics of the dental pathology of chronic schizophrenic patients'. *Isr J Psychiatry Relat Sci* 1982; 19: 255–61.

Moraes, N., Moraes, E., Cunha Marques, H. H., 'Dental anomalies in mental patients'. *Bull Pan Am Health Organ* 1975; 9: 325–8.

Odutuga, A. A., Prout, R. E., 'Fatty acid composition of neutral lipids and phospholipids of enamel and dentine from rat incisors and molars'. *Arch Oral Biol* 1973; 18: 689–97.

—, —, 'Effect of essential fatty acid deficiency on the fatty acid composition of individual lipids from enamel and dentine of the rat'. *Arch Oral Biol* 1974; 19: 911–20.

—, —, 'Lipid analysis of human enamel and dentine'. *Arch Oral Biol* 1974; 19: 729–31.

—, —, 'Fatty acid composition of carious molar enamel and dentine from rats deficient in essential fatty acids'. *Arch Oral Biol* 1975; 20: 49–51.

Prout, R. E., Atkin, E. R., 'Effect of diet deficient in essential fatty acid on fatty acid composition of enamel and dentine of the rat'. *Arch Oral Biol* 1973; 18: 583–90.

—, Shutt, E. R., 'Analysis of fatty acids in human root dentine and enamel'. *Arch Oral Biol* 1970; 15: 281–6.

—, Tring, F. C., 'Periodontal changes in the rat induced by a fat-free diet'. *J Periodontal Res* 1971; 6: 182–7.

Prout, R. E. S., Odutuga, A. A., 'The effect on the lipid composition of enamel and dentine of feeding a corn oil supplement to rats deficient in essential fatty acids'. *Arch Oral Biol* 1974; 19: 955–8.

—, —, 'In vivo incorporation of (1-14C)-linoleic acid into the lipids of enamel and dentine of normal and essential fatty acid deficient rats'. *Arch Oral Biol* 1974; 19: 1167–70.

Rabinowitz, J. L., Gregg, J. R., Nixon, J. E., Schumacher, H. R., 'Lipid composition of the tissues of human knee joints. I. Observations in normal joints (articular cartilage, meniscus, ligaments, synovial fluid, synovium, intra-articular fat pad and bone marrow)'. *Clin Orthop* 1979; 260–5.

Rosebury, T., Karshan, M., 'Susceptibility to dental caries in the rat. V. Influence of Ca, P, vitamin D, and corn oil'. *Arch Pathol* 1935; 20: 697–707.

—, —, 'Susceptibility to dental caries in the rat. VIII. Further studies of the influence of vitamin D and of fats and fatty oils'. *J Dent Res* 1939; 18: 189–202.

Schweigert, B. S., Potts, E., Shaw, J. H., Zepplin, M., Phillips, P. H., 'Dental caries in the cotton rat. VIII. Further studies on the dietary effects of carbohydrate, protein and fat on the incidence and extent of carious lesions'. *J Nutr* 1946; 32: 405–12.

—, Shaw, J. H., Zepplin, M., Elvehjem, C. A., 'Dental caries in the cotton rat. VI. The effect of the amount of protein, fat and carbohydrate in the diet on the incidence and extent of carious lesions'. *J Nutr* 1946; 31: 439–47.

Thomas, A., Lavrentzou, E., Karouzos, C., Kontis, C., 'Factors which influence the oral condition of chronic schizophrenia patients'. *Spec Care Dentist* 1996; 16: 84–6.

RELATIONSHIP BETWEEN HUMAN EVOLUTION AND WATER

Buchanan, W. F., 'Shellfish in prehistoric diet: Elands Bay S.W. Cape Coast, South Africa'. *Bar Intern Series* 455: Oxford, 1988.

Crawford, M. A., Kirby, E., Morgan, E. (eds), 'The aquatic ape: selected papers'. *Nutrition Health* 1993; 9: 157–235.

DeHart, R. L., *Fundamentals of Aerospace Medicine.* 2nd edn. Williams and Wilkins: Baltimore, Md., 1996.

Editorial, 'Human evolution: the first seaside holiday?' *The Economist* 2000; 6 May.

Gebbie, D. A. M., *Reproductive Anthropology: Descent Through Woman.* Wiley: Chichester, 1981.

Kennedy, G. E., 'The relationship between auditory exostoses and cold water: a latitudinal analysis'. *Am J Phys Anthropol* 1986; 71: 401–15.

Langdon, J. H., 'Umbrella hypotheses and parsimony in human evolution: a critique of the aquatic ape hypothesis'. *J Human Evolution* 1997; 33: 479–94.

Montgomery, D., *Aquatic Ape and African Eve: A Search for the Origins and Evolution of Humankind in Africa.* http://homepages.tesco.net/~sondela/index.html: Chedburgh, 1999.

Morgan, E., *The Descent of Woman.* Stein and Day: New York, 1972.

—, *The Aquatic Ape: A Theory of Human Evolution.* Souvenir Press: London, 1982.

—, *The Scars of Evolution: What Our Bodies Tell Us about Human Origins.* Souvenir Press: London, 1990.

Rhys Evans, P. H., 'The paranasal sinuses and other enigmas: an aquatic evolutionary theory'. *J Laryngology Otology* 1992; 106: 214–25.

Roede, M., Wind, J., Patrick, J., Reynolds, V. (eds), *The Aquatic Ape: Fact or Fiction?* Souvenir Press: London, 1991.

Sandweiss, D. H., McInnis, H., Burger, R. L., *et al.*, 'Quebrada Jaguay: early South American maritime adaptations'. *Science* 1998; 281: 1830–2.

Scholander, P. F., 'Rhapsody in science'. *Annu Rev Physiol* 1978; 40: 1–17.

Schusterman, R. J., Thomas, J. A., Wood, F. G., Hubbs Marine Research Institute, *Dolphin Cognition and Behavior: a Comparative Approach.* L. Erlbaum Associates: Hillsdale, NJ, 1986.

Stewart, K. M., *Fishing Sites of North and East Africa in the Late Pleistocene and Holocene Environmental Change and Human Adaptation.* BAR: Oxford, 1989.

Sutton, J. E. S., 'The aquatic civilisation of middle Africa'. *J African History* 1974; 15: 527–46.

—, 'The African aqualithic'. *Antiquity* 1977; 51: 25–34.

Terman, L. M., *Genetic Studies of Genius.* Stanford University Press: Stanford, Calif., 1926.

Walter, R. C., Buffler, R. T., Bruggemann, J. H., *et al.*, 'Early human occupation of the Red Sea coast of Eritrea during the last interglacial'. *Nature* 2000; 405: 65–9.

Yellen, J. E., Brooks, A. S., Cornelissen, E., Mehlman, M. J., Stewart, K., 'A middle stone age worked bone industry from Katanda, Upper Semliki Valley, Zaire'. *Science* 1995; 268: 553–6.

FAT BIOCHEMISTRY AND THRIFTY GENES

Anon., *The Mongongo/Manketti nut.* http://Naturalhub.Com/Natural_Food_Guide_Nuts_Uncommon_Ricinodendron_Rautanenii.Htm: 2000.

Barkai, A. I., Bazan, N. G., 'Arachidonic cid metabolism in the nervous system'. *Ann NY Acad Sci* 1989; 559: 1–504.

Basalingappa, S., Badami, R. C., Kudari, S. M., 'The gross fatty acid composition of the body fat from the termite (*Odontotermes Assmuthi*) queen'. *Biochem J* 1972; 128: 44p–45p.

—, Kudari, S. M., Badami, R. C., Gandhi, M. R., Tharabai, P., 'Fatty acid composition of body fat from the queens of the termite *Odontotermes (Assmuthi) Obesus (Termitidae: Isoptfra)*'. *Indian J Comp Anim Physiol* 1985; 3: 12–16.

Broadhurst, C. L., 'Balanced intakes of natural triglycerides for optimum nutrition: an evolutionary and phytochemical perspective'. *Med Hypotheses* 1997; 49: 247–61.

—, 'Nutrition and non-insulin dependent diabetes mellitus from an anthropological perspective'. *Alt Med Rev* 1997; 2: 378–99.

Carter, F. L., Dinus, L.A., Smythe, R. V., 'Fatty acids of the eastern subterranean termite *Reticulitermes P Flavipes Isopters Rhinotermitidae*'. *Ann Entomol Soc Am* 1972; 65: 655–8.

Clandinin, M. T., 'Dietary lipids and evolution of the human brain'. *Br J Nutr* 1998; 80: 299–300.

Crawford, M., Marsh, D., *The Driving Force: Food, Evolution and the Future.* Heinemann: London, 1989.

Eaton, S. B., 'Humans, lipids and evolution'. *Lipids* 1992; 27: 814–20.

—, Konner, M., 'Paleolithic nutrition: a consideration of its nature and current implications'. *N Engl J Med* 1985; 312: 283–9.

Editorial, 'Evolution and development: dietary wisdom of paleolithic man reaffirmed'. PUFA Newsletter 2000; 4: 8.

Fernandez-Real, J. M., Ricart, W., 'Insulin resistance and inflammation in an evolutionary perspective: the contribution of cytokine genotype/phenotype to thriftiness'. *Diabetologia* 1999; 42: 1367–74.

Gurr, M. I., 'Dietary lipids and evolution of the human brain'. *Br J Nutr* 1998; 79: 389–90.

Hillbrand, M., Spitz, R. T., *Lipids, Health, and Behavior.* American Psychological Association: Washington, DC, 1997.

Kuzawa, C. W., 'Adipose tissue in human infancy and childhood: an evolutionary perspective'. *Yearbook Phys Anthropol* 1998; 41: 177–210.

Mann, N. J., 'The paleolithic diet, meat intake and insulin resistance: relevance to Western lifestyle diseases'. *Proc Nut Soc Aust* 1998; 22: 107.

Murray, I., Havel, P. J., Sniderman, A. D., Cianflone, K., 'Reduced body weight, adipose tissue, and leptin levels despite increased energy intake in female mice lacking acylation-stimulating protein'. *Endocrinology* 2000; 141: 1041–9.

Neel, J. V., 'Diabetes mellitus: a "thrifty" genotype rendered detrimental by "progress"?' *Am J Hum Genet* 1962; 14: 353–62.

—, Weder, A. B., Julius, S., 'Type II diabetes, essential hypertension, and obesity as "syndromes of impaired genetic homeostasis": the "thrifty genotype" hypothesis enters the 21st century'. *Perspect Biol Med* 1998; 42: 44–74.

Onigbinde, A. O., Adamolekun, B., 'The nutrient value of *Imbrasia belina Lepidoptera: Saturnidae (madora)*'. *Cent Afr J Med* 1998; 44: 125–7.

Oyarzun, S. E., Crawshaw, G. J., Valdes, E. V., 'Nutrition of the Tamandua: 1. Nutrient composition of termites (*Nasutitermes spp.*) and stomach contents from wild Tamanduas (*Tamandua tetradactyla*)'. *Zoo Biology* 1996; 15: 509–24.

Peet, M., Glen, I., Horrobin, D. F. (eds), *Phospholipid Spectrum Disorder in Psychiatry.* Marius Press: Carnforth, 1999.

Pond, C. M., *The Fats of Life.* Cambridge University Press: Cambridge, 1998.

Siegel, G., Agranoff, B., Albers, R., Molinoff, P., *Basic Neurochemistry: Molecular, Cellular, and Medical Aspects.* Raven Press: New York, 1994.

Simopoulos, A. P., 'Evolutionary aspects of omega-3 fatty acids in the food supply'. *Prostaglandins Leukot Essent Fatty Acids* 1999; 60: 421–9.

Sinclair, A. J., O'Dea, K., 'The significance of arachidonic acid in hunter-gatherer diets: implications for the contemporary Western diet'. *J Food Lipids* 1993; 1: 143–57.

Speake, B. K., Thompson, M. B., McCartney, R. J., 'Lipid composition of eggs of an oviparous lizard (*Bassiana duperreyi*)'. *Lipids* 1999; 34: 1207–10.

Surai, P. F., Royle, N. J., Sparks, N. H. C., 'Fatty acid, carotenoid and vitamin A composition of tissues of free living gulls'. *Comp Biochem Physiol* [A] 2000; 126: 387–96.

Thompson, M. B., Speake, B. K., Russell, K. J., McCartney, R. J., Surai, P.F., 'Changes in fatty acid profiles and in protein, ion and energy contents of eggs of the Murray short-necked turtle, *Emydura macquarri* (*Chelonia, Pleurodira*) during development'. *Comp Biochem Physiol* [A] 1999; 122: 75–84.

Vardi, P., Pinhas-Hamiel, O., 'The young hunter hypothesis: age-related weight gain – a tribute to the thrifty theories'. *Med Hypotheses*: forthcoming.

Wendorf, M., 'Thrifty gene and hunting as a way of life are evident in a Paleoindian burial'. *Diabetes Care* 1999; 22: 176.

Wood, B., Brooks, A., 'Human evolution – we are what we ate'. *Nature* 1999; 400: 219–20.

Zaheer, K., 'Fatty acid composition of total lipids and effects of some insecticides upon them in termite *Odontotermes obesus* (Rambur)'. *Biologia* 1986; 32: 29–38.

—, 'Fatty acid analysis of total lipids in the soldier caste of termite, *Odontotermes obesus* (Rambur)'. *Pakistan J Zoology* 1994; 26: 86–9.

—, Iqbal, Q. J., Athar, F., Iqbal, H., 'Fatty acid composition of phospholipids and effect of insecticides on them in the termite *Odontotermes obesus* (Rambur)'. *Pakistan J Zoology* 1985; 17: 349–56.

Zenebe, T., Ahlgren, G., Boberg, M., 'Fatty acid content of some freshwater fish of commercial importance from tropical lakes in the Ethiopian Rift Valley'. *J Fish Biol* 1998; 53: 987–1005.

LANGUAGE AND SPEECH

Adler, R., 'Voices from the past'. *New Scientist* 2000; 28 February: 36–40.

Basser, L. S., 'Hemiplegia of early onset and the faculty of speech with special reference to the effects of hemisperectomy'. *Brain* 1962; 85: 427–60.

Bishop, D. V. M., 'Can the right hemisphere mediate language as well as the left? A critical review of recent research'. *Cognitive Neuropsychol* 1988; 5: 353–67.

Burne, J., 'Finding the key to language'. *Sunday Times* 2000; 28 May.

Calvin, W. H., 'The unitary hypothesis: a common natural circuitry for novel manipulations, language, plan-ahead and throwing?' In *Tools, Language and Cognition in Human Evolution*, Gibson, K. R., Ingold, T. (eds), Cambridge University Press: Cambridge, 1992; 230–50.

—, 'The emergence of intelligence'. *Scientific American* 1994; 271: 79–85.

—, Bickerton, D., 'Lingua ex machina: reconciling Darwin and Chomsky with the human brain'. MIT Press: Cambridge, Mass., 2000.

Crow, T. J., 'Twin studies of psychosis and the genetics of cerebral asymmetry'. *Br J Psychiatry* 1999; 175: 399–401.

—, 'Schizophrenia as the price that *Homo sapiens* pays for language: a resolution of the central paradox in the origin of the species'. *Brain Res Rev* 2000; 31: 118–29.

Deacon, T., *The Symbolic Species: The Co-evolution of Language and the Human Brain*. Allen Lane: New York, 1997.

DeGusta, D., Gilbert, W. H., Turner, S. P., 'Hypoglossal canal size and hominid speech'. *Proc Natl Acad Sci USA* 1999; 96: 1800–4.

Dunbar, R., *Grooming, Gossip and the Evolution of Language*. Faber and Faber: London, 1997.

Dunbar, R. I. M., 'Coevolution of neocortical size, group size and language in humans'. *Behavioural Brain Sci* 1996; 16: 681–735.

Forrest, D. V., 'Nonsense and sense in schizophrenic language'. *Schizophr Bull* 1976; 2: 286–301.

Higgs, P. G., 'The mimetic transition: a simulation study of the evolution of learning by imitation'. *Proc Royal Soc Lond* B 2000; 267: 1355–61.

Landahl, K. L., Ziolkowski, M., 'Speech production and intelligibility given anomolous vocal tracts'. *Am J Phys Anthropol* 1989; 78: 258.

Leiber, J., 'Coming of age in Olduvai and the Zaire rain forest'. *J Behavioral Brain Sci* 1995; 18: 196–7.

Lieberman, P., *Eve Spoke: Human Language and Human Evolution*. W. W. Norton: New York, 1998.

Meier, R. P., 'Diminishing diversity of signed languages'. *Science* 2000; 288: 1965.

Negus V., *The Mechanism of the Larynx*. Heineman: London, 1929.

Nichols, J., *Linguistic Diversity in Space and Time*. University of Chicago Press: Chicago, 1992.

Noble, W., Davidson, I., *Human Evolution: Language and Mind*. Cambridge University Press: Cambridge, 1996.

Ogden, J. A., 'Language and memory functions after long recovery periods in left-hemispherectomized subjects'. *Neuropsychologia* 1988; 26: 645–59.

Parker, S. T., Gibson, K. R., 'A developmental model for the evolution of language and intelligence in early hominids'. *Behavioural Brain Science* 1979; 2: 367–408.

—, —, *'Language' and Intelligence in Monkeys and Apes: Comparative Developmental Perspectives*. Cambridge University Press: Cambridge, 1990.

Pepperberg, I. M., *The Alex Studies: Cognitive and Communicative Abilities of Grey Parrots*. Harvard University Press: Cambridge, Mass., 1999.

Peterson-Falzone, S. J., Caldarelli, D. D., Landahl, K. L., 'Abnormal laryngeal vocal quality in ectodermal dysplasia'. *Arch Otolaryngol* 1981; 107: 300–4.

Pinker, S., *The Language Instinct: The New Science of Language and Mind*. Allen Lane: London, 1994.

Previc, F. H., 'A general theory concerning the prenatal origins of cerebral lateralization in humans'. *Psychol Rev* 1991; 98: 299–334.

Ramus, F., Hauser, M. D., Miller, C., Morris, D., Mehler, J., 'Language discrimination by human newborns and by cotton-top tamarin monkeys'. *Science* 2000; 288: 349–51.

SCHIZOPHRENIA, BIPOLAR DISORDER AND SCHIZOTYPY – GENERAL DESCRIPTIONS

Abed, R. T., 'Psychiatry and Darwinism: time to reconsider?' *Br J Psychiatry* 2000; 177: 1–3.

Altschuler, E., 'Shakespeare knew the layered clothing sign of schizophrenia'. *Br Med J* 1999; 319: 520–1.

American Psychiatric Association, *DSM-IV. Diagnostic and Statistical Manual of Mental Disorders*. 4th edn. American Psychiatric Association: Washington, DC, 1994.

Andreasen, N. C., *Schizophrenia: From Mind to Molecule*. American Psychiatric Press: Washington, DC, 1994.

Bates, C., Horrobin, D. F., Ells, K., 'Fatty acids in plasma phospholipids and cholesterol esters from identical twins concordant and discordant for schizophrenia'. *Schizophr Res* 1991; 6: 1–7.

Bayley, R., 'First person account: schizophrenia'. *Schizophr Bull* 1996; 22: 727–9.

Bennett, C. N., Horrobin, D. F., 'Gene targets related to phospholipid and fatty acid metabolism in schizophrenia and other psychiatric disorders: an update'. *Prostaglandins Leukot Essent Fatty Acids* 2000; 63: 47–59.

Cawte, J., *The Last of the Lunatics*. Melbourne University Press: Melbourne, 1998.

Claridge, G., *Origins of Mental Illness*. Basil Blackwell: Oxford, 1985.

—, *Schizotypy: Implications for Illness and Health*. Oxford University Press: Oxford, 1997.

—, 'The schizophrenias as nervous types'. *Br J Psychiatry* 1972; 121: 1–17.

Eaton, W. W., Romanoski, A., Anthony, J. C., Nestadt, G., 'Screening for psychosis in the general population with a self-report interview'. *J Nerv Ment Dis* 1991; 179: 689–93.

Essen-Moller, E., 'The concept of schizoidia'. *Monatschr Psychiat Neurol* 1946; 112: 258–71.

Gattaz, W. F., Hafner, H., *Search for the Causes of Schizophrenia. IV. Balance of the Century*. Steinkopff Verlag: Darmstadt, 1999.

Georgotas, A., Cancro, R. (eds), *Depression and Mania*. Elsevier: New York, 1988.

Gerland, G., *A Real Person: Life on the Outside*. Souvenir Press: London, 1997.

Glen, A. I. M., Glen, E. M., Horrobin, D. F., *et al.*, 'A red cell membrane abnormality in a subgroup of schizophrenic patients: evidence for two diseases'. *Schizophr Res* 1994; 12: 53–61.

Goodnick, P. J. (ed), *Mania: Clinical and Research Perspectives*. American Psychiatric Press: London, 1998.

Goodwin, F. K., Jamison, K. R., *Manic-Depressive Illness*. Oxford University Press: Oxford, 1990.

Gottesman, I. I., Shields, J., *Schizophrenia: the Epigenetic Puzzle*. Cambridge University Press: Cambridge, 1982.

Gottesman, I. I., Wolfgram, D. L., *Schizophrenia Genesis: the Origins of Madness*. Freeman: New York, 1991.

Greenblat, L., 'First person account: understanding health as a continuum'. *Schizophr Bull* 2000; 26: 243–5.

Hall, L. L. (ed), *Genetics and Mental Illness: Evolving Issues for Research and Society*. Plenum: London, 1996.

Hemmings, G., *Inside Schizophrenia: A New Comprehensive Guide for Sufferers and Their Families*. Sidgwick and Jackson: London, 1989.

Hirsch, S. R., Weinberger, D. R. (eds), *Schizophrenia*. Blackwell Science: Oxford, 1995.

Horrobin, D. F., 'Essential fatty acids and prostaglandins in schizophrenia and alcoholism'. *Biol Psychiatry* 1985; 1163–5.

—, 'Fatty acids, phospholipids, and schizophrenia'. In *Handbook of Fatty Acid Biology,. Yehuda, S., Mostofsky, D. I. (eds), Totowa, NJ: Humana Press 1997; 245–56.

—, 'Lipid metabolism, human evolution, and schizophrenia'. *Prostaglandins Leukot Essent Fatty Acids* 1999; 60: 431–7.

—, 'Lithium, essential fatty acids (Efas) and eicosanoids'. In *Lithium: 50 Years of Psychopharmacology*, Birch, N. J. (ed), Weidner Publishing: Cheshire, Conn., 1999; 154–67.

—, 'Niacin flushing, prostaglandin E and evening primrose oil: a possible objective test for monitoring therapy in schizophrenia'. *J Orthomolecular Psychiatry* 1980; 9: 33–4.

—, 'Nutritional supplementation in schizophrenia'. Schizophrenia Association of Great Britain Newsletter. 1999; 27: 12–16.

—, 'Prostaglandin deficiency and endorphin excess in schizophrenia: the case for treatment with penicillin, zinc, and evening primrose oil'. *J Orth Psychol* 1979; 8: 13–19.

—, 'Prostaglandins and schizophrenia'. *Lancet* 1979; 1: 1031–2.

—, 'Prostaglandins and schizophrenia'. *Lancet* 1980; 1: 706–7.

—, 'Schizophrenia as a membrane lipid disorder which is expressed throughout the body'. *Prostaglandins Leukot Essent Fatty Acids* 1996; 55: 3–7.

—, 'Schizophrenia as a prostaglandin deficiency disease'. *Lancet* 1977; 1: 936–7.

—, 'Schizophrenia: reconciliation of the dopamine, prostaglandin, and opioid concepts and the role of the pineal'. *Lancet* 1979; 1: 529–31.

—, 'Schizophrenia: the illness that made us human'. *Med Hypotheses* 1998; 50: 269–88.

—, 'The membrane phospholipid hypothesis as a biochemical basis for the neurodevelopmental concept of schizophrenia'. *Schizophr Res* 1998; 30: 193–208.

—, 'The relationship between schizophrenia and essential fatty acid and eicosanoid metabolism'. *Prostaglandins Leukot Essent Fatty Acids* 1992; 46: 71–7.

—, Ally, A. I., Karmali, R. A., Karmazyn, M., Manku, M. S., Morgan, R. O., 'Prostaglandins and schizophrenia: further discussion of the evidence'. *Psychol Med* 1978; 8: 43–8.

—, Bennett, C. N., 'Depression and bipolar disorder: relationships to impaired fatty acid and phospholipid metabolism and to diabetes, cardiovascular disease, immunological abnormalities, cancer, aging and osteoporosis: possible candidate genes'. *Prostaglandins Leukot Essent Fatty Acids* 1999; 60: 217–34.

—, —, 'New gene targets related to schizophrenia and other psychiatric disorders: enzymes, binding proteins and transport proteins involved in phospholipid and fatty acid metabolism'. *Prostaglandins Leukot Essent Fatty Acids* 1999; 60: 111–67.

—, —, 'The membrane phospholipid concept of schizophrenia'. In *Search for the Causes of Schizophrenia*, Gattaz, W. F., Hafner H. (eds), Steinkpoff Verlag: Darmstadt, 1999; 261–77.

—, Glen, A. I., Vaddadi, K., 'The membrane hypothesis of schizophrenia'. *Schizophr Res* 1994; 13: 195–207.

—, —, Hudson, C. J., 'Possible relevance of phospholipid abnormalities and genetic interactions in psychiatric disorders: the relationship between dyslexia and schizophrenia'. *Med Hypotheses* 1995; 45: 605–13.

Horrobin, D. F., Manku, M. S., Hillman, H., Iain, A., Glen, M., 'Fatty acid levels in the brains of schizophrenics and normal controls'. *Biol Psychiatry* 1991; 30: 795–805.

—, —, Morse Fisher, N., *et al.*, 'Essential fatty acids in plasma phospholipids in schizophrenics'. *Biol Psychiatry* 1989; 25: 562–8.

—, —, 'Possible role of prostaglandin E1 in the affective disorders and in alcoholism.' *Br Med J* 1980; 280: 1363–6.

Howe, G., *Working with Schizophrenia: A Needs Based Approach*. Jessica Kingsley Publishers: London, 1995.

Hudson, C. J., Kennedy, J. L., Gotowiec, A., *et al.*, 'Genetic variant near cytosolic phospholipase A2 associated with schizophrenia'. *Schizophr Res* 1996; 21: 111–16.

—, Lin, A., Horrobin, D. F., 'Phospholipases: in search of a genetic base of schizophrenia'. *Prostaglandins Leukot Essent Fatty Acids* 1996; 55: 119–22.

Jamison, K. R., *An Unquiet Mind: A Memoir of Moods and Madness*. Picador: London, 1995.

Kellett, J. M., 'Evolutionary theory for the dichotomy of the functional psychoses'. *Lancet* 1973; 1: 860–3.

Lachenmeyer, N., *The Outsider: A Journey into My Father's Struggle with Madness*. Broadway Books: New York, 2000.

Leudar, I., Thomas, P., *Voices of Reason, Voices of Insanity: Studies of Verbal Hallucinations*. Routledge: London, 2000.

McKenna, P. J., *Schizophrenia and Related Syndromes*. Psychology Press: Hove, 1997.

Nasar, S., *A Beautiful Mind*. Simon and Schuster: New York, 1998.

Nissen, A. A., Spencer, K. A., 'The psychogenic problem (endocrinal and metabolic) in chronic arthritis'. *New Eng J Med* 1936; 214: 576–81.

Pantelis, C., Nelson, H. E., Barnes, T. R. E. (eds), *Schizophrenia: A Neuropsychological Perspective*. Wiley: Chichester, 1996.

Pauling, L. C., Hawkins, D., *Orthomolecular Psychiatry: Treatment of Schizophrenia*. W. H. Freeman: San Francisco, 1973.

Peet, M., Brind, J., Ramchand, C. N., Shah, S., Vankar, G. K., 'Two double-blind placebo-controlled pilot studies of eicosapentaenoic acid in the treatment of schizophrenia'. *Schizophr Res* 2000; forthcoming.

—, Glen, I., Horrobin, D. F. (eds), *Phospholipid Spectrum Disorder in Psychiatry*. Marius Press: Carnforth, 1999.

—, Horrobin, D. F., EPA Multicentre Trial Group, 'Eicosapentaenoic acid in the management of treatment-unresponsive schizophrenia'. *Br Assoc Psychopharmacol* 2000; Summer Meeting, 16–19 July, Cambridge, UK: PG43.

—, Laugharne, J., Rangarajan, N., Horrobin, D. F., Reynolds, G., 'Depleted red cell membrane essential fatty acids in drug-treated schizophrenic patients'. *J Psychiatr Res* 1995; 29: 227–32.

—, —, Horrobin, D. F., Reynolds, G. P., 'Arachidonic acid: a common link in the biology of schizophrenia?' *Arch Gen Psychiatry* 1994; 51: 665–6.

Pivnicki, D., Christie, R. G., 'Body build characteristics in psychotics'. *Compr Psychiatry* 1968; 9: 574–80.

Price, J. S., Stevens, A., 'The human male socialization strategy set: co-operation, defection, individulism and schizotypy'. *Evol Hum Behav* 1998; 19: 57–70.

Puri, B. K., Richardson, A. J., 'Sustained remission of positive and negative symptoms of schizophrenia following dietary supplementation with poly-unsaturated fatty acids'. *Arch Gen Psychiatry* 1998; 55: 188–9.

—, —, Horrobin, D. F., *et al.*, 'Eicosapentaenoic acid treatment in schizophrenia associated with symptom remission, normalisation of blood fatty acids, reduced neuronal membrane phospholipid turnover and structural brain changes'. *Int J Clin Pract* 2000; 54: 57–63.

Raine, A., Lencz, T., Mednick, S. A., *Schizotypal Personality*. Cambridge University Press: Cambridge, 1995.

Richardson, A. J., 'Dyslexia, handedness and syndromes of psychosis-proneness'. *Int J Psychophysiol* 1994; 18: 251–63.

Rollin, Henry, R., McDonald, Fiona, National Schizophrenia Fellowship, *A Tragedy of Schizophrenia: The Wife's Tale*. National Schizophrenia Fellowship: Surbiton, 1980.

Shorter, E., *A History of Psychiatry: From the Era of the Asylum to the Age of Prozac*. Wiley: New York, 1997.

Soares, J. C., Gershon, S., *Bipolar Disorders – Basic Mechanisms and Therapeutic Implications*. Marcel Dekker: New York, 2000.

Stevens, A., Price, J., *Prophets, Cults and Madness*. Duckworth: London, 2000.

Stevens, L. J., Zentall, S. Z., Deck, J. L., *et al.*, 'Essential fatty acid metabolism in boys with attention-deficit hyperactivity disorder'. *Am J Clin Nutr* 1995; 62: 761–8.

Strauss, J. S., 'Hallucinations and delusions as points on continua function: rating scale evidence'. *Arch Gen Psychiatry* 1969; 21: 581–6.

Templeton, W. L., 'The effect of malaria fever upon dementia praecox subjects'. *J Ment Sci* 1924; 92.

Thullier, J., *Ten Years that Changed the Face of Mental Illness*. Martin Dunitz: London, 1999.

Torrey, E. F., *Out of Shadows: Confronting America's Mental Illness Crisis*. Wiley: New York, 1997.

—, *Schizophrenia and Civilisation*. Jason Aronson: New York, 1980.

Tsuang, M. T., *Schizophrenia: The Facts*. Oxford University Press: Oxford, 1997.

Vaddadi, K. S., Courtney, P., Gilleard, C. J., Manku, M. S., Horrobin, D. F., 'A double-blind trial of essential fatty acid supplementation in patients with tardive dyskinesia'. *Psychiatry Res* 1989; 27: 313–23.

Van Os, J., Gilvarry, C., Bale, R., *et al.*, 'A comparison of the utility of dimensional and categorical representations of psychosis. UK700 Group'. *Psychol Med* 1999; 29: 595–606.

—, Hanssen, M., Bijl, R. V., Ravelli, A., 'Strauss (1969) revisited: a psychosis continuum in the general population?' *Schizophr Res* 2000; 45: 11–20.

—, Marcelis, M., Sham, P., Jones, P., Gilvarry, K., Murray, R., 'Psycho-pathological syndromes and familial morbid risk of psychosis'. *Br J Psychiatry* 1997; 170: 241–6.

Verdoux, H., Maurice Tison, S., Gay, B., Van Os, J., Salamon, R., Bourgeois, M. L., 'A survey of delusional ideation in primary-care patients'. *Psychol Med* 1998; 28: 127–34.

Vonnegut, M., *The Eden Express*. Bantam: New York, 1976.

Ward, P. E., Sutherland, J., Glen, E. M. T., Glen, A. I. M., 'Niacin skin flush in schizophrenia: a preliminary report'. *Schizophr Res* 1998; 29: 269–74.

Warner, R., *Recovery from Schizophrenia: Psychiatry and Political Economy*. 2nd edn. Routledge: New York, 1994.

Whitrow, M., *Julius Wagner-Jauregg (1857–1940)*. Smith Gordon: London, 1993.

Winokur, G., Tsuang, M. T., *The Natural History of Mania, Depression, and Schizophrenia*. American Psychiatric Press: Washington, DC, 1996.

Yao, J. K., Leonard, S., Reddy, R. D., 'Membrane phospholipid abnormalities in postmortem brains from schizophrenic patients'. *Schizophr Res* 2000; 42: 7–17.

SCHIZOPHRENIA, BIPOLAR DISORDER AND SCHIZOTYPY – GENETIC AND FAMILY STUDIES

Alanen, Y. O., 'The family in the pathogenesis of schizophrenic and neurotic disorders'. *Acta Psychiatr Scand* 1966; S189: 1–654.

Allen, J. S., 'Are traditional societies schizophrenogenic?' *Schizophr Bull* 1997; 23: 357–64.

Barondes, S., *Mood Genes*. Freeman: San Francisco, 1998.

Berrettini, W. H., 'Are schizophrenic and bipolar disorders related? A review of family and molecular studies'. *Biol Psychiatry* 2000; 48: 531–8.

—, 'Genetics of psychiatric disease'. *Annu Rev Med* 2000; 51: 465–79.

—, 'Susceptibility loci for bipolar disorder: overlap with inherited vulnerability to schizophrenia'. *Biol Psychiatry* 2000; 47: 245–51.

Cardno, A. G., Gottesman, II., 'Twin studies of schizophrenia: from bow-and-arrow concordances to star wars mx and functional genomics'. *Am J Med Genet* 2000; 97: 12–17.

Cook, E., 'Genetics of psychiatric disorders: where have we been and where are we going?' *Am J Psychiatry* 2000; 157: 1039–40.

DeLisi, L. E., Craddock, N. J., Detera-Wadleigh, S., *et al.*, 'Update on chromosomal locations for psychiatric disorders: report of the Interim Meeting of Chromosome Workshop Chairpersons from the VIIth World Congress of Psychiatric Genetics, Monterey, California, October 14–18, 1999'. *Am J Med Genet* 2000; 96: 434–49.

Faraone, S. V., Seidman, L. J., Kremen, W. S., Toomey, R., Pepple, J. R., Tsuang, M. T., 'Neuropsychologic functioning among the nonpsychotic relatives of schizophrenic patients: the effect of genetic loading'. *Biol Psychiatry* 2000; 48: 120–6.

Freedman, R., Adams, C. E., Adler, L. E., *et al.*, 'Inhibitory neurophysiological deficit as a phenotype for genetic investigation of schizophrenia'. *Am J Med Genet* 2000; 97: 58–64.

Hammer, M., Salzinger, K., Sutton, S., Zubin, J., *Psychopathology: Contributions from the Social, Behavioral, and Biological Sciences*. Wiley-Interscience: New York, 1973.

Heston, L. L., 'The genetics of schizophrenic and schizoid diseases'. *Science* 1970; 167: 249–56.

Ingraham, L. J., Kety, S. S., 'Adoption studies of schizophrenia'. *Am J Med Genet* 2000; 97: 18–22.

Kaplan, A. R., *Genetic Factors in 'Schizophrenia'*. Thomas: Springfield, Il.l, 1972.

Kretschmer, E. (trans. Sprott, W. J. H.), *Physique and Character: An Investigation of the Nature of Constitution and of the Theory of Temperament*. Kegan, Trench and Trubner: London, 1925.

Kringlen, E., *Heredity and Environment in the Functional Psychoses*. William Heinemann Medical Books: London, 1967.

Kuttner, R. E., 'The prudence of suboptimal biological performance'. *Proc Inst Med Chic* 1982; 35: 130.

—, —, Swan, D. A., 'Schizophrenia and evolution'. *Eugen Q* 1966; 13: 355–6.

—, —, 'Additional comments on schizophrenia and evolution'. *Eugen Q* 1967; 14: 160–61.

Kuttner, R. E., Lorincz, A. B., Swan, D. A., 'The schizophrenia gene and social evolution'. *Psychol Rep* 1967; 20: 407–12.

Meltzer, H. Y., 'Genetics and etiology of schizophrenia and bipolar disorder'. *Biol Psychiatry* 2000; 47: 171–3.

Morris, K., 'Viewing the mind's maladies through Darwin's eyes'. *Lancet* 1999; 354: 228.

Pierson, A., Jouvent, R., Quintin, P., Perez-Diaz, F., Leboyer, M., 'Information processing deficits in relatives of manic depressive patients'. *Psychol Med* 2000; 30: 545–55.

Ray, I., *Mental Hygiene*. Hafner: New York, and Kingston upon Thames, 1968.

Richter, D., *Schizophrenia: Somatic Aspects*. Pergamon Press: London, 1957.

Roe, A., 'A psychological study of eminent psychologists and anthropologists and a comparison with biological and physical scientists'. *Psychol Monogr* 1953; 67: 2.

Rosenthal, D., Kety, S. S., Foundations' Fund for Research in Psychiatry, 'The Transmission of Schizophrenia Proceedings of the Second Research Conference of the Foundations' Fund for Research in Psychiatry, Dorado, Puerto Rico, 26 June to 1 July 1967'. Pergamon Press: Oxford, New York, 1968.

Slater, E., May, J., Shields, J., Medical Research Council, *Psychotic and Neurotic Illnesses in Twins*. HMSO: London, 1953.

Sullivan, R. J., Allen, J. S., 'Social deficits associated with schizophrenia defined in terms of interpersonal Machiavellianism'. *Acta Psychiatr Scand* 1999; 99: 148–54.

Tsuang, M. T., *Genes and the Mind: Inheritance of Mental Illness*. Oxford University Press: Oxford, 1980.

Tsuang, M. T., Stone, W. S., Faraone, S. V., 'Toward reformulating the diagnosis of schizophrenia'. *Am J Psychiatry* 2000; 157: 1041–50.

Vinogradov, S., Adcock, R. A., Fischer, A., Poole, J. H., 'Neurocognitive findings in schizophrenic subjects with above average IQ'. *Biol Psychiatry* 2000; 47: 1S–173S.

CREATIVITY, ACHIEVEMENT AND MENTAL DISORDERS

Addad, M., 'Stigma, creativity, crime and madness'. *Deviant Behavior* 1985; 6: 67–81.

Albert, R. S., *Genius and Eminence: The Social Psychology of Creativity and Exceptional Achievement*. Pergamon: Oxford, 1983.

Alias, A. G., 'Schizotypy and leadership: a contrasting model for deficit symptoms and a possible therapeutic role for sex hormones'. *Med Hypotheses* 2000; 54: 537–52.

Andreasen, N. C., 'Creativity and mental illness: prevalence rates in writers and their first-degree relatives'. *Am J Psychiatry* 1987; 144: 1288–92.

Austin, J. H., *Chase, Chance and Creativity: The Lucky Art of Novelty*. Columbia University Press: New York, 1985.

Babcock, W. L., 'On the morbid heredity and predisposition to insanity of the man of genius'. *J Nerv Mental Dis* 1895; 20: 749–69.

Barron, F., *Creativity and Personal Freedom*. Van Nostrand: Princeton, NJ, and London, 1968.

—, *Creativity and Psychological Health: Origins of Personal Vitality and Creative Freedom*. Van Nostrand: Princeton, NJ, 1963.

Becker, G., *The Mad Genius Controversy*. Sage: Beverly Hills, Calif., 1978.

Behrens, R. R., 'Lunatics, lovers and poets: on madness and creativity'. *J Creative Behaviour* 1975; 9: 228–32.

Beveridge, A., ' "Teetering on the verge of complete sanity": Boswell's life of Boswell'. *J R Soc Med* 2000; 93: 434–7.

Boden, M. A., *Dimensions of Creativity*. MIT: Cambridge, Mass., 1994.

Cattell, R. B., Butcher, H. J. (eds), *The Prediction of Achievement and Creativity*. Bobbs-Merrill: Indianapolis, Ind., 1968.

—, Drevdahl, J. E., 'A comparison of the personality profile (16 P.F.) of eminent researchers with that of eminent teachers and administrators and of the general population'. *Br J Psychology* 1955; 46: 248–61.

Chadwick, P. K., *Schizophrenia: The Positive Perspective*. Routledge: London, 1997.

David, A. S., 'Intelligence and schizophrenia'. *Acta Psychiatr Scand* 1999; 100: 1–2.

Davis, R. D., *The Gift of Dyslexia*. Ability Workshop Press: Burlingame, Calif., 1995.

Drevdahl, J. E., 'Factors of importance for creativity'. *J Clin Psychology* 1956; 12: 21–6.

Drevdahl, J. E., Cattell, R. B., 'Personality and creativity in artists and writers'. *J Clin Psychology* 1958; 14: 107–11.

Dudek, S. Z., 'The artist as person: generalizations based on Rorschach records of writers and painters'. *J Nerv Ment Dis* 1970; 150: 232–41.

Dykes, M., McGhie, A., 'A comparative study of attentional strategies of schizo-phrenic and highly creative normal subjects'. *Br J Psychiatry* 1976; 128: 50–6.

Ellis, H., *A Study of British Genius*. Hurst and Blackett: London, 1904.

Eysenck, H. J., *Genius the Natural History of Creativity*. Cambridge University Press: Cambridge, 1995.

Galton, F., Wozniak, R. H., *Classics in Psychology, 1874 Vol 12: English Men of Science*. Thoemmes: Bristol, 1998.

—, —, *Classics in Psychology, 1883 Vol 19: Inquiries into Human Faculty and Its Development*. Thoemmes: Bristol, 1998.

Glover, J., Ronning, R., Reynolds, C., *Handbook of Creativity*. Plenum: New York, 1989.

Hasenfus, N., Magaro, P., 'Creativity and schizophrenia: an equality of empirical constructs'. *Br J Psychiatry* 1976; 129: 346–9.

Haynal, A., *Depression and Creativity*. International Universities Press: New York, 1985.

Henney, J. H., Pressel, E., Goodman, F. D., *Trance, Healing, and Hallucination: Three Field Studies in Religious Experience*. Wiley: New York, 1974.

Hershman, D. J., Lieb, J., *Manic Depression and Creativity*. Prometheus Books: New York, 1998.

—, —, *The Key to Genius*. Promethus Books: New York, 1988.

Heston, L. L. 'Psychiatric disorders in foster-home-reared children of schizophrenic mothers'. *Br J Psychiatr* 1966; 122: 819–25.

—, Denney, D., 'Interactions between early life experience and biological factors in schizophrenia'. In *The Transmissions of Schizophrenia*, Rosenthal, D., Kety, S. (eds), Pergamon Press: Oxford, 1968; 363–76.

Hilts, P. J., *Scientific Temperaments: Three Lives in Contemporary Science*. Simon and Schuster: New York, 1982.

Holden, C., 'Creativity and the troubled mind'. *Psychology Today* 1987; 21: 9–10.

Horrobin, D. F., 'Schizophrenia: the illness that made us human'. *Med Hypotheses* 1998; 50: 269–88.

Isohanni, I., Jarvelin, M. R., Jones, P. et al., 'Can excellent school performance be a precursor of schizophrenia?' *Acta Psychiatr Scand* 1999; 100: 17–26.

Jamison, K. R., *Touched with Fire: Manic-depressive Illness and the Artistic Temperament*. Free Press: New York, 1993.

Juda, A., 'The relationships between highest mental capacity and psychic abnormalities'. *Am J Psychiatry* 1949; 106: 296–304.

Karlsson, J. L., 'Creative intelligence in relatives of mental patients'. *Hereditas* 1984; 100: 83–6.

—, 'Genetic association of giftedness and creativity with schizophrenia'. *Hereditas* 1970; 66: 177–81.

—, 'Genetic basis of intellectual variation in Iceland'. *Hereditas* 1981; 95: 283–8.

—, 'Genetic relationship between giftedness and myopia'. *Hereditas* 1973; 73: 85–7.

—, *Inheritance of Creative Intelligence*. Nelson-Hall: Chicago, 1978.

—, 'Inheritance of schizophrenia'. *Acta Psychiatr Scand Suppl* 1974; 274: 1–116.

—, *The Biologic Basis of Schizophrenia*. Thomas: Springfield, Ill., 1966.

Keefe, J. A., Magaro, P. A., 'Creativity and schizophrenia: an equivalence of cognitive processing'. *J Abnorm Psychol* 1980; 89: 390–8.

Krebs, H., Shelley, J., *The Creative Process in Science and Medicine. Proceedings of the CH Boehringer Sohn Symposium. Kronberg, Taunus, 16–17 May 1974*. American Elsevier: New York, 1975.

Lange-Eichbaum, W. (trans. Paul, E. and Paul, C.), *The Problem of Genius*. Macmillan: New York, 1932.

Le Souef, P. N., Goldblatt, J., Lynch, N. R., 'Evolutionary adaptation of inflammatory immune responses in human beings'. *Lancet* 2000; 356: 242–4.

Littlewood, R., 'The imitation of madness: the influence of psychopathology upon culture'. *Soc Sci Med* 1984; 19: 705–15.

Lucas, C. J., Stringer, P., 'Interaction in university selection, mental health and academic performance'. *Br J Psychiatry* 1972; 120: 189–95.

Ludwig, A. M., *The Price of Greatness*. Guilford Press: New York, 1995.

MacKinnon, D. W., *In Search of Human Effectiveness*. Creative Education Foundation: Buffalo, NY, 1978.

—, 'The nature and nurture of creative talent'. *Am Psychol* 1962; 17: 484–95.

McNeil, T. F., 'Prebirth and postbirth influence on the relationship between creative ability and recorded mental illness'. *J Pers* 1971; 39: 391–406.

Miller, A. I., *Insights of Genius: Imagery and Creativity in Science and Art.* Copernicus: New York, 1996.

Murphy, H. B., 'Cultural aspects of the delusion'. *Stud Gen* (Berl) 1967; 20: 684–92.

Myerson, A., Boyle, R. D., 'The incidence of manic-depressive psychosis in certain socially important families'. *Am J Psychiatry* 1941; 98: 11–21.

Nesse, R. M., Williams, G. C., *Evolution and Healing: The New Science of Darwinian Medicine.* Weidenfeld and Nicolson: London, 1995.

Nisbet, J., *The Insanity of Genius: And the General Inequality of Human Faculty Physiologically Considered.* Stanley Paul: London, 1912.

Nordau, M. S., *Degeneration.* D. Appleton: New York, 1895.

Ochse, R., *Before the Gates of Excellence: The Determinants of Creative Genius.* Cambridge University Press: Cambridge, 1990.

—, 'The relation between creative genius and psychopathology: an historical perspective and a new explanation'. *S African J Psychology* 1991; 21: 45–53.

Planansky, K., 'Conceptual boundaries of schizoidness: suggestions for epidemiological and genetic research'. *J Nerv Ment Dis* 1966; 142: 318–31.

Prentky, R. A., *Creativity and Psychopathology, a Neurocognitive Perspective.* Praeger: New York, 1980.

Price, J. S., Stevens, A., 'An evolutionary approach to psychiatric disorders: group splitting and schizophrenia'. *Hum Evol Behav Intell* 1999; 197–207.

Richards, R. L., 'Relationships between creativity and psychopathology: an evaluation and interpretation of the evidence'. *Genet Psychol Monogr* 1981; 103: 261–324.

Sandblom, P., *Creativity and Disease: How Illness Affects Literature, Art and Music.* Marion Boyars: New York, 1992.

Simonton, D. K., *Genius and Creativity: Selected Papers.* Ablex: Greenwich, Conn., 1997.

Singh, M. M., Gang, R. G., 'An ethological model of schizophrenia – a preliminary investigation'. *Dis Nervous Systems* 1974; 35: 157–65.

—, Kay, S. R., Pitman, R. K., 'Territorial behavior of schizophrenics: a phylogenetic approach'. *J Nerv Ment Dis* 1981; 169: 503–12.

Stearns, S. C., *Evolution in Health and Disease.* Oxford University Press: Oxford, 1999.

Stevens, A., Price, J., *Evolutionary Psychiatry.* Routledge: New York, 1996.

Storr, A., *The School of Genius.* André Deutsch: London, 1989.

Taylor, C. W., Barron, F. (eds), *Scientific Creativity: Its Recognition and Development.* Wiley: New York, 1966.

Treffert, D. A., *Extraordinary People.* Bantam Press: London, 1989.

Tsanoff, R. A., *The Ways of Genius.* Harper: New York, 1949.

Vernon, P. E. (ed), *Creativity: Selected Readings.* Penguin Books: Harmondsworth, 1970.

Weeks, D. J., Ward, K., *Eccentrics: The Scientific Investigation.* Stirling University Press: London, 1988.

Wilson, B. R., *The Noble Savages: The Primitive Origins of Charisma and Its Contemporary Survival.* University of California Press: Berkeley, 1975.

INDEX

AA (arachidonic acid): brain function, 78, 79, 99-100; brain growth, 90-3, 96-7, 169-70; brain structure, 78, 88; formation, 78-9; inflammatory response, 158; in milk, 92; release of, 88, 99, 158-60; in schizophrenia, 158-62, 215; sources, 93-6, 188, 190-1, 201, 230
Acheulian tools, 235
acylation stimulating proteins, see ASPs
adoption studies, 137-9, 142-4
Africa, 40, 175
Africans, 40
agriculture: development, 44, 188; effects, 188, 190, 192; schizophrenia, 202, 237
Aiello, Leslie, 55
albumins, 73
ALA (alpha-linolenic acid), 77-9, 92, 190-1, 200-1, 202
alpha-linolenic acid, see ALA
Alport syndrome, 90, 162
Altamira, cave paintings, 5-9
amino acids, 16
Ampère, André Marie, 147
ancestors, 174-5
Andersen, Hans Christian, 148
Andreasen, Nancy, 147
apes: brain size, 20; diet, 50; differences from humans, 12-13, 228-9; DNA sequences,

21; genome, 186
apolipoproteins, 73, 230
arachidonic acid, see AA
Ardrey, Robert, 45, 49, 53
art: cave paintings, 5-9, 13, 174; emergence, 7-9, 43, 173, 174, 178; link with schizophrenia, 182-3
arthritis, 151-2, 157, 215
artists, 147-8
ASPs (acylation stimulating proteins), 74, 97, 230
asylums, 198, 208, 209
Australian Aborigines, 119, 122, 176-7
Australopithecines, 25-7, 28, 30, 55, 231
Australopithecus afarensis, 26
Australopithecus garhi, 28
autism, 164-5, 166
autosomal DNA, 17, 19, 21, 39, 122, 175
axons, 82-3, 166-7

babies: fat at birth, 22; premature, 92-3, 96-7
Balzac, Honoré de, 148
Baroda, University of, 221
Baudelaire, Charles, 147
Beethoven, Ludwig van, 129, 147
Bell, Alexander Graham, 148
Berlioz, Hector, 147
Bern, Howard, 2, 63-4, 65, 100